JESUS OF NAZARETH

This is the work of a master teacher—a lifetime of study, travel, reflection, and teaching distilled in lively prose for beginning students of the New Testament. It is an ideal textbook for courses on Jesus and the Gospels: comprehensive, balanced, and constructive. Students will find new insights about Jesus, his times, and the Gospels on every page.

R. Alan Culpepper
Dean, McAfee School of Theology
Mercer University

More than twenty-five years ago Gerald Borchert taught me to study Jesus and the gospels within their cultural and historical contexts. This wisdom was life-altering for me. He offers that wisdom to a broader audience in this book as he "sets" Jesus in the soil of first century Palestine where Jesus and his people were impacted by Roman occupation and Jewish tradition. In so doing, Borchert presents a compelling understanding of Jesus as a flesh-and-blood person living out a transformative mission from God in a difficult world. No "plastic" Jesus here! Rather, Borchert's careful, analytical, faithful study helps readers relate to Jesus' revolutionary living and appreciate anew the testimonies to his life and significance in the gospels. Believers who wish both to think and believe will welcome Borchert's effort as his students have been doing for decades.

Mitzi L. Minor
Professor of New Testament, Memphis Theological Seminary
Author of *2 Corinthians* in the Smyth & Helwys Bible Commentary Series

In *Jesus of Nazareth* Gerald Borchert guides readers into historical encounter with the Jesus of the Gospels. Displaying wisdom and skill developed over decades of teaching the New Testament in Christian colleges and seminaries, Borchert blends descriptions of the ancient contexts of the Gospels with a literary survey analysis that utilizes methods of careful critical study of the texts. In this era when debates over Jesus too often shed more rhetorical heat than kindly light, Borchert offers a trustworthy guide to Christians seeking deeper understanding of Jesus and the testimonies of the Gospels.

Charles J. Scalise
Professor of Church History
Fuller Theological Seminary

JESUS OF NAZARETH

BACKGROUND, WITNESSES, AND SIGNIFICANCE

Gerald L. Borchert

MERCER UNIVERSITY PRESS

MACON, GEORGIA

MUP/P438

© 2011 Mercer University Press
1400 Coleman Avenue
Macon, Georgia 31207
All rights reserved

First Edition

Books published by Mercer University Press are printed on acid-free
paper that meets the requirements of American National Standard for
Information Sciences—Permanence of Paper for Printed Library
Materials.

Mercer University Press is a member of Green Press Initiative
(greenpressinitiative.org), a nonprofit organization working to help
publishers and printers increase their use of recycled paper and
decrease their use of fiber derived from endangered forests. This book
is printed on recycled paper.
Library of Congress Cataloging-in-Publication Data

Borchert, Gerald L.
 Jesus of Nazareth : background, witnesses, and significance / by
Gerald L. Borchert. -- 1st ed.
      p. cm.
 Includes bibliographical references and index.
 ISBN 978-0-88146-266-1 (pbk. : alk. paper)
 1. Jesus Christ. 2. Bible. N.T. Gospels--Criticism, interpretation, etc. 3.
Bible. N.T. Gospels--Hermeneutics. I. Title.
 BT205.B59 2011
 232--dc23
                                    2011024427

For my dear wife Doris

MERCER
UNIVERSITY PRESS

Endowed by
TOM WATSON BROWN
and
THE WATSON-BROWN FOUNDATION, INC.

CONTENTS

Abbreviations   xiii

Preface   xvi

INTRODUCTION   1

  A. Encountering Jesus and the Gospels   1

    1. A Little Task for the Reader   1

    2. The Issue of Communication   2

    3. Organization of this Work   3

    4. The Goal of this Work   5

  B. Patterns of Reading the Bible   6

  C. Key to the Map   10

Map of Israel in the Time of Jesus   12

PART I: THE HISTORICAL, GEOGRAPHICAL, AND SOCIAL
  BACKGROUND FOR THE COMING OF JESUS   13

CHAPTER 1: THE HISTORICAL SETTING FOR THE COMING OF JESUS   15

  1. Alexander the Great and His Successors   15

  2. The Maccabees and Their Hasmonean Successors   18

  3. The Romans and Their Herodian Agents   22

  Recommended for Further Study   37

CHAPTER 2: THE PALESTINIAN SETTING AND THE VARIOUS
  ASPECTS OF JUDAISM IN THE TIME OF JESUS   38

  1. The Geographical Context   39

  2. A Brief Introduction to Most of the People and

Where and How they Lived 40

3. The Language Context 42

4. The Crucial Nature of the Jewish Rabbinic Context 43

5. Other Important Written Sources that Provide a
Context for Understanding Jesus 47

6. The Temple, the Priesthood, and the Jewish Festivals 51

7. The Synagogue 55

8. The Jewish Parties in the Time of Jesus 59

9. The Dreamers and Their Apocalyptic Expectations 66

10. The Diaspora and Its Significance 69

Recommended for Further Study 72

PART II: UNDERSTANDING THE GOSPELS AS TESTIMONIES 73

CHAPTER 3: THE WITNESS OF MARK TO JESUS: WHO IS HE? 77

1. The Introduction: Mark 1:1–13 79

2. The Southern Galilean Ministry: Mark 1:14–7:23 80

3. The Ministry of Jesus in the North: Mark 7:24–9:50 86

4. Conflict and Conclusion in Judea: Mark 10:1–16 89

Recommended for Further Study 96

CHAPTER 4: THE WITNESS OF MATTHEW TO JESUS AS
EMMANUEL ("GOD WITH US") AND THE FULFILLMENT
OF OLD TESTAMENT PROPHECIES 98

1. Introduction of Emmanuel—Fulfillment through
the Coming of the Messianic King: Matthew 1:1–2:23 99

2. The Preparation of Jesus, the King, for Ministry:
Matthew 3:1–4:11 100

3. Introduction to Jesus' Teaching Ministry of the
Kingdom: Matthew 4:12–7:29 102

4. The Kingdom, Jesus' Miraculous Mission, and

His Commission to His Followers: Matthew 8:1–11:1   106

5. Hostility, the Parables, and the Mystery of the
Kingdom: 11:2–13:53   108

6. Revealing the Nature of the Kingdom:
Matthew 13:54–19:2   109

7. The Climax to the Kingdom Ministry of Jesus
in Judea: Matthew 19:1b–26:1   111

8. The Death and Resurrection of the King:
Matthew 26:2–28:20   113

Recommended for Further Study   117

CHAPTER 5: THE WITNESS OF LUKE TO THE JESUS WHO
CARES FOR THE HURTING AND DISPOSSESSED   118

1. Introduction: The Coming of God's Caring
Messenger: Luke 1:5–2:52   121

2. The Preparation of Jesus for Ministry:
Luke 3:1–4:13   125

3. The Beginning of the Caring Ministry of Jesus:
Luke 4:14–7:17   127

4. Ministry and the Winds of Hostility Begin to Blow:
Luke 7:18–9:55   129

5. Jesus' Ministry of Caring on the Long Way to Jerusalem:
Luke 9:56–19:27   131

6. The Entry into Jerusalem and the Death of Jesus:
Luke 19:28–23:56   138

7. The Startling Resurrection Stories and Waiting
for the Promised Gift: Luke 24:1–53   141

Recommended for Further Study   143

CHAPTER 6: THE WITNESS OF JOHN TO THE DIVINE

WORD WHO BECAME FLESH   144

1. The Prologue to the Witness of John: John 1:1–18   145

2. John the Baptist and Three Cameos of

Witness: John 1:19–51   147

3. The Cana Cycle and the Importance of

Believing: John 2:1–4:54   150

4. The Festival Cycle and the Fulfillment of the

Jewish Religious Calendar: John 5:1–11:57   153

5. The Centerpiece of the Gospel: The Beginning

of the End: John 12:1–50   160

6. The Farewell Cycle: The Model of Jesus and

the Promise of the Spirit: John 13:1–17:26   162

7. The Johannine Death Story: John 18:1–19:42   164

8. The Amazing Resurrection Stories:

John 20:1–21:14   167

9. The Epilogue: 21:15–25   172

Recommended for Further Study   172

CHAPTER 7: NON-CANONICAL AND REJECTED WITNESSES TO JESUS 175

A. The Coptic "Gnostic" Gospels   176

1. The Gospel of Thomas   176

2. The Gospel of Philip   179

3. The Gospel of Truth (*Evangelium Veritatis*)   182

4. Other Gnostic Documents   184

B. The Infancy Gospels   185

1. The Protoevangelium of James   185

2. The Gospel of Thomas the Israelite:

Concerning the Childhood of the Lord   186

C. Conclusion   188

1. The Fiasco Concerning the Gospel of Judas   188

2. A Summation   189

Recommended for Further Study   190

PART III: AN INTRODUCTION TO GOSPEL METHODOLOGY   191

CHAPTER 8: METHODOLOGICAL TOOLS FOR THE

STUDY OF JESUS AND THE GOSPELS   193

1. Concerning Presuppositions   193

2. Orality and Deconstruction   196

3. Textual Analysis   197

4. Source or Synoptic Analysis   199

5. Form Analysis (or the Analysis of Pericopes)   202

6. Redaction Analysis and the Quests for the Historical Jesus 204

7. Narrative Analysis   206

8. Sociological Analysis   207

9. Conclusion   209

Recommended for Further Study   210

PART IV: CONCLUDING REFLECTIONS AND IMPLICATIONS   211

CHAPTER 9: THE SIGNIFICANCE OF JESUS:

CONSIDERING HIS IMPORTANCE   213

A. What about the Context and Time?   213

B. Who Is this Jesus?   216

1. The Virginal Conception and the Incarnation   217

2. The Issue of Temptation and Sin

Concerning Jesus (and Others)   220

3. The Dependence of Jesus on God

(the Father)   224

4. The Messianic Consciousness of Jesus:

A Brief Reflection on His Words and Works   225

5. The Nature of Jesus' Messiahship   228

6. The Death of the Messiah   230

7. The Resurrection of the Messiah   233

8. The Church and the Return of Jesus in Power   235

C. Reviewing the Integrity of Our Understanding of Jesus   237

Recommended for Further Study   240

CHAPTER 10: IMPLICATIONS CONCERNING THIS
MYSTERIOUS PERSON CALLED JESUS   241

1. Doubt and Rejection of Jesus   241

2. The Worship of Jesus   243

3. Living and Witnessing for Jesus   245

4. Conclusion   248

Subject Index   251

Modern Name Index   257

ABBREVIATIONS

Gen	Genesis	Mic	Micah
Exod	Exodus	Nah	Nahum
Lev	Leviticus	Hab	Habakkuk
Num	Numbers	Zeph	Zephaniah
Deut	Deuteronomy	Hag	Haggai
Josh	Joshua	Zech	Zechariah
Judg	Judges	Mal	Malachi
Ruth	Ruth	Matt	Matthew
1, 2 Sam	1, 2 Samuel	Mark	Mark
1, 2 Kgs	1, 2, Kings	Luke	Luke
1, 2 Chr	1, 2 Chronicles	John	John
Ezra	Ezra	Acts	Acts
Neh	Nehemiah	Rom	Romans
Job	Job	1, 2 Cor	1, 2 Corinthians
Ps, Pss	Psalm(s)	Gal	Galatians
Prov	Proverbs	Eph	Ephesians
Song	Song of Songs/	Phil	Philippians
	Song of Solomon	Col	Colossians
Isa	Isaiah	1, 2 Thess	1, 2 Thessalonians
Jer	Jeremiah	1, 2 Tim	1, 2 Timothy
Lam	Lamentations	Titus	Titus
Ezek	Ezekiel	Phlm	Philemon
Dan	Daniel	Heb	Hebrews
Hos	Hosea	Jas	James
Joel	Joel	1, 2 Pet	1, 2 Peter
Amos	Amos	1, 2, 3 John	1, 2, 3 John
Obad	Obadiah	Jude	Jude
Jonah	Jonah	Rev	Revelation

Ancient Greek And Latin Authors

Sources quoted are rendered in English translations although the citations used normally refer to the standard titles and abbreviations used by the Society of Biblical Literature in *The SBL Handbook of Style* (Hendrickson, 1999).

Other Ancient And Modern Abbreviations

EvV	The Coptic Gospel of Truth
GP	The Coptic Gospel of Philip
GT	The Coptic Gospel of Thomas
LXX	The Main Greek Version of the Hebrew Old Testament

AB	Anchor Bible
BAR	*Biblical Archaeology Review*
BBC	*Broadman Bible Commentary*
Herm	Hermeneia
KJV	King James Version
MCB	*Mercer Commentary on the Bible*
MDB	*Mercer Dictionary of the Bible*
NAC	New American Commentary
NIB	*New Interpreter's Bible*
NLT	New Living Translation
R&E	*Review and Expositor*
RSV	Revised Standard Version
WBC	Word Biblical Commentary

Diatessaron.	*Tatian's Diatessaron.* Edited by Erwin Preuschen. Heidelberg: Carl Winters U–Heidelberg, 1926. (Also known as J. H. Hill, ed., *The Earliest Life of Christ ever compiled from the Four Gospels being the Diatessaron of Tatian* [Edinburgh: T & T Clark, 1894].)

John 1–11, John 12-21   *John 1–11*; *John 12–21*. Gerald L. Borchert.
                             Volumes 25A and 25B in the New American
                             Commentary. Nashville: Broadman &
                             Holman, 1996, 2002.

Millennium Matrix   *The Millenium Matrix*. M. Rex Miller. San
                             Francisco: Jossey Bass, 2004.

N.T. Background Documents *The New Testament Background: Selected
                             Documents*. C. K. Barrett. New York: Harper
                             & Brothers, 1956.

O.T. Pseudepigrapha   *The Old Testament Pseudepigrapha*: *Apocalyptic
                             Literature and Testaments,* volume 1, and
                             Expansions of the Old Testament, volume 2.
                             Edited by James H. Charlesworth. Garden
                             City NY: Doubleday, 1983, 1985.

Worship in the NT   *Worship in the New Testament: Divine Mystery
                             and Human Response*. Gerald L. Borchert. St.
                             Louis: Chalice Press, 2007.

PREFACE

The invitation from Mercer University Press via Marc Jolley, the publisher, to write a work on Jesus and the Four Gospels was a welcomed request. It came at a time when I was just finishing my work on *Worship in the New Testament*, and I was pondering what to tackle next. The task of writing this work has been nothing but a joy for me because it focuses on Jesus, whom I consider to be crucial not merely in my own life but also in the lives of others who seek authentic guidance in relating to God and their neighbors.

Writing this work on Jesus comes after many years of teaching the New Testament at levels from the baccalaureate to the doctorate in schools around the world, as well as in church settings from those that are magnificent in structure to those that have mud floors. It also comes after having written or edited at least twenty other books and countless articles on various subjects pertinent to the New Testament and to Christian life and witness. On the one hand, this present work is written, I trust, in an unencumbered manner so that those who are beginning their study of Jesus will not be overwhelmed. On the other hand, I have included ideas that I have been contemplating for many years. All biblical translations are mine unless otherwise noted.

I have tried purposely not to follow the pattern of engendering complexity for the sake of seeming scholarly. I confess that I have little patience with those who seek to create theological fog. I remember vividly what one of the outstanding scholars of the Old Testament said in a crowded meeting of the Society of Biblical Literature when he spoke on Daniel some years ago. He stated that because scholars had not paid attention to writing for the church in an understandable manner, the interpretation of Daniel had been left to people who developed and proclaimed strange ideas and methods that were completely foreign to that document.

I have earnestly attempted to provide a balanced approach to the subject of Jesus and the Gospels purposely within the context of a faith commitment, yet recognizing the reality of doubt and imbalance in all humans. I also understand that some people have rejected and will reject Jesus. Moreover, I have included reflections on what I think are dead ends in the study of Jesus and the Gospels as well as additions to the canonical witnesses that I consider are unacceptable from both inside and outside the church. Furthermore, I have given insights into how I have reached my present positions, and in the final part I have tried to evaluate them as best as I am able.

My goal is to be as transparent as possible so that you, my readers, can decide for yourselves what path you will take in your analysis of the Gospels. May you experience new insights as you study, and, as you peruse my work, please keep an open copy of the Bible at your fingertips so that you can prayerfully and honestly weigh my remarks. Using the Bible in this manner has been my practice throughout my career, and I strongly recommend it to you. Also, to aid you in your study, the introduction offers reflections on methods of reading the Bible, and chapter 8 presents methods of analyzing the Gospels. Welcome to this study of Jesus.

I now come to the portion of the preface where I must express my gratitude to others. First, I am deeply thankful to my dear wife, Doris, who is God's wonderful gift to me. She has been my partner in theological education as a professor in Christian education and of supervised ministry for many years, and she has read most of my many manuscripts, including this one. Her insistence that I eliminate the unnecessary and that I try not only to be theologically clear but also sensitive to the needs of my audiences has been significant in both my teaching and writing. I gratefully dedicate this work to her.

I am also exceedingly grateful to the many students who have taught and continue to teach me as I instruct them in matters pertaining to the New Testament and the Christian faith. Their questions and concerns are the fodder that keeps me pondering ideas and learning from them. In addition, I am particularly delighted at this stage of my career that I am now able to teach alongside my sons in academic settings and in the church, as well as alongside several of my former doctoral students in several schools. It is a special blessing to spend time with them over lunches and to visit them in their teaching roles around the world.

I also express a special thank you to Mercer University Press and to Marc Jolley for the opportunity to write this work on Jesus.

Finally, in this season of Advent and at the beginning of a new Christian year, I express my foremost gratitude to God in Christ Jesus who came to this cosmos in order that we might understand more clearly the will of God for humanity and for the world.

—Gerald L. Borchert, Advent 2010
Thesis Director, The Robert E. Webber Institute for Worship Studies and Senior Professor of New Testament, Carson Newman College (Retired Dean and Director of Doctoral Studies, Northern Baptist Theological Seminary, and Retired Chair and Coleman Professor of New Testament, Southern Baptist Theological Seminary)

INTRODUCTION

A. Encountering Jesus And The Gospels

Welcome to an exciting encounter with an ancient pattern of communication and the ageless testimonies concerning Jesus of Nazareth. Many
have asked in the past and continue to do so today, "Who is he?" The
four canonical Gospel writers would answer, "He is the one chosen by
God Almighty to be the Messiah of the Jews and the Savior of the
world." But with the exception of a brief sojourn during his childhood in
the land of Egypt and an apparent brief visit to what today would be
southern Lebanon, this unique person called Jesus lived almost all of his
short physical life within the context of a small region now known as
Israel and Palestine. The ancient geographical setting was known as the
Roman province of *Palestina*, an area encompassing less than 200 miles
from north to south and less than 70 miles from east to west. For many
contemporary westerners, that area seems confining. Yet that same Jesus
has affected the lives of innumerable people around the world and
throughout the millennia, even changing the way most humans reckon
time.[1]

1. A Little Task for the Reader

On the first day of my New Testament classes on the Gospels, I
normally ask my students to see how many places they can identify that
are marked by numbers and the first letters of place names on a map of
the so-called "Holy Land." As you begin this encounter with Jesus and
the communication vehicles of the early church, I offer you, the reader,

---

[1] The usual chronological designations are B.C. (before Christ) or in other
sources B.C.E. (before the common era), and A.D. (anno Domini, "in the year of
our Lord") or in other sources C.E. (in the common era).

the same opportunity. Why not test yourself by copying the place numbers and letters from the map and filling in your suggestions for the names. This quiz is just a thought starter. It is not an evaluation of how brilliant you are. It is a friendly quiz. The identifying answers to the numbers are supplied at the end of this introduction on page 12. But I suggest that you do not consult the answers until you finish the test quiz. For your own sake, such an understanding of the geography will be an invaluable aid to your study of the Gospel testimonies.

2. The Issue of Communication

In reflecting on Jesus and the communication patterns of the early church, I want to remind you who sit at your computers receiving e-mail messages from around the world and searching through millions of web sites in nanoseconds that the first century was steeped in the tradition of *oral communication*. The early disciples loved to communicate their testimonies orally. "Tell me the stories of Jesus I love to hear" would undoubtedly represent the first line of communication for the early church. Written documents recorded important decisions, but they were the people's second line of communication, a confirmation of the oral testimonies. Here is the reason the New Testament writers repeat the statement "Whoever has ears to hear, let him hear" (e.g., Matt 11:15; 13:9, 43; Mark 4:23; cf. Rev 2:7, 11, 17, 29; 3:6, 13, 22). When God spoke, it carried power (cf. Gen 1:3–26). His Son was called "the Word" (John 1:1, 18), indeed "the Word of God" (Rev 19:13), the epitome of God's self. Hearing about the electrifying Word and his work carried not only the power of human declaration but a sense of the divine presence (cf. Rev 13:9) that is foreign to many of us in our desperately lonely generation, which longs for community in the midst of our impersonalized busyness. Thus, when the Council of Jerusalem met and decided that the Gentiles did not have to become Jews in order to be Christians, the council not only wrote a message concerning their decision but also sent representatives with Paul and Barnabas to present the decision orally to the Gentiles (Acts 15:22).[2]

---

[2] For a discussion of oral culture, see M. Rex Miller, *The Millennium Matrix* (San Francisco: Jossey-Bass, 2004) 19–34.

The primary oral witnesses to Jesus' life, death, and resurrection did not continue for long. They soon began to die or were killed, and their powerful testimonies needed to be preserved. At that point, Mark introduced a new literary genre—a gospel—to fill the gap of the dying witnesses. At the end of John's Gospel, a concluding postscript by the community of the evangelist attests to the passing of the apostolic period (21:23–24). It bears solid witness to the end of an era and the need to preserve authentic testimonies concerning Jesus. With this rationale concerning the Gospels in mind, I turn to the format for this present study.

3. Organization of this Work

In organizing this brief work on Jesus and the authentic written witnesses/testimonies called Gospels, I will discuss in Part I the context into which Jesus came. For those who live in an era when change is occurring exponentially and history is being made daily, the contrast between Jesus' context and the twenty-first century is great, and the early setting needs to be understood by the contemporary reader. In chapter 1 I will attempt to provide an introduction to the Hellenistic and Jewish contexts that are foundational for understanding Jesus and the early church that proclaimed him to be "the Lord." To do so, it is necessary to begin briefly with one of the great transition periods in the history of the world—the rise of Alexander the Great and his successors. These leaders made an indelible impact upon Israel and the Mediterranean world, a region that has since experienced repeated upheavals. Next, I will turn to the Maccabees and their Hasmonean heirs as they struggled for an identity. I will conclude this section of the book with the coming of the Romans and their Herodian puppets before, during, and following the time of Jesus.

In the second chapter, I will treat the geographical context of Jesus in the land of Palestine, the common people known as the *am haeretz*, the language context, the rabbinic context, and the literary sources before I turn specifically to the Jewish religious and cultural context during that period. I include a discussion of the elements of that society's fabric—the temple setting and the festivals, the representative parties, the apocalyptic dreamers, and the significance of the Diaspora.

In Part II I will deal with the Gospels as authentic testimonies concerning Jesus. In chapters 3 through 6, I will focus on the nature and special characteristics of each individual Gospel and how they differ in witnessing to Jesus. In chapter 7, I will also provide a brief outline of the later non-canonical portraits of Jesus and why the church did not accept them.

In Part III (chapter 8), I will briefly introduce the analytical methods that have been used to interpret the Gospels, including textual, source, form, redactional, narrative, and social and cultural approaches to these documents. Understanding the methodologies should assist readers in their personal approaches to these testimonies of Jesus. I should add that in scholarship, the terms "criticism" and "critical" are often applied to these methodologies. While I do not use these terms in this work, they should generally not be understood in a pejorative manner but as shorthand substitutes for technical analytical studies. Both rationalists and sensitive believers can of course employ such methodologies. Readers are therefore cautioned to distinguish the perspectives of the users. I realize that some professors prefer to begin their teaching of the Gospels with the type of discussion found in chapter 8. I have placed it after a review the of the Gospels because I find that students are more receptive to analysis once they find out what is in the Gospels and can go back and look at them analytically.

In Part IV (chapter 9), I will provide a few insights in formulating a picture of the significance of Jesus that emerges from the study of the four canonical testimonies. I do not try to harmonize the various portraits of Jesus by eliminating different perspectives in these testimonies. Such a harmonizing was first introduced by the early Christian defender Tatian, a second-century logician who did not understand the nature of an eastern testimony. In effect, he turned the Gospels into one combined picture of Jesus. By doing so, he tried to ensure that no one could criticize the legitimacy of the Christian presentations of Jesus. I often ask my beginning students and people in churches how many of them have heard about Tatian. Most of them shake their heads in a negative response. But then I tell them that even though they have not heard of him, they may be using his methods.[3] In contrast, I try to examine the stories of Jesus by maintaining their unique perspectives. In closing this chapter, I will attempt to evaluate the integrity of our portrait of Jesus.

Finally, in chapter 10 I will briefly state some implications in our study of Jesus for the church and the world today. I will review why some people have doubts concerning Jesus and why many have rejected the testimonies about him. Then I will turn to our Christian theological confessions of him in terms of worship, living, and witnessing. The authentic church confesses this Jesus as "Savior" and "Lord." These theological confessions are of incredible importance. They affect our understanding of humanity, of the confessing church, of the fractured world, of our narcissistic society, of our view and treatment of others, and of our expectations of the future and our ultimate hope for people and the world.

4. The Goal of this Work

I recognize that the task I have been given with only a few pages is monumental. But I view this work as a concise summary of the various fields involved. At the end of each chapter, I will refer to several representative works that should be helpful for those who wish to pursue this study further. My hope and prayer is that in this presentation I may be able to challenge most of you as readers to visualize an encounter with Jesus. I will do my best to share with you the results of my many years of teaching the New Testament as well as lecturing on other subjects including counseling, sociology of religion, homiletics, and worship. In writing this book, I have tried to provide a work that will be both clear and stimulating enough to encourage your further reflection and investigation of Jesus and the Gospels.

With these initial remarks in mind, then, I approach the subject of Jesus. Even though this book by design is quite small, I trust that its size

---

[3] For example, people often talk about two cleansings of the temple, but there is only one cleansing in any Gospel. The point is that people have to understand how the stories or pericopes are used by each evangelist. (Note: I am using "evangelist" in this work to refer to the Gospel writers.) Tatian's patterns are still frequently copied today.

will hardly be a representation to the reader of the importance of Jesus and the Gospels. The writer of the Fourth Gospel has given the proper perspective to this issue. He forcefully reminded us that if one were to reflect further on the subject of Jesus, then the whole world could hardly contain the books that could be written (John 21:25). The life and extended ministry of Jesus continues to be the foundation of the church and is crucial to the heart and motivating impetus of every follower of the one whom his disciples appropriately called "Lord."

B. Patterns of Reading the Bible

To begin our analysis of the Gospels, it may be helpful to review a few of the ways we read and study the Bible or the New Testament.

The first method is reading the Bible primarily for its spiritual direction and immediate application to one's personal needs. Such an approach does not require the reader to delve into matters of historical significance or to deal with questions of the type of literature that is in the Bible. The focus is on a text's usefulness (utility). The significance sought is generally devotional and spiritually enlightening. Such was the method I employed in the memorization of countless Bible verses during the early stages of my life and with some of the Christian organizations I attended while in university. This method often highlights certain strategic passages (I call them purple or royal passages). It frequently excises texts or verses from their contexts and often leads the reader to give a foreign or inappropriate context to the text. While the method can be personally rewarding, it can also encourage subjectivity.[4]

---

[4] One of my experiences in this type of study took place on a visit to the west coast of the United States where I was leading a series of Bible studies. I was invited by the owner of a local business to attend a Monday morning Bible group. The folks at the business had been studying Romans, and each person read one verse and tried to indicate its personal value. I must say that in that study I learned a great deal about what was enlightening to them, but I was troubled by what was being read into the verses of Romans. The dear people were trying desperately to make difficult verses apply to their lives. I wished they had used some resources that might have provided a contextual understanding for the passages before they tried to apply these texts.

The second method is the study of the factual content of the Bible. In this method, the goal is the study of historical and other facts as a support basis for one's spiritual life. The facts in this case become the primary focus, and the person studying may be able to quote or identify all kinds of facts such as how many books are in the Bible, the dates when David and Solomon probably ruled over Israel, how many times Jesus healed people, and where those events are located in the Bible. Indeed, one may even know where all the biblical sites are located on a map like the ones I earlier asked you to identify.[5] Knowing "facts" about the Bible is important, but without the other two methods discussed here, this type can become a vehicle for advocating a closed or dead system of Christianity. As such, on the one hand it can function without spiritual life (dead orthodoxy). On the other hand it can be part of an unwillingness to look honestly at the nature of the Bible as a literary document.

The third type of Bible study involves bringing to the interpretation of the text all the methodologies available in analyzing the writings as literature. Such a concern will be part of our focus in chapter 8. This method of study can be enlightening as we discover the types and forms of literature in the Bible and especially in the Gospels. In this pattern of investigation, an examination is also made of the kind of social and cultural settings that were present among the people when the events took place. Equally important, the method considers the setting that was present during the later time when the stories were actually set in their canonical form. Such study also helps us understand how the stories circulated orally before they were put in written form, and it can enable us to relate our social conditions to those of the biblical period. This process can help in interpreting the point of each story or pericope that was intended by the evangelist.

There is, however, an important danger to avoid in this approach. We can assume that, when we understand the technical details of the

---

[5] This method can be extended so that one can reason with some teachers (I will not mention) about how many times the cock crowed during Peter's denial. The result of counting all the "crowings" in the four Gospels can become a curious one.

written document, we can also stand above the text and judge the legitimacy of the message delivered in the writings. This type of study may thus suffer from an academic smothering, the results of which are not unlike the deadness that can be evident in the earlier type of factual study, especially if it is linked with a rationalistic perspective that tells the text what it has to mean in a given literary context.

My conclusion to this brief review is that in order for us to achieve an adequate hermeneutic (method of interpretation), we must be able to synthesize all three methods of Bible study. More to the point, it is essential in our task for us not to tell the biblical writers what they *should* mean but to try to understand what they *did* mean. This task is of course quite difficult because we do not think like the ancient writers, and so we must maintain a humble attitude of seeking to learn from their communication methods when we try to determine the meaning of any biblical text. I would also add that whether interpreters are on the right wing (conservative) or the left wing (liberal) of biblical studies, it is important to realize that we are all tempted to argue that Scripture means what our presuppositions imply it should mean. Thus, we must remember that when people insist that their understanding of meaning is the only authentic one, such an approach can be divisive and lead to a superiority in dealing with the texts. Accordingly, it can engender an attitude that is foreign to what it means to be a follower of Jesus.

As we approach the biblical texts, we also need to remember constantly that we have inherited many ideas and views from our homes as well as our social and religious contexts. These ideas and views provide us with an assumed or *imbedded theology*. Our task as growing people in the Lord is to develop a *deliberative theology* that is based on learning and analyzing the legitimacy of our theological perspectives. It implies not a defensive modality but an open and receptive modality that is prepared to examine our preconceptions and to analyze how we acquired our views.

For example, many in the past assumed that slavery was theologically a legitimate Christian practice, and they refused to examine that position. Indeed, they often offered "proof-texts" for its legitimacy. Most Christians today regard that position as theologically erroneous. But I challenge you think about what enabled Christians to change their imbedded views. Was it just the result of a restudy of the biblical texts and a reassessment of theology? Or was it also a series of other issues? Did social conditions, economics, war, and other matters such as social integrity enable Christians to reassess and abandon their old imbedded theologies? A similar analysis could be done with polygamy and other social concerns.

When you study the life of Jesus, consider seriously why so many Jews did not accept him. Were they willing to subject their old imbedded Jewish theologies to a deliberative reassessment? Think about what it meant for the brilliant rabbi Paul to change his commitments, and then ask yourself if you are willing to subject your imbedded views to a serious examination with God's help. Jesus and the Gospels can easily suggest that we do so. The questions of course remain: Would I be willing to contemplate doing so? What might be the cost or implications of a reexamination of my views?

Welcome, then, to this study of Jesus and to the four precious testimonies concerning him. Let me give you, my reader, a little advice concerning this study before you launch into it: I recommend again that you have a Bible open to the Gospels and that you begin your readings each day with the prayer that God, your creator, would enlighten your mind concerning Jesus. Hopefully your study of Jesus will make an indelible impact on your life and your relationships with others. I mention this practice because I myself seek to follow that pattern. The reason is because I, a mere human being, need divine assistance in order to live my life authentically each day. Therefore, in good Jewish tradition, I invoke praise and blessing upon God, and then I pray that the ruler of the universe would bless you in your examination of and reflection into these testimonies. May the triune God be with you in your study, and may you become more like Jesus as the result of your encounter with these magnificent Gospel texts.

C. Key to the Map

1. Damascus
2. Sidon
3. Tyre
4. Mt. Hermon
5. Caesarea Philippi / Panias / Banias
6. Tel Dan
7. Tel Hazor
8. Bethsaida
9. Chorazim / Korazim
10. Capernaum
11. Tabgah
12. Kursi
13. Acco (Acre) / Ptolemais
14. Haifa
15. Mt. Arbel
16. Tiberias
17. Mt. Carmel
18. Cana
19. Sephoris / Zippori
20. Nazareth
21. Gaddara
22. Tel Megiddo
23. Jezreel and Nain
24. Beth Shean / Scythopolis
25. Caesarea Maritma
26. Pella and Jerash
27. Shechem, Samaria (Sebastia), Sychar, and Mt. Gerazim
28. Bethel
29. Beth Horon Pass
30. Tel Aviv / Jaffa (Yaffo) & Lydda (Lod)
31. Gezer and Antipatris
32. Emmaus
33. Jericho and Qumran
34. Jamnia / Yavneh
35. Amman

36. Jerusalem and Bethany
37. Ashdod or Azotus
38. Bethlehem/Ephratah and the Herodian
39. Ashqelon
40. Mt. Nebo and Madaba
41. Hebron/Mamre
42. Gaza
43. Ein Gedi
44. Machaerus
45. Beersheba
46. Petra
47. Eilat/Aqaba

An Introductory Friendly Map Quiz
(To Remind You of Some Important Sites You Should Know)

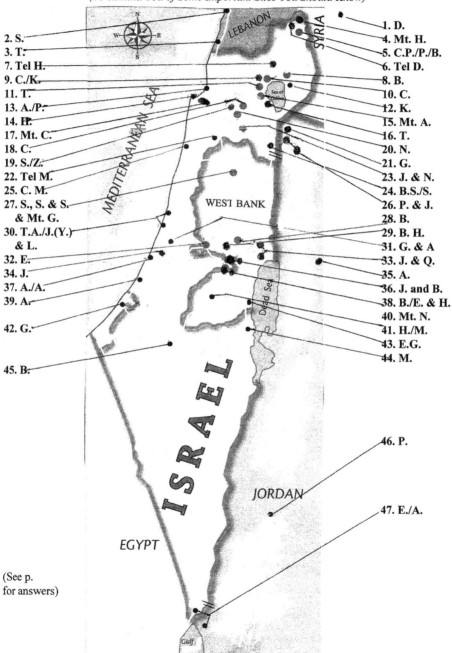

2. S.
3. T.
7. Tel H.
9. C./K.
11. T.
13. A./P.
14. H.
17. Mt. C.
18. C.
19. S./Z.
22. Tel M.
25. C. M.
27. S., S. & S.
  & Mt. G.
30. T.A./J.(Y.)
  & L.
32. E.
34. J.
37. A./A.
39. A.

42. G.

45. B.

1. D.
4. Mt. H.
5. C.P./P./B.
6. Tel D.
8. B.
10. C.
12. K.
15. Mt. A.
16. T.
20. N.
21. G.
23. J. & N.
24. B.S./S.
26. P. & J.
28. B.
29. B. H.
31. G. & A
33. J. & Q.
35. A.
36. J. and B.
38. B./E. & H.
40. Mt. N.
41. H./M.
43. E.G.
44. M.

46. P.

47. E./A.

(See p.
for answers)

PART I

THE HISTORICAL, GEOGRAPHICAL, AND SOCIAL
BACKGROUND FOR THE COMING OF JESUS

THE HISTORICAL SETTING FOR THE COMING OF JESUS

Every person is born into an environmental context that affects a person and has an impact upon how he or she is received. In writing to the Galatians, Paul indicated that when the time (*chronos*) had reached its "fullness" (*pleroma*), God sent his Son into the world (Gal 4:4). Many Christians have pondered these words and reflected about how many conditions were conducive for the beginning of Christianity at that time. It is not my intention to exegete the text of Galatians at this point; I have done so in one of my commentaries.[1] My point is to indicate that, historically in the coming of Jesus, God was fulfilling the divine intentions not only in the Jewish context (4:4) but also in the broader Hellenistic context so that even Gentiles like the Galatians could accept the gift of his Son (cf. John 3:16). Indeed, God provided a strategic historical womb for the coming of the Savior of the world (cf. John 4:42).

1. Alexander the Great and His Successors

The world at the time of Jesus had been indelibly affected by the short life of Alexander of Macedon more than three centuries before Jesus' coming. Alexander's father, Philip of Macedon, had been advised by Isocrates, the philosopher, that once he had subjected the Persians to his control, nothing would be left except for him "to become a god." However, Philip was killed (perhaps by instigation of his son) before the realization of such a predicted conquest. Alexander then claimed the crown, suppressing his rivals. Historians debate whether an oracle

---

[1] See my commentary on Galatians concerning this verse in Roger Mohrlang and Gerald L. Borchert, *Romans, Galatians*, Cornerstone Biblical Commentary (Carol Stream IL: Tyndale House Publishers, 2007) 301–303.

actually communicated to Alexander that he was the son of a god and was destined to unite the world.[2] It is known that his tutor Aristotle clearly taught him that if he could make conquered people become Greek, he could rule his world.

Alexander's goal soon became clear. After uniting Greece, he turned his attention eastward, and with a force of some 35,000 men and gold from the mines in Philippi, he challenged the Persian Empire both on the land and the sea. He won a strategic face-off with the Persian navy in the sea off Athens and followed it with an impressive battle at the mountain pass of Issus (between Tarsus and what later became known as Antioch) in 333 B.C. The astuteness of Alexander as a military commander obviously concerned his Persian rival, Darius III, who in an attempt to counter this victorious Macedonian general offered large gifts to an oracle for blessing him in the battle. The oracle responded in a brilliant model of slippery communications when the priestly interpreter told Darius that if he went to war, a great general would be defeated. In full confidence, Darius then entered the battle with Alexander, and as you probably guessed—he lost!

Alexander's strategy for world domination was to place Greeks in charge of conquered people and institute superior Greek cultural patterns into their societies. Among these innovations were the insistence on the use of the Greek language for commerce; the wearing of Greek-type clothing for acceptability; the installation of the theatre for enjoyment and the communication of ideas; the employment of the gymnasium for learning, recreation, and physical development; and the athletic games that served for entertainment and proof of vitality. The strategy worked with an incredible success that matched the military genius of the conqueror.

Alexander continued his march south from Issus along the eastern shore of the Mediterranean through Syria and Israel to Egypt, and when he had conquered them, he returned north to take all of Mesopotamia from Darius. He finally entered India and desired to move on to China.

---

[2] For elaborate myths concerning Alexander and especially of the serpent who was found lying near his mother Olympia(s) as she slept and afterward suspected of making her pregnant, see Plutarch, *Life of Alexander II*.

His soldiers, however, became weary and were unwilling to venture into the land of the dragon, fearing the myths of an encounter with the end of the world. At the same time, Alexander became ill and was unable to continue his trek. He reversed his course and began his return, but he soon died at the age of thirty-two (323 B.C.) in Babylon en route to his homeland. During this time, he had traversed approximately 11,000 miles from Greece in about eleven years, and his conquests altered the patterns of world history.

Alexander left no viable heirs except a young offspring and a mentally challenged brother. As a result, his five generals agreed to divide his kingdom (cf. Dan 11:4). After a series of battles for power between the five leaders, only three were left in charge of the divided realm. Cassander[3] held Greece and parts of Europe, Ptolemy controlled Egypt and the land of Israel, and Seleucus ruled in Mesopotamia and Asia Minor. But Seleucus believed that in the agreement between the generals he had been allotted Israel, even though he was not strong enough to wrest it from Ptolemy. As a result, the land bridge of Israel between Mesopotamia and Egypt became the scene of constant battles. Daniel 11, which is one of the best history records in the Bible, recounts the continuing battles between the Seleucids (the kings of the north) and the Ptolemies (the kings of the south). Anyone with a little knowledge of history can readily identify the figures and events in this blow-by-blow record.

That chapter, however, focuses on the acts of a despicable Seleucid ruler, Antiochus (IV) Epiphanes, who thought he was "divine" (Dan 11:36). Even his subjects, the citizens of Antioch, who were known for their wit and for giving nicknames to people,[4] despised him. So they referred to him as *Epimanes*—"madman." Thinking he was as competent as his predecessor, Antiochus (III) the Great, Epiphanes tried to despoil Egypt, but he was met there with a force that he could not handle. That

---

[3] Cassander's wife was Saloniki, the sister of Alexander after whom Thessaloniki (Thessalonica) was named. Today the city of Saloniki(a) is the second largest in Greece.

[4] Cf. Acts 11:26 where the "followers of the Way" received their nickname "Christians" in Antioch.

force was the new power on the horizon—the ships of the "Kittim" (the Romans; see Dan 11:30).

2. *The Maccabees and Their Hasmonean Successors*

Before detailing the fateful coming to Israel of these Romans with Pompey in 63 B.C., it is imperative to recount a few of the episodes involving the Maccabees and their successors (known as the Hasmoneans). In revenge and to assuage his tattered pride, Antiochus Epiphanes returned to Israel and made the Jews pay for their refusal to obey him. He deposed the Jewish high priest (Dan 11:22), slaughtered a pig on an altar of sacrifice, and set up a statue of Zeus in the Most Holy Place of the Temple (which became known as the desolating desecration/sacrilege; 11:31).[5] The Syrians/Seleucids imposed harsh restrictions on the Jews so that owning a copy of the Torah, observing *shabbat* (Sabbath), celebrating the Jewish festivals, and circumcising Jewish sons were punishable by death. The enforcers were also commissioned to travel throughout the land of Israel and to insist that the Jews and especially their priests sacrifice to the Greek gods on pain of death.

The turning point in this narrative came in the little town of Modein where Mattathias, a faithful priest, refused to accept the oppressive Hellenizing policies of the Seleucids. He killed a conforming priest and the enforcers. This blow of resistance in 167 B.C. was like "the shot that sounded around the world" in the American Revolution. The rebels headed for the hills and instigated a new strategy—guerilla warfare. Almost every Jewish child knows the story of these Jewish patriots. The patriots gathered a group of like-minded insurgents who continually raided the Syrian convoys, encampments, and checkpoints. The effect of this Jewish resistance strategy was devastating for the Seleucids, who sent repeated reinforcements to counteract the terrorism of the rebels but could not succeed in routing them.

During this period, the Jewish descendantsof Abraham struggled to regain control of the land bridge. The courage of Mattathias and his five sons (John, Simon, Judas, Eleazar, and Jonathan) birthed a new spirit of

---

[5] See the helpful account in the Apocrypha at 1 Maccabees 1:54ff.

"messianism" among the descendants of Israel. When the father died in 166 B.C., the role of leadership fell upon his heroic third son, Judas, who was nicknamed "the hammerer" (*Maccabeus*). Judas led the Jewish resisters to recapture Jerusalem and rededicate or cleanse the temple on the twenty-fifth of *Kislev* (about the middle of our December in 165/164 B.C.). This act resulted in the establishment of the second major non-Mosaic festival of Hanukkah (*chanukah*) in the Jewish calendar.[6] The torches that lit up Jerusalem at the rededication celebration became symbolized in a festival of lights and in the development of a special Hanukkah candelabra. Epiphanes died in 164 B.C., and although the hostility was thereafter not quite so severe, the Syrians did not desist in their Hellenizing goals.

Accordingly, even though Rome apparently sent a missive indicating support for the Jews against the Syrians (cf. 2 Macc 11:34–38), the Jews continued in their struggle without much assistance from outsiders. When Judas was killed (160 B.C.), his place was taken by Jonathan and then by Simon (142–134 B.C.). The Seleucids were finally expelled at the beginning of Simon's priesthood. Simon's son, John Hyrcanus, was a vigorous fighter, and by the time of Jannaeus, his successor, the Jews had recaptured most of the territory once held by David, including the half-Jewish people of Idumea whom they forced to convert to Judaism (the group that would later haunt them since they were the people from whom Antipater and his despotic son, Herod, hailed). The Maccabees functioned as military leaders and high priests but refused to cross the line of uniting the high priesthood with the monarchy, even though they generally lived like kings. Such was true especially of John Hyrcanus, the first in the Hasmonean dynasty.

That situation, however, changed after John Hyrcanus died in 104 B.C. He apparently wished for his wife to succeed him, but his sons had other ideas. The two eldest were Judas (Judah) Aristobulus (104–103 B.C.) and Antigonus. Aristobulus seized power and demanded his brother appear before him. But Salome Alexandra (Salina, the wife of

---

[6] The other non-Mosaic festival involves the three days of Purim in our February, a time that recalls the attempted Jewish pogrom during the time of Esther.

Aristobulus) manipulated the order, and Antigonus came dressed in full armor and was promptly seized and eliminated. Aristobulus died soon thereafter (some suggest by intrigue but probably from a bloody congestion), and he was succeeded by Alexander Jannaeus (103–76 B.C.), a much younger son of John Hyrcanus. He had been imprisoned and conspired with the shrewd Salome Alexandra (Aristobulus's wife) to free him and enthrone him. Alexandra (like the Egyptian beauty, Cleopatra) recognized the potential for power. After the death of her husband, she married Jannaeus. The marriage was duly celebrated, but the Pharisees were distraught for a number of reasons, including the fact that the high priest was supposed to marry a virgin. Obviously Salome Alexandra hardly fit that model! The ruthless Jannaeus also claimed the right to be the "king of the Jews," and this move to unite the kingship and high priesthood was viewed as an abomination by the Pharisees. The Pharisees (who were politically and sociologically conservative but more liberal theologically) reacted to these moves of Jannaeus by opposing his political manipulations. The Sadducees, however (who were more liberal politically but theologically conservative),[7] supported Jannaeus in his moves to strengthen the Jewish state.

The conflict reached a boiling point at the Festival of Tabernacles. The Pharisees advocated the inclusion of a water ceremony within the older Mosaic celebration, but the Sadducees regarded it as being revisionist. The task of the high priest during this new ceremony was to lead a liturgical parade by carrying a tray of water from the Pool of Siloam (*Shiloah*) to the temple and presenting the water to God along with a prayerful petition for the return of the rainy season. Since Jerusalem is situated on the edge of the desert, this ceremony was vital to the Pharisees, who were mostly city dwellers and saw their cisterns empty after a hot summer. Jannaeus favored the Sadducees and instead of raising the water in prayer to God, he dumped the water at his feet. Flavius Josephus, the Jewish historian, indicates that the reaction of the Pharisees was immediate. They pelted the high priest with citrons (a small lemon-like fruit). Jannaeus quickly summoned the temple guard to protect him, and many Pharisees were slaughtered within the temple

---

[7] See the later discussion on the Pharisees and Sadducees for more clarity.

precincts. Indeed, Jannaeus later executed some 800 by crucifixion and thousands of other non-cooperating Jews. From that point, there was little cooperation between the Pharisees and the Sadducees. For Jannaeus, these moves were major political, religious, and communication disasters. Thereafter, he was unable to garner united Jewish support from the Pharisees. (As an aside, I often ask my students in New Testament to read the account of Jesus' appearance at the popular Festival of Tabernacles in John 7 [especially at verses 37–38] and in the light of Jewish history consider whether or not they think Jesus knew how to preach relevantly to the Jewish people.)

At his death, Jannaeus agreed with his cunning wife, Salome Alexandra,[8] that she should make peace with the Pharisees if she wanted to remain queen. The Pharisees welcomed her overtures for peace, and in return for the crown she agreed that political royalty should be separated from the high priesthood. She readily accepted the division since in the Jewish minds of the time a woman could hardly become a priest anyway. The arrangements were made and her older (but weaker) son, Hyrcanus II, was installed as high priest. The apportionment suited Alexandra perfectly because she was in power and could manipulate Hyrcanus. According to Josephus, she also permitted the Pharisees to exercise considerable authority in the religious realm, to the dismay of the Sadducees.[9] But the brother of Hyrcanus, Aristobulus II, thought he should have the power and curried favor with the Sadducees.

Following the death of Alexandra, Aristobulus gathered forces in an attempt to seize the crown and priesthood. After Hyrcanus was defeated in an opening battle at Jericho, he was in dread of being deposed and sought to negotiate with Aristobulus but was also open to support from others. Waiting in the wings to help him was the Idumean strong man, Antipater (the father of Herod the Great). Hyrcanus accepted Antipater's overtures and sought assistance from the Nabatean king (Aretas III) and his forces on the east side of the Jordan. This decision to align with

---

[8] For an excellent discussion on Salome Alexandra, see Kenneth Atkinson, "The Salome No One Knows," *BAR* 34/4 (July/August 2008): 60–65, 72.

[9] For further information on this period, see Josephus, *Antiquities* xiii.14–15.

Antipater, however, had far-reaching implications that the Jews would sadly come to regret.

3. *The Romans and Their Herodian Agents*

Typical of the Romans and their strategies, they waited for times of unrest and upheaval in a region, and then they moved into that area with their forces and took control.

a. Pompey, Julius Caesar, and Antipater. Pompey was already in the vicinity, and Aristobulus sought and won the support of Pompey's assistant, Scarus. Unfortunately for Aristobulus, however, when Pompey came on the scene with his forces, he did battle with the supporters of Aristobulus and defeated them in 63 B.C. Then, after consulting with both parties, Pompey was convinced that Hyrcanus would give him less trouble than Aristobulus. Accordingly, he accepted the succession of Hyrcanus and permitted him to continue as the high priest. But instead of allowing Hyrcanus to retain the kingship he had assumed on the death of Alexandra, Pompey gave him a reduced title of ethnarch (a local ethnic ruler subservient to Rome). Antipater, however, was recognized as a powerful potential ally by Pompey and was granted the actual administrative power in the land. Aristobulus, on the other hand, was treated as an enemy and shipped to Rome as a prisoner of war, thus freeing Antipater from an obvious opponent.

Pompey's conquest of Jerusalem at that point effectively ended the Jewish messianic hopes in the Hasmonean dynasty. But in his brashness, Pompey committed an act for which the Jewish people never forgave him (or the Romans). Having heard stories of how the Jewish God had defeated the Egyptians centuries before, Pompey was anxious to see "this god," assuming that a statute of him would be housed in the Jewish temple. Despite the pleas of the Jews, he forcibly marched into the Most Holy Place of the temple and was shocked to find nothing there but a great stone block (the ark had been lost during the Babylonian conquest in 586/585 B.C.). When Pompey emerged from the Jewish sacred shrine, about all he could say was that the Jews were "atheists"—which for him meant they had no visible god! The pathos in the Jewish sense of lost political independence and their grief at the desecration of the temple by the Romans is expressed vividly in the Pharisaic *Psalms of Solomon*, which was written in the mid-first century B.C.[10]

When Julius Caesar gained power in Rome, Pompey's supporters were either eliminated or lost authority (48 B.C.), and Pompey himself was assassinated in Egypt. That change of power left Antipater without Roman support in Judea. But the power broker of Idumea was not without a strategy and boldly approached Caesar, declaring his loyalty to Rome and his new leader. The result was that Caesar promoted Antipater to Procurator of Judea. At the behest of Antipater, Caesar tried to conciliate the Jews by remitting many of the harsh taxes on them as a conquered people. Caesar also had the Jews declared to be an *ethnos*, an accepted ethnic group within the Roman judicial and religious systems. That declaration was exceedingly significant because it entitled the Jews to their own court system on matters not touching Roman policy, and it opened the way for them to retain their religious practices (a situation that would later greatly affect the Christians). In spite of the Roman concessions, however, the Jews continued to hate Antipater and regarded him merely as a deceptive Idumean Roman puppet.

The security of Antipater did not last long, and he was again threatened as a result of the assassination of Caesar by Brutus and Cassius in 44 B.C. Antipater quickly realized his need to change loyalties again, but with Cassius in the region and two new powerful "consuls" (military supermen) arising in Rome (Mark Antony and Octavian), the situation in Judea was chaotic. Unfortunately for Antipater, before he could regroup, he was murdered by his enemies in 43 B.C. Then Brutus and Cassius were defeated by Antony and Octavian in the decisive battle at Philippi in Macedonia (42 B.C.) that spelled the end of the old Roman Republic.

b. Mark Antony, Octavian, and Herod the Great. The demise of Antipater was followed by the ascendancy of his son Herod, who like his father was exceedingly shrewd in his dealings with Rome. He won the confidence of Mark Antony, who controlled Egypt and the southern half of the Mediterranean, but Herod had little respect for the wily Egyptian

---

[10] See James H. Charlesworth, ed., *O. T. Pseudepigrapha*, vol. 2 (Garden City NY: Doubleday & Company, 1983) 639–70.

beauty, Cleopatra. Like his father, the son also suffered from the changes in the Roman political arena. His patron, Antony, was probably Rome's most brilliant and able general, but he fell to the craftiness of Cleopatra, and in that fall he lost the admiration of his trusted soldiers as well as the respect of the citizens of Rome. Thus, in the great Mediterranean battle at Actium in 31 B.C., Antony lost to Octavian, who later became known as Augustus. The defeat of Antony created a great blow to the status of his loyal supporter, Herod, who quickly realized that his position and life were in jeopardy. Following the pattern of his father, Herod boldly traveled to Rhodes and pledged his loyalty to Octavian. He declared that as he had been unquestionably faithful to Antony, his former Roman authority, he would likewise serve his new master. Octavian was so taken with Herod's brash approach that he accepted his allegiance and ultimately established him as the unquestioned Roman authority in the land of Israel (the Roman province of *Palestina*).

Scores of books have been written about this megalomaniac who feared for his safety but who arguably became the greatest builder of his time. Like an ancient potentate, Herod acquired ten wives and had many children in his attempt to appease disparate elements throughout his realm and beyond. His favorite wife was Mariamne, a Maccabean princess whom he thought would bring him acceptance with the Jews. But as an Idumean, he was badly out of touch with Jewish thinking. Thus, in an effort to forestall the possibility that the son of the princess (Herod Aristobulus) might contemplate usurping his place, Herod killed him, but his son who would become Herod Agrippa I escaped. Along the way, Herod disposed of three other sons of various wives. He also had Mariamne's brother, the high priest, drowned in the pool during a swimming party at the winter palace in Jericho. Captivated by his own importance, Herod named his sons "Herod" in honor of himself. Accordingly, we are forced with the biblical writers to distinguish between all of them by referring to their additional designations, such as Archelaus, Antipas, and Philip (of which there were more than two).

Herod never forgot the Jewish assassination of his father and the early attempts to eliminate him before he escaped to the security of the Romans. Thus, many of his great building accomplishments were actually oriented to his own safety and to providing fortified shelters for him during possible Jewish uprisings.[11] Among these protective sanctuaries to the south and east were the Herodian, Masada, and Machaerus (on the east side of the Jordan). To the north was Sabaste (a rebuilt Samaria named for Augustus) and the palatial fortress in the magnificent harbor city of Caesarea Maratima. In Jerusalem itself, he built several fortresses, including the observatory fortress of the Antonio (named after his patron Mark Antony) on the northern wall of the temple and the Citadel on the western wall of Jerusalem. But Herod was also architecturally both creative and practical. His harbor at Caesarea still amazes archaeologists today, and the feat of developing underwater hardening cement is still a wonder. Indeed, while I was teaching in Israel, Jewish archaeologists dumped some great stones (like those used by Herod for the breakwater of his harbor) into the Mediterranean near Caesarea to test whether they would remain, but in no time they disappeared, lost in the backwash of the currents. Herod's aqueducts in Caesarea for bringing water from the Carmel range and in Jerusalem for bringing water from the springs in Bethlehem were also no minor feats. For those of us who have been involved in archaeological work in Israel, his winter palace at Jericho, his three-tiered palace on Masada, and his magnificent palace on the shores of the Mediterranean at Caesarea testify to his great talent for assembling brilliant contractors who could build awe-inspiring structures.

The Romans did not usually bestow the title of "king" on national leaders of conquered people unless they were both unquestionably loyal and clearly able to maintain the peace (the *Pax Romana*). But in spite of all his eccentricities, Herod certainly earned the title Herod "the Great." For many readers of the Bible, most of what they know about Herod is that the Jews were exceedingly fearful of him (Matt 2:3) and that he killed the infants of Bethlehem (2:16–18). These reports certainly fit his historical profile. But it is imperative for readers to understand more about this

---

[11] See T. Mueller, "The Holy Land's Visionary Builder: Herod," in *National Geographic* 214/6 (December 2008): 34–59. See also my discussions on Herod's buildings in Gerald L. Borchert, *The Lands of the Bible* (Cleveland TN: Mossy Creek Press, 2011) 25, 40–42, 47, 66, 78, 87, 93–94, 167.

man than those few verses one encounters about him in the New Testament.

c. Augustus, the Herodian Successors, and the Setting for the Coming of Jesus. I must pause at this point before mentioning the death of Herod and the birth of Jesus to reflect briefly on Octavian, who was later declared to be the supreme "Augustus." Roman poets lauded him, including the renowned Virgil in his fourth *Eclogue.* He described Augustus as "sent from heaven," and his reign was regarded as the "golden age" of Rome marked by the "reign of peace in the world."[12] Roman historians like Seutonius detailed Octavian's birth as marked by wonders in the heavens and reported that he was regarded as the "son of Apollo."[13] Contemporary writers remind us that Octavian declared that the presence of a "comet" at the death of Julius was "proof of his adopted father's divinity," namely that "Julius ascended after his death into heaven to sit at the right hand of the god Zeus."[14] Such an argument, of course, meant that Augustus himself was the "son of a god." Indeed, in the collection known as the *Res Gestae,* Augustus in a propaganda move proclaimed that the Senate had commemorated "my return, ordered an altar to Pax Augusta to be consecrated in the Campus Martius…[and decreed] that the magistrates, priests, and Vestal Virgins should celebrate an anniversary sacrifice."[15] He was in fact declared "the most divine Caesar" and was acknowledged to be "equal to the Beginning of all things" because before him all things were tending to chaos. With his coming, it was said, the whole world experienced the "beginning of good news, *euangelion,* concerning him, therefore [it was proclaimed] let a new era begin from his birth."[16] For many Christians

---

[12] See Virgil, *Eclogue IV,* 5–23. Readers can consult anthologies such as C. K. Barrett, ed., *N. T. Background Documents* (New York: Harper & Brothers, 1956) 4–5 for such records.

[13] See Seutonius, *Divus Augustus* in *Lives of the Caesars,* iii.94.3–4. Readers can consult anthologies like David R. Cartlidge and David L Dungan, eds., *Documents for the Study of the Gospels* (Philadelphia: Fortress Press, 1980) 132–33.

[14] See Mike Erre, *The Jesus of Suburbia: Have we Tamed the Son of God to Fit Our Lifestyles?* (Nashville: W. Publishing Group, 2006) 4–5.

[15] See the *Res Gestae,* 8–11 in Barrett, *N. T. Background Documents,* 2.

[16] From an inscription dated about 9 B.C., see Richard A. Horsley, *Jesus and Empire* (Minneapolis: Fortress Press, 2003) 24–25.

who are unaware of such records, these statements at first glance may be disturbing since they seem rather similar to the biblical texts such as John 1:1–18; Matthew 2:2; Luke 2:10–14; and Hebrews 1:3. Yet the greater reality is that the world and the time that cradled Jesus was an electrifying period that anticipated the dawning of a new era. That era was indeed initiated by God's divine intervention in sending the Savior of the world (cf. Gal 4:4).

Now we return to Herod. He died on the Ides of March in 4 B.C., which has created another concern for some Christians in reference to our calendars. Jesus was not born in A.D. 1 (or 1 C.E. [the common era]), there being no zero in the early analysis. But as I have told my students repeatedly, the mistake is the result of poor calculation on the part of Dionysius Exegiuus (for our purposes I call him Dennis the Little) in the sixth century of our era. Starting with the Roman calendar A.U.C. (*ab urbe condita* = "from the founding of the city [of Rome]"), Dennis figured that 753 A.U.C. would have been the date of Jesus' birth, but in actuality it was at least five years earlier (749) and probably six or seven years earlier (we will return to this matter later).

Herod's death ended an era of a unified *Palestina*. Herod left instructions that at his death, scores of eminent Jews were to be put to death so that all Palestine would mourn at the same time. Those instructions were clearly not implemented. In addition, Herod's will proposed that the ruthless Archelaus (cf. Matt 2:22)—his favorite son by Malthace, the Samaritan—should be his successor. The Romans, however, did not let their captured subjects make such decisions. Instead, in reviewing the situation at Herod's death, Augustus and his advisors were not convinced that any of the sons were as trustworthy as their father, and so the territory of the province was split into three parts. The Romans assigned the southern part of the province (the largest portion), namely Judea and Samaria, to Archelaus and designated him merely as an ethnarch (the lowest office because a delegation of the Jewish emissaries reported his irrational cruelty to Rome). The central part of Galilee and Perea went to his full brother, Antipas, as a tetrarch (one step above an ethnarch), and the northern area of Iturea, Trachonitis, and related regions was given to their half-brother Philip (by

Cleopatra of Jerusalem) as a tetrarch.[17] None of the sons were elevated to the position of king.

When Archelaus returned to Israel, he was exceedingly bitter and killed many of his opponents both in Judea and Samaria.[18] Archelaus's ruthlessness is noted by Matthew when Joseph refuses to return to Judea but heads for the realm of his brother, Antipas, in Galilee (Matt 2:22). The Romans received a second delegation of Jews concerning the bitter actions of Archelaus and the growth of hostility in the region, and they exiled the tyrant to their "Siberia" (the wilds of Gaul) in A.D. 6, thus ending Herodian rule in that southern area during the time of Jesus. In his place, the Romans began the appointment of Roman military officers as governors (procurators/*praefects*) in the sub-province.

The fifth of these governors was Pontius Pilate (A.D. 26–36), who was appointed by Emperor Tiberias and who almost immediately upon his arrival alienated the Jews by bringing insignia of Caesar (ensigns) into Jerusalem during the night. When the Jews protested, Pilate threatened them with death, but they all kneeled down awaiting their end, whereupon Pilate relented.[19] The relationship between him and the Jews remained strained during his entire tenure, and the Jews used this tension during the condemnation of Jesus by questioning whether he was in fact a "friend of Caesar" (cf. John 19:12), a technical status that his sponsor Sejanus had acquired and that Pilate clearly desired.

d. The Roman Provincial System. To understand the Roman provincial system, it is important at this point to take a brief digression. The Romans under Augustus were masters of government and divided their provincial system into two segments: senatorial provinces and imperial provinces. As the system reached its zenith in New Testament times, the Romans had thirty-two provinces. Eleven of these provinces were administered by the Senate and were generally regarded as "peaceful."

---

[17] See Josephus, *Antiquities* 17.11.1–5.

[18] It may be helpful to remind readers of the intriguing brief statements of Jesus in Luke 19:12 and 27 concerning the nobleman who went to a foreign country to receive a kingship. When the nobleman returned, he quickly dispatched the lives of his enemies. The statements that seem to come out of nowhere in the parable certainly must have their reference point to this event.

[19] See the accounts of Josephus in *Antiquities* 18.3.1 and *Jewish Wars* 2.9.2–4.

They were governed locally by a "proconsul" who was a senior senator and was normally appointed for one year with the possibility of a reappointment for another year. He had at his disposal a small army for policing the region, and he was expected to collect the taxes for Rome and also enhance the collection as a means for ensuring a good retirement for himself. Two such governors/proconsuls are mentioned in the New Testament: Sergius Paulus who was assigned to Cyprus at Paphos (see Acts 13:7), and Gallio who was assigned to Achaia with its capital at Corinth (see Acts 18:12). An inscription discovered at the sacred city of Delphi mentions Lucius Junius Gallio as proconsul of Achaia in the 26th acclamation of Claudius Caesar. This reference has furnished scholars with an important tool in dating the presence of the Apostle Paul at Corinth sometime around A.D. 52–54.[20]

In contrast to the senatorial provinces, the imperial provinces were under the strict authority of the emperor, and the governors, who were leaders in the military, held their offices at the will of the emperor for as long as he wished. The titles and positions of these governors usually varied in importance according to their rank. Among those mentioned in the New Testament holding superior governorships is Quirinius, who held the high rank of "legate" as the governor of the huge province of Syria (cf. Luke 2:2). These legates were dispatched with large armies for the purpose of quelling major difficulties or of collecting taxes. Those in charge of troublesome sub-provinces were designated as "praefects" or "procurators," and these officers included Pontius Pilate, the fifth procurator (cf. Luke 3:1; 23:1; etc.), as well as Felix (cf. Acts 23:26 ff.), and Porcius Festus (Acts 24:27ff.), the fourth and fifth in the second series of procurators after Herod Agrippa I.

e. The Herodians and the Procurators. The two northern provinces remained in control of the Herodian sons during the lifetime of Jesus. When the irenic Philip died in A.D. 34, his region was added to the authority of Pilate, but in A.D. 36 Pilate's sponsor, strong-man Sejanus, fell out of favor in Rome and Pilate was recalled from the province. In

---

[20] For a translation and reconstruction of the Delphic inscription, see Barrett, *N. T. Background Documents*, 48–49. Acclamations were made periodically in honor of a reigning caesar.

A.D. 37 the territory was assigned by the new emperor Gaius Caligula (the grandson of Augustus) to his friend, Agrippa I, the Hasmonean grandson of Herod the Great, who was the son of Herod Aristobulus by Marianne. He was made "king" like his grandfather. The Jews rejoiced in his appointment since he was a descendant of the Maccabees, and they hoped for further indications that their heritage was being restored. Their hopes began to return in earnest when the jealous Herodias (wife of Herod Antipas and divorced wife of the other Herod Philip [Boethus]—the instigator of John the Baptist's death [cf. Matt 14:1–12; Mark 6:14–29]) pushed her husband to seek a kingship like her brother Agrippa I. She did not realize that her brother had poisoned the ear of Caligula by suggesting that Antipas was collecting and storing arms. Accordingly, instead of gaining more power and prestige, Antipas and Herodias in A.D. 39 were shown the door to exile in Gaul, and the territory of Antipas was added to that of Herod Agrippa I.

Then Caligula became enamored with his own importance and took to himself divine accolades (much like Agrippa I is said to have done in Acts 12:22). When Gaius Caligula heard that the Jews resisted honoring him as a god in Egypt, he ordered that a statue of himself be set up in the Jerusalem temple, but his friend Agrippa pleaded for him to change his mind. The emperor agreed in part but insisted that shrines be built to honor him outside of Jerusalem. Fortunately for the Jews, Caligula was assassinated before the order was effected, but Agrippa at that point had also been given control of the southern third of the province. So, in A.D. 41 the entire province of *Palestina* including Judea and Samaria was reunified under Agrippa I (a descendant of the Maccabees) who sought in many ways to please the Jews (cf. Acts 12:1–3).

Unfortunately for the Jews, however, Agrippa I died early, apparently of some horrible internal distress. Luke, the Christian writer, identified Agrippa as "eaten by worms" (Acts 12:23), an ancient designation for a divine curse upon tyrants, such as was applied to Herod the Great. Based on Josephus's record of Herod's putrid smelly body, physicians today suspect that he either suffered from chronic kidney disease or a case of Founier's gangrene (rare in our time) perhaps brought on by gonorrhea. The agony suffered by Herod, Paul Maier suggested, turned the "house of Herod into a can of worms."[21]

When Agrippa I died in A.D. 44, he left a young son who would eventually become Agrippa II, the one before whom Paul appeared in Acts 25:13–26:32. But the new emperor, Claudius, a brilliant but physically challenged statesman, was hesitant to take chances immediately on the seventeen-year-old and placed the entire province under a second set of procurators. In A.D. 53, however, Claudius gave control of the province's northern third to Agrippa II, and in A.D. 57 and 61 he gave over some parts of the central third. But Judea and Samaria were never again returned to the Herodians.

f. The Downward Spiral of Events in Palestina. The second set of procurators (governors) were hardly the best representatives that Rome produced, but Palestine was also regarded by most Romans as among the least attractive assignments (indeed, the dregs). So it is not surprising that Cumanus and Felix were both self-centered and incompetent procurators. In the fifties under Cumanus, during a temple Passover celebration, one of the Romans on duty on the wall displayed his disgust for the Jews by pretending to defecate on them. They responded by pelting the soldier with rocks. The troops were immediately summoned, and many Jews were slaughtered in the riot.[22] Felix was hardly better in controlling the situation, and his morals were questionable by any description. After he divorced his wife, he married Drusilla (Acts 24:24), the sister of both Agrippa II and Agrippa's seedy sister Bernice, who married their uncle Herod Chalcia (25:13). The inciting of negative reactions among the Jews by these procurators certainly contributed to the formation of Jewish bands of assassins known as *sicarii* ("dagger men" from *sicae*, cf. Acts 21:38) who were insurrectionists and frequently stabbed Romans with weapons concealed under their cloaks.

Rome sought to rectify the dismal situation by removing Felix and replacing him with the more competent Festus, but by that time the

---

[21] See Amanda Onion's report, "Researchers Diagnose Herod the Great: Miserable End," 24 January 2002, http://abcnews.go.com/Technology/story?id=98107&page=1 (accessed 28 January 2002).

[22] See Josephus, *Jewish Wars* 2.12.1, who reported that ten thousand Jews were killed.

downward spiral was practically irreversible. Anarchy began to reign in Jerusalem and throughout the entire province. The Sadducean high priest at the time, Annas (the son of the "godfather" Annas), was as scheming as his father.[23] He eliminated those whom he regarded as opponents to his authority, including Christians such as James, the half-brother of Jesus.[24] The Pharisees were distressed by his dismal actions and sought recourse from both Agrippa II and the then-new procurator, Albinus, who eventually had this Annas deposed. But the situation in Jerusalem and throughout the province continued to deteriorate into chaos as bands of Jewish radicals rose in defiance against Rome.

Gessius Florus, a ruthless reprobate himself, replaced Albinus in A.D. 64, and with his coming the end was predictable. He plundered the temple to pay the taxes, and when the Jews protested he countered the resistance with fierce reprisals including a host of crucifixions. The slaughter of Jews by Gentiles in Caesarea (Maritima) united resistance in the north. In Jerusalem the situation became violent. Eleazar, the son of Annas, mounted a counter move in the temple by terminating the daily sacrifices for the emperor (clearly a sign to Rome of rebellion). The moderate Jews, including the Pharisees, were unable to stem the tide of hostility, especially when Eleazar and the Zealots captured the garrison in Jerusalem and executed the Romans there. The reaction in Antioch was immediate. The legate/governor, Cestius Gallus, mobilized his troops to quash the rebellion, but he was unprepared for the fierce resistance and was defeated.

Word of the Jewish victory spread throughout the province and beyond with the result that patriots emerged from the hills and valleys of the province. A rebel army was quickly formed to kick the foreign

---

[23] Annas, the "godfather," who conducted a preliminary trial of Jesus (cf. John 18:13), had earlier been deposed by the Romans, but he kept his title since high priests were so chosen by the Jews for life. During his lifetime he controlled his priestly family, including his son-in-law and successor, Caiaphas, who arranged for the condemnation of Jesus (cf. John 11:49–53; 18:14, 24, 28; Matt 26:57–68; cf. Mark 14:55–65 and Luke 22:66–71).

[24] While in some Christian traditions Mary is said to have remained a perpetual virgin, James was probably not merely a cousin of Jesus as is claimed but his half-brother by Joseph.

"dogs" (a term used for Gentiles) out of the country with "generals" appointed in each region. The messianic dream of a free state was reborn, and moderate Jews, Christians, and those who cooperated with the Romans fearfully fled the rebellious centers.

But the dream of victory was short lived because the new emperor, Nero, dispatched his supreme commander, Vespasian, with a huge force of 60,000 elite fighting men to Caesarea in order to stamp out the revolution. Although the Jews fought bravely, their defeats multiplied.

One story emerged (which could be somewhat apocryphal) involving the commanders of the north who recognized that their fight was hopeless. They gathered in a cave to plan their demise. In typical Jewish fashion they chose lots for the one who would kill them and then prayerfully committed suicide (similar to the later experience on Masada). The lot apparently fell to Flavius Josephus, the commander of the forces at Caesarea. He killed his colleagues as agreed but then failed to kill himself and instead surrendered to Vespasian. In the interview that followed, he assumed the posture of a seer and predicted that the commander would shortly become emperor. When news arrived shortly thereafter that Nero had been murdered, Vespasian quickly assembled his troops and returned to Rome to claim the purple robe. He rewarded Josephus for his prediction and gave him a handsome retirement, enabling him to pursue his avocation of writing a history of the Jewish people as well as his account of the Jewish War. While Josephus wrote his works to affirm the Jewish ways for his Roman readers, the Jews did not widely accept his works because he was despised as a traitor. The Christians, however, were the ones who preserved his fascinating writings, which have become a strategic source for our understanding of this entire period.

The hasty departure of Vespasian and his Roman forces was viewed by the Jews as another miracle of divine deliverance. But their hopes were soon dashed because, as soon as Vespasian had secured his position in Rome, he dispatched his son Titus with a full force to return to Palestine with the singular purpose of wiping out Jewish resistance. When the fall of Jerusalem and the destruction of the temple finally came in A.D. 70, it was not the Romans but the Jews themselves who killed their despised high priest and his clan, holding them responsible for the loss of Jerusalem and the temple. The tragic story of the final days of Jerusalem is recorded by Josephus. People did the unimaginable to avoid starvation (drinking their urine and eating babies). Josephus also argued that Titus did not intend to destroy the magnificent temple, but in storming it the buildings were torched by overanxious soldiers, and Titus knew he could not then extinguish the flames. It is impossible to confirm this story in Josephus's writings.

g. The Significance of Jerusalem's Fall. The fall of Jerusalem in A.D. 70 was exceedingly important, and its significance needs to be understood by contemporary readers. From the Roman point of view, it was obviously a strategic event. Indeed, it was so significant that it was marked by a triumphal arch dedicated to Titus that was erected in the central precincts of the Roman Forum. The Romans had won many battles, but triumphal arches were not built for most of those victories. It is somewhat like the Viet Nam memorial in Washington, D.C. Israel was a mini-state, but it represented an incredible problem for Rome. The Romans honestly believed that the victory (*"Judaea Capta"* minted on coins) and the arch would serve as an indication of the ultimate power of Rome and a warning to all subservient states of their destiny if they challenged mighty Rome.

For the Jews, the fall of Jerusalem and the destruction of the temple meant that they had lost their center of worship. But the destruction did not mean the end of Judaism because the Jews had developed an alternate institution that enabled the people to continue their faith. That institution was the *synagogue*. During the siege of Jerusalem, the elite Jewish rabbis had earlier left or escaped through a hidden tunnel. Then, during a series of council meetings (circa A.D. 75ff.) sometimes designated by the term "Bet Din of Jamnia" (the Jewish site of Yavneh, near Joppa and modern Tel Aviv), they continued the long process of defining and reformulating their decisions for the faithful of "Judaism." The codification of their "opinions" was ultimately published as the *Mishnah*. Later, the rabbinic center was moved to the interior region of Sephoris and Tiberias, where it continued for several centuries.

For the Christians, the fall of Jerusalem represented a release from the restrictive bonds of Judaism. The apocalyptic statements of Jesus (cf. Mark 13:14; Matt 24:15; and Luke 21:20) that predicted the coming of a "desolating abomination" like the one noted in Daniel 11:31 were taken seriously by early Christians in *Palestina* so that when the Roman legions began their war on the Jews, the Christians in the region retreated to the Decapolis (the ten free Greek cities), particularly in Pella, and were not found in Jerusalem during the crisis or the fall (cf. Mark 13:14–19). Moreover, when the rabbis added the "curse of the heretics" to the eighteen benedictions,[25] which the Jews repeated in their synagogues, it was then used as a test for judging "true" Jewish people and as a basis for excommunicating Christians.[26] The curse thus became a convenient means to designate Jewish Christians as being illegitimate Jews and thus no longer protected them under Jewish rights that excluded Jews from the necessity of engaging in Roman worship practices to prove their loyalty. Such a removal of status as members of a protected *religio licita* (a licensed religion) meant that the Jews could report Christians to the Roman authorities as lacking in patriotism. That scenario soon led to the persecution of Christians and undoubtedly was the reason why John in Revelation condemned the Jewish institution as a "synagogue of Satan" (Rev 3:9; 4:9).[27]

h. The Continuing Resistance and the End. But the Jewish resistance did not end with the fall of Jerusalem. The zealots continued their opposition in various places as they seized fortresses like the Herodian and moved to the hills and caves such as those around Qumran for protection. The final phase of the war was fought at Masada, where the rebels/patriots were highly protected from attack. At Masada the possibility of starvation or lack of water was exceedingly remote because of the magnificent storage facilities built by Herod the Great. The

---

[25] For the addition of the curse to the twelfth benediction, see Barrett, *N. T. Background Documents*, 166–67.

[26] The story of the blind man being excommunicated from the synagogue for confessing Jesus in John 9:22, 34 was probably viewed by early believers as a pattern for the treatment experienced by Christians in later decades at the time when the Gospel was written.

[27] For further insights on this issue, see the description of the testing of Christians in Bithynia (Asia Minor) by the Romans in the correspondence between Pliny the Younger and the emperor, Trajan, about the first decade of the second century in Henry Bettenson, ed., *Documents of the Christian Church* (London: Oxford University Press, 1943) 3–6.

fascinating story of resistance at Masada is today stamped on the memories of most loyal Jews, and it is important to note that on its flat summit, currently many of Israel's new recruits after basic training are inducted into military service with the vow that "Never again shall Masada fall!" Because the ancient fighters were able to resist the Romans scaling the fortress, a plan was devised in which the Romans used captured Jews as slaves to support building a ramp to the top of Masada so that a siege machine could enable entrance through the perimeter wall. As the Roman plan proved to be successful and the Jewish zealots refused to kill their fellow Jews by hurling rocks or hot oil and hot water on them, the resisters on Masada concluded that their only course of action was to kill their families so they would not be molested and paraded in victory as captives of mighty Rome. Eleazar ben Ya'ir and the rebel leaders met and drew lots to determine the man who would kill the rest of the patriots and also kill himself in a sacrificial suicide.[28] When the Romans reached the top, they were deprived of their victory celebration and found plenty of food and water, but all the zealots were dead except for a woman and some children who had hidden in a storage facility.

The Romans expected that the Jewish resistance had thus reached its end. But to their dismay, it rose again under Simon ben-Kosebah, who became known as *Bar Kokbah* (son of a star; cf. Num 24:17). He and his rebels mounted a substantial fight against Rome but were finally eliminated in A.D. 135. The Romans under Hadrian decided to settle the problem by completely reconstructing Jerusalem as a Roman colony and eliminating it as the center for the Jews. They rebuilt it as a Roman city and named it *Aelia Capitolina*. It was configured according to the typical grid plan with a magnificent cardo (main street) and a temple dedicate to Hadrian. The Jews were strictly forbidden on pain of death to enter their former holy city. Thus, the Jewish hope for an independent state with its capital at Jerusalem ended until the twentieth century.

---

[28] For a helpful study on Ben Ya'ir, the patriots, and the archaeological work done at Masada including the finding of the possible ostraca used in the casting of the lots, see Yigael Yadin's well-known report on *Masada; Herod's Fortress and the Zealots' Last Stand* (London: Cardinal–Sphere Books, 1973) especially at 195–99.

Recommended for Further Study

Barrett, C. K., editor. *N. T. Background Documents.* New York: Harper & Row, 1956.

Davies, W. D., L. Finkelstein et al., editors. *The Cambridge History of Judaism.* 4 volumes. London: Cambridge U. Press, 1984–2006.

Horsley, R. A. *Jesus and the Empire.* Minneapolis: Fortress, 2003.

Schürer, E. *A History of the Jewish People in Time of Jesus Christ.* 5 volumes. Peabody MA: Hendrickson, 1995.

Whiston, W. *The Works of Josephus*, complete and unabridged, new updated edition [with several dissertations added]. Peabody MA: Hendrickson, 1987. For a scholarly Greek and English translation of Josephus, consult the Loeb Classical Library in thirteen volumes published by Harvard University Press.

THE PALESTINIAN SETTING AND THE VARIOUS
ASPECTS OF JUDAISM IN THE TIME OF JESUS

Having concluded our brief survey of the history of the region that prepared for the cradling of Jesus and the beginning of the people known as Christians, I turn now to focus on the setting of Palestine together with the people known as Jews and their ways in the time of Jesus.

1. The Geographical Context

The land of Palestine, as I have noted earlier, is a narrow land bridge between Egypt and Mesopotamia, which should suggest to the reader that the area is a mountainous country. Indeed, there are few places that one can travel for any distance without negotiating significant hills and deep cuts in the terrain except (i) in the coastal plains that once were swampy, (ii) in the great Jezreel Valley north of the Carmel range, (iii) in the steadily falling Jordan Valley, and (iv) in a few other smaller plains.

a. The Topography. From the top of Mount Hermon in the north at approximately 9,100 feet above sea level (snow-capped much of the year and open to skiing), the Jordan Valley continually drops through the Hulah Valley so that by the time the Jordan River reaches the sea of Galilee (Kinneret or Tiberias), the great rift has fallen to nearly 700 feet below sea level with the hills around it soaring to more than 1,500 feet above sea level, making the area appear like great bowl where the winds howl through the passes and still today can often whip the sea into fierce waves that swamp even modern motor boats (which testifies to the disciples' earlier fears). From that point the river continues to drop until it reaches the Dead Sea, which is more than 1,290 feet below sea level at its surface, and the deepest pit of the sea plunges another 1,300 feet. In this region is located the site of *Sedom* (perhaps Sodom), regarded as the lowest spot on the earth's surface at 390 meters below sea level.[1]

This Rift Valley, so designated, is part of one of the deepest cracks in the earth's surface where the meeting of two tectonic plates has produced what is popularly known as part of the pan-African fault that runs through the Gulf of Aqaba/Elat and joins the crack at Lake Victoria in Africa. (To swim as I have done off the tip of Sinai at Sharem esh-Sheikh is to see marine life similar in colors to those I saw at the Great Barrier Reef off the coast of Australia.)

b. The Road Systems. Running north to south through the region are two major ancient highways and a third more local one. (i) On the west near the Mediterranean Sea is the great Via Maris that joins Mesopotamia with Egypt and that was traversed by countless armies as they frequently met for battle. Seeking to stop foreign forces crossing Israel's territory, Solomon is described in the Bible as fortifying three important sites on the highway (cf. 1 Kgs 9:15): *Hazor* in the north on the edge of the Hulah Valley to halt if possible the Syria and Mesopotamia armies; *Meggido* in the center at the major pass through the Carmel mountain range where much blood was spilled and where the faithful Josiah was slain by the army of Pharaoh Neco (2 Kgs 23:29); and *Gezer* in the south to slow the advance of the Egyptians. (ii) On the west side of the Jordan rift running through the Jordanian highlands (the Gilead) is the ancient caravan route called the King's Highway where Joseph was sold to mercenaries and carried off to Egypt (Gen 37:25–28). (iii) In middle of the country is the so-called Ridge Road or the Way of the Patriarchs. It is the route Jesus no doubt took as he traveled through Samaria and visited with the woman at Jacob's well in Sychar (John 4:1–42).

c. The Climate. With such a variety in geography, you undoubtedly guessed that there are great differences in climate throughout this region. One can experience blistering heat and chilling cold on the same day in the desert (the Negev and Sinai), and when the torrid *Hamseen*

---

[1] See Zev Vilnay, *The Guide to Israel* (Jerusalem: Ahiever, 1978) 13.

winds are blowing in from Arabia, I have witnessed the blossoming desert dry up in a single day (cf. Isa 40:7). But Jerusalem and other places are in the mountains, and it can be both windy and cold. Moreover, I have seen several inches of snow on a winter day in Jerusalem, but it can also melt quickly when the sun comes out. At Mount Carmel it can rain more than 50 inches a year, but some places near the Dead Sea may receive only 4 to 8 inches of rain in a year.

Along the Jordan rift one will encounter many deep sandy "wadis," which are dry riverbeds that look like they have been parched for years. But if a rain comes, the water will rush down through those wadis (valleys) like torrents because the sandy ground will not absorb the water. So the people understood what Jesus meant when he said it is foolish to build a house on the sandy soil because when the rains come the house will collapse (cf. Matt 7:26–27).

2. A Brief Introduction to Most of the People and Where and How They Lived

The land of Palestine during the time of Jesus was primarily a rural setting in contrast to much of modern Israel and the Palestinian territories of today. The estimates of the local population at that time range anywhere from 700 thousand to 2 million, but the smaller estimate may be closer to reality. In addition to this number, one should add hundreds of visitors to the "Holy Land" and many Romans who were stationed there to "keep the peace" and to ensure that the taxes were raised.

The primary cities and towns of Jesus' day would include such places as Jerusalem, the great sea port of Caesarea Maritima (and its little sister, Joppa), the prosperous Zippori (Sepphoris) in Galilee (near the little towns of Cana and Nazareth), Caesarea Philippi (ancient Panias, the old worship center of Pan, near the ancient site of Dan in the north at the foot of Mt. Hermon and at the headwaters of the Jordan River), Capernaum (on the north edge of the Sea/Lake of Galilee/ Kinneret/Tiberias) and its sister towns of Bethsaida and Chorazim, the growing Gentile city of Tiberias (on the west side of the Sea), Beth Shean (the only Decapolis city on the west side of the Jordan), Sebaste (ancient Samaria near Sychar and ancient Shechem), Jericho (the winter playground near the Dead Sea), Hebron (and small towns such as Bethlehem to the south of Jerusalem), and Azotus (ancient Ashdod and the Philistine cities on the Via Maris, the ancient highway by the sea). These centers represented the larger population areas.

Most of the people, the *am haeretz* (the people of the land), however, lived in small villages and eked out a living. They were basically farmers (raising grapes, olives, vegetables, and grains), sheep herders, fishermen, and small craftsmen such as carpenters, stone cutters, and builders. Many, however, did not even have regular work and sought day jobs to finance their living (cf. the parable of Jesus in Matt 20:1–15). Many were exceedingly poor and sick. Most were taxed beyond their means and on the verge of slavery or a debtor's prison (cf. the story of two debtors in Matt 18:23–34).

Often these peasants felt that their situation was hopeless, and they longed for a change. They prayed for relief from their plights and sought liberation from oppressors, whether they were Romans, Herodians, or the Jewish religious elite. They dreamed of the coming of a "messianic savior" who would provide them with physical sustenance and offer them a future. They would readily join groups whose leaders promised them at least some type of hope. Readers need to recognize the implications of the large crowds that followed this Jesus who fed them and preached to them (cf. Matt 14:13–21 and 15:32–38). The crowds were like many in the world today who are poor and ill and who grasp at any promise of hope, even joining terrorist organizations in the expectation of a new life—if not for themselves, then for their families or a wonderful life hereafter.

The stories and teachings of Jesus frequently deal with such people who lacked adequate food and medical attention. There is little doubt that the poor and those who were ill perceived Jesus as a captivating answer to their prayers and heartfelt longings. He must have seemed to be such an amazing contrast to the religious leaders of their day. As you read the Gospels, then, please do not forget that Jesus and the evangelists dealt with people who probably had needs far beyond most that you normally encounter unless you have lived in the Middle East, India, Haiti, or other places where poverty is rampant. When you read the Gospels, you might get a quick impression from the stories that most of the people in Palestine would have been members of the various parties such as the Pharisees or Sadducees or that they were members of a profession such as scribes, lawyers, or tax collectors. But it is imperative to understand that these people were actually the elite and represented much less than 10 percent of the general population. Most people worked with their hands and were therefore disparagingly designated by the rabbis as the *am haeretz*, "the people of the land." They were viewed as "unstudied and amateurish/ignorant" (*agrammatoi kai idiotai*) like Peter and John (cf. Acts 4:13), but they were the people who heard Jesus gladly (cf. Mark 12:37). If you keep in mind this picture of the common people as you read the Gospels, it should give you an important perspective on Jesus. It could even change the way you think about Jesus!

3. The Language Context

During the time of Jesus, many strangers visited the temple mount and stayed in Jerusalem on a regular basis (but especially during the great festivals such as Passover and Tabernacles) as can be witnessed when Peter preached his Pentecost sermon (see Acts 2:9–11). Many of the poor people in Palestine probably used *Aramaic* (a cognate or related language to Hebrew) in their homes. They would attend synagogue services where the Hebrew Scriptures were read and where the comments in the service were spoken in Aramaic. This interpretive or commentary pattern in the synagogue led the rabbis to develop a series of Aramaic Targums (interpretive commentaries) on the Hebrew Bible.

But not all families spoke Aramaic. Since *Greek* was the foundational language of commerce, many Jews used Greek in their homes. Therefore, many Greek synagogues were formed (even in Jerusalem) where the reading of the Torah could be done either from Hebrew or from the Septuagint (the Greek version of the Old Testament often designated as LXX), but the interpretations would certainly have been made in Greek.

The concern that arose in the early church of Jerusalem that the Greek-speaking widows were not being given proper attention in the regular distribution of assistance (a pattern of care used in the synagogues) is a witness to the presence of a Greek-speaking Jewish population in Israel. The seven who were appointed to assist the apostles in the task of financial service to these widows were basically Hellenists themselves (cf. Acts 6:1–6).[2]

The third major language used in Israel during the time of Jesus was the language of the military/government—namely *Latin*. If anyone wanted to be accepted and to relate appropriately to the governing officials, it would probably have been judicious to use Latin. Therefore, residents of Palestine would be conversant with a number of Latin words. It is intriguing to note that in the Gospels, several Latin words find their way into the Greek texts, such as *praetorium, census, denarius, centurion, legion*, etc., indicating some familiarity of the Christian audience with such words.

Of course, a number of questions can be raised at this point: Did Jesus need a translator in his conversation with Pilate? Did they converse in Greek? Since Jesus spent much of his life in "Galilee of the Gentiles" (cf. the quotation in Matt 4:15), did Jesus speak Greek? Readers may wish to speculate on these intriguing queries, but what can be said for certain is that these languages were present in Jerusalem at the time of Jesus. Their presence is confirmed by the fact that the charge against Jesus on the cross was written in Hebrew (or Aramaic), Latin, and Greek (cf. John 19:20).

4. The Crucial Nature of the Jewish Rabbinic Context

Understanding the intensity of the conflict between Jesus and the rabbis in the Gospels necessitates at least a brief introduction to the subject of the Jewish rabbis and their teachings. This dimension of our study concerning the context of Jesus' life is a crucial aspect in our background investigation for non-Jewish western readers to understand. To present the rabbinic system adequately, however, would require many pages. What can be offered here is merely an overview that will serve to provide readers with some insight into the reason behind the conflict the rabbis had with Jesus and later with the early Christians.

---

[2] Readers of the Gospels and Acts should be aware that the word that appears for serving "tables," the Greek *trapeza*, is used to designate financial administration (cf. John 2:15; Acts 6:2). Those who visit Greece today will discover that the word *trapeza* is used to denote a bank.

a. The Jewish Rabbinic Traditions. Following the return from exile, Ezra had confronted the Jews with the seriousness of their failure to obey the Law of Moses. As the system developed, the scholars of the Hebrew Bible committed themselves to rectifying that failure by intensely studying the Scripture and by seeking to clarify the meanings of the ancient biblical texts, primarily focusing on the Torah (the five books attributed to Moses). But within the Torah as a whole, the scholars sought to identify the particular verses that functioned as precise commands that were to be obeyed. In that process they were able to select 248 verses/statements that they categorized as positive commands (basically "thou shalt" imperatives) and 365 negative statements ("thou shalt not" imperatives) for a total of 613 command statements.

These imperatives then became the subject of intense discussion and debate among the rabbis as to their meaning and as to the gradation of their significance in relation to each other. It should not be difficult to imagine that various schools of opinion would emerge from these debates, some of which would differ significantly from one another. Supporting these various views were a number of capable teachers who were recognized as experts in the Law. Their students gave them the accolade "rabbi," meaning "my master" or "my great one." The views of these "great ones" were then precisely memorized by their students and quoted in discussions/debates concerning obedience to the Law.

The next stage became important in the development of the traditions. Because Moses could hardly have envisioned every imaginable law that would be needed in the development of the community, a theory was asserted that, along with the Written Law, Moses passed on to Joshua and the Elders of Israel (cf. Josh 24:31) the Oral Law (Oral Torah), which the rabbis were in fact enunciating in their formulations. The elders in turn passed these prescriptions to the prophets, and the prophets passed them to the "Men of the Great Synagogue," who promulgated them following the important commission of Ezra. These traditions were then received in the third century B.C. by Simeon the Just and after him given to Antigonus of Soko and others until they came to the last great pair of debaters, Shammai (the forceful conservative) and Hillel (the captivating liberal).[3] The great successor of Hillel was Gamaliel (see his wisdom in Acts 5:33–39), who was also the teacher of the Apostle Paul (Acts 22:3).

From my experience as a lawyer, I would argue that the conclusive stage in this development was the formulation of a protective defense of the system that is enunciated clearly in the *Mishnah* (*Sanh.* 11:3), namely that "Greater stringency applies [to the observance of] the words of the Scribes than to [the observance of] the [written] Law."[4] The phrase "greater stringency" would condemn all those who would argue for the priority of written formulation (Torah) above oral traditions (Oral Torah).

The process that was set in motion by the rabbis, who were also designated as the *Tannaim,* has popularly been known as the "fencing of the Torah." Around the written Torah of Moses the rabbis placed the protective fence of the Oral Law. After the fall of Jerusalem and following the restructuring of Judaism by the Jamnia (Yavneh) councils (in last decades of the first century A.D.), the Oral Law was codified or set in written form as the *Mishnah.* But the *Mishnah* was not the end of the process because the Jewish society kept developing in two primary places (Israel and Babylon) where the traditions of the rabbis continued to be enhanced orally. These enhancements came to be known as the *Gemarah* ("supplement"or "completion"). These oral traditions were then codified and added to the tractates of the *Mishnah.* The result was two written combinations of the *Mishnah* plus the *Gemarah* called Palestinian (Jerusalem) Talmud from the fifth century and the shorter but for some the more authoritative Babylonian Talmud from the sixth century.

In both the *Mishnah* and particularly in the Talmuds, two types of material are present. The most important parts are the legal prescriptions that are designated as *Halakah* and for which obedience is required. The other parts are termed *Haggadah,* which involve comments, stories,

---

[3] For the official tradition of the Jews concerning this history see 'Abot 1:1ff. For a discussion of this tradition see the introduction in Herbert Danby, ed., *The Mishnah* (London: Oxford University Press, 1933) xvii.

[4] *The Mishnah,* 400.

liturgical forms, and many other historical notes that can be helpful in encouraging Jewish spirituality, but they are not prescriptive (e.g., the Passover *Haggadah*). To be able to determine which are in fact prescriptive and which are advisory took/takes considerable insight, learning, and experience.

   b. The Confrontational Jesus. With these brief comments concerning the significant authority given to the Oral Law, I turn to the conflict between Jesus and the rabbis. When Jesus is reported to have proclaimed in no uncertain terms his "halakic" interpretations in the well-known six antitheses of the Sermon on the Mount—"You have heard that it was said by men of old...But I say unto you..." (Matt 5:21, 27, 33, 38, 43, and the shortened form in 31)—he was challenging the entire structure of rabbinic tradition directly by asserting that he had divine authority to do so. In other words, Jesus was calling the people (and the rabbis) back not to "halakic *words*" but to the "halakic *intentions*" of God for Law or Torah. And he was doing it by using a higher method than rabbinic logic. He was claiming not the authority of Moses but his authority as the direct representative of God. By doing so, Jesus was not acting like the "sweet namby-pamby Jesus" that is often presented in the church. He was more like the warrior God of the Old Testament as he called down a series of blistering "woes" upon the Pharisees in Matthew 23:1–36. He was the confrontational Jesus of John 8:44 when he called his opponents the sons of the devil. Do you think Jesus' turning over the "banking tables" in the temple and using a whip (cf. John 2:13–16) is an uncharacteristic picture of Jesus? Think again! His perspective in the Gospels is that the methods of the rabbis and God cannot coexist in true worship.

   Please do not think I am advocating an anti-Semitic approach to the Gospels. I love Israel and have taught in Jerusalem. I have been in the Mediterranean world more than forty times and have studied, taught, and lectured on both sides of the so-called military "Green Line" that separates Israel and the Palestinian territories as well as in other Muslim countries. In making these statements, I am neither anti-Jewish nor anti-Muslim. I am pro-Jesus and his genuine way of understanding the intentions of God both for believers and for those in the world who doubt him.

The transformed rabbi, Paul, understood the difference between Jesus and the traditions of the rabbis, and in his forceful letter to the Galatians he was willing to declare an "anathema" (curse of condemnation; Gal 1:6–8) on the "stupid" Galatians (3:1), the pillars/authorities of the early church (2:9), himself, or even an angel from heaven (1:8) if anyone would try to combine or identify such human traditions and the intentions of God.

The question of course is whether Christians today are trying to resurrect such legalistic methods in developing their new traditions for the church. The Jesus of the Gospels was and is not an easy person to routinize or nationalize. He shattered the formulas of the Jews, and he refused to be "bottled" and distributed for easy consumption by the religious leaders of that day. And like God, he refuses to be programmed today and demands from his current obedient servants not easy formulas for acceptability but true reformation and renewal!

5. *Other Important Written Sources that Provide a Context for Understanding Jesus*[5]

I pause here to mention a few other significant written works that have been preserved for us from the centuries near the time of Jesus since they can provide helpful insights to readers concerning the context into which Jesus came.

a. The Apocrypha and Pseudepigrapha. Between the close of the Old Testament and the writing of the New Testament documents, the literary world was not asleep. During this period the Jews were producing other literature such as the Apocrypha and the Pseudepigrapha. Some of this literature was written in Hebrew, but for the people of the Diaspora (the Jews who lived outside of Palestine) it was translated into Greek. Other documents were seemingly penned in Greek or at least the revisions were written in Greek. Because this literature was similar to the various books of the Old Testament but was not regarded as authoritative by the rabbis, it was not preserved primarily by the Jews but by Christians who

---

[5] For a helpful resource on these sources consult a work such as George W. E. Nickelsburg, *Jewish Literature Between the Bible and the Mishnah* (Philadelphia: Fortress Press, 1981).

knew the literature. Many of these writings were then rendered into Latin. Indeed, some of these books (e.g., the Old Testament Apocrypha) found their way into the "canon" (the authoritative books) of some parts of the later church so that they are included, for instance, in the Bibles of the Roman Catholics and others. Most Protestants have excluded them as a whole from such recognition as lacking biblical canonicity. These writings can, however, provide significant contextual insights into the way the Jews were thinking in the centuries surrounding the life of Jesus.

One of the unique phenomena in the New Testament that can cause frustrations for some Christians concerns the canonical book of Jude. Martin Luther rejected this book as not authoritative in matters of doctrine and faith for a number of reasons, not the least of which is that Jude (and 2 Peter) quotes or cites as authentic support stories that are not merely from the Apocrypha but are from books that could be designated as from the Pseudepigrapha (another set of Jewish books that no Christian church recognizes as authoritative). These stories involve the disobedient angels that had been chained in the darkness or heavy gloom (Jude 6 and 2 Pet 2:4) cited from the book of Enoch (12:4; 10:6; and 22:11) and the apparent dispute over the body of Moses (Jude 9) that is probably from a lost segment of the Assumption of Moses.

Serious students of the New Testament should certainly possess a copy of the Apocrypha and should become familiar with the Pseudepigrapha.[6] As I indicated in the historical review, the books of Maccabees (from the Apocrypha) can be helpful in giving a Jewish perspective on the battles with the Syrians and others as they sought to reestablish their identity as a free state. The Pseudepigraphic[7] works also

---

[6] The books of the Apocrypha are 1–2 Esdras, Tobit, Judith, Additions to Esther, Wisdom of Solomon, Ecclesiasticus (Ben Sirach), Baruch, Epistle of Jeremiah, Prayer of Azariah, Song of the Three Young Men, Susanna, Bel and the Dragon, Prayer of Manasseh, and 1–2 Maccabees. Some lists also include Additions to Daniel and 3–4 Maccabees. See for example *The Apocrypha of the Old Testament: Revised Standard Version* (New York: Thomas Nelson & Sons, 1957) or any other version of it. See also the *SBL Handbook of Style* , ed. P. H. Alexander et al. (Peabody MA: Hendrickson, 1999) 74.

[7] The term "pseudepigrapha" literally means "false writings" (a western interpretation of the books), but the names attached to these books were not regarded as attempts at fraud. The books were viewed by the Jews as written by

capture the spirit of the people not only in their eschatological hopes and expectations in God as their deliverer but also in their pains and sorrows at the loss of their freedom and identity. Reading these works can provide insight into messianic expectations of the Jewish people who awaited the coming of their predicted deliverer in the time of Jesus and yet missed his presence (cf. John 1:11).

b. Flavius Josephus. In the black hole of the history of Palestine around the time of Jesus there is no more important source than the Jewish historian, Flavius Josephus, about whom I narrated important details earlier concerning his surrender, his prediction concerning Vespasian, and his comfortable retirement. He lived from A.D. 37 to the turn of the century and produced two substantial works (*Jewish Antiquities* and *Jewish Wars*) plus his counterattack against Hellenizing pressures on the Jews in *Against Apion* and his own autobiography.[8] His reports have generally proven to be reliable where it is possible to check him. His perspectives, however, are colored by his propaganda goals of communicating to his Roman readers a rather rosy view of both Jewish history and the loyalty to Rome of most Jews.

c. Philo Judaeus. The Alexandrian philosopher Philo (circa 20 B.C.–A.D. 50, the son of substantial wealth), overlapped in time with Jesus and most of the Herodians. Educated in the best Greek school systems, he was hardly regarded by the rabbis as a spokesperson for Orthodox Judaism. Because he was a member of the Diaspora and of Hellenistic Judaism, his writings help us gain insights into how loyal Hellenistic Jews sought to make Jewish ideas palatable in the Greek world. A prodigious writer, he was skilled in the art of allegorical interpretation, which is evident in his comments on the Scripture and which gradually

---

later authors who were restricted (because of the concept of a "closed canon") and attempted to communicate in the spirit of earlier patriarchs and prophets both warnings and important spiritual perspectives for their contemporaries. For the best source on the Pseudepigrapha, see James H. Charlesworth, ed., *O. T. Pseudepigrapha*, 2 vols. (Garden City NY: Doubleday & Company, 1983, 1985).

[8] Readers will find a helpful edition of Josephus's first three works, an extract concerning the Greek view of Hades, and seven earlier dissertations about his writings in William Whiston, trans., *The Works of Josephus: Complete and Unabridged*, new updated ed. (Peabody MA: Hendrickson, 1987).

seeped into the methods of the rabbis who were looking for means to make the Hebrew texts applicable to the lives of people.

The Apostle Paul evidences the use of this allegorical method in his analysis of Hagar and Sarah, the two wives of Abraham, and their children (cf. Gal 4:21–31). In succeeding generations, Christian interpreters of the Gospels developed this art to such an extreme extent that most texts were given a fourfold meaning. Indeed, parables such as the Good Samaritan succumbed to such interpretations so that the medicinal oil and the wine were viewed from multiple perspectives, including being indications that the Holy Spirit and the blood of Christ were present in the story.

d. The Dead Sea Scrolls. The cliffs around Qumran and beyond have given up countless fragments, some of which are amazingly intact manuscripts of the Bible and commentary materials. In addition, instructions concerning the life and activities of the "covenantors" have been recovered. As a result, scholars have often linked the people of the scrolls with the ancient Essenes. The early assumption was that the people were perhaps more like the Pharisees because of their rejection of the temple priesthood, but more recently some scholars have posited that the texts suggest the covenantors were somewhat like the Sadducees. The remains of the buildings at Qumran below the mountains were early regarded by many as a monastery where "monks" lived and copied the scrolls. That conclusion has been called into question by recent archaeologists who have proposed that the buildings housed a pottery factory instead and that the scrolls had nothing to do with the buildings.[9] These debates point out just how complex is the task of reconstructing the Jewish society in the time of Jesus, and care must be taken not to assume that we have a full understanding of the Jewish parties in the time of Jesus.

What can be said is that the scrolls provide evidence that the people of the community lived as an eschatologically expectant group and were undoubtedly prepared as the "sons of light" to fight the sons of darkness (Romans? Syrians? Other Jews? Perhaps a combination of all of them?).

---

[9] See the report "Qumran–The Pottery Factory" in *BAR* 32/5 (September–October 2006): 26–32.

The community members were clearly opposed to Hellenistic syncretistic patterns arising among the Jews, and they had become disheartened with the secular patterns of leadership evidenced in the temple as far back as the second century B.C. The covenantors accordingly had separated themselves from society as a whole. They obviously perished in the onslaught of the Romans, probably prior to A.D. 70, and they never returned to the caves to recover their treasured scrolls.

The scrolls are enlightening for their expectation of two Messiahs, a priestly one (the Messiah of Aaron) and a Davidic one (the Messiah of Israel), with priority of status being given to the priestly Messiah (see 1QSa =1Q28a 11–14, 20 and the blessings in 1QSb=1Q28b Cols 3 and 4).[10] When one compares Paul's concept of Jesus as a Davidic Messiah (cf. Rom 1:3) with the expectation in Hebrews of a Priestly Messiah (Heb 4:14–5:10 and 7:1–17), one becomes immediately aware that the scrolls provide us with a fascinating window into the intriguing context of Jewish eschatological expectations in the time of Jesus.

Intriguingly, a stone slab with ink writing sometimes called a "Dead Sea Scroll in Stone" or designated as "Gabriel's Revelation" has also been found. It seems to suggest a Jewish expectation of a non-militant messiah who would suffer and after three days would live.[11]

6. The Temple, the Priesthood, and the Jewish Festivals[12]

a. A Brief Introduction to Jesus and the Temple. According to the accounts in Luke, the temple was a solemn symbol for Jesus and his

---

[10] For convenient translations of the Dead Sea Scrolls see either Geza Vermes, *The Dead Sea Scrolls in English*, 4th ed. (New York: Penguin Books, 1995) or Florentino Garcia Martinez, *The Dead Sea Scrolls Translated*, 2nd ed. (Grand Rapids: Wm. B. Eerdmans, 1996), particularly at 127 and 432–33 for the messianic expectations.

[11] For a report of this artifact see Israel Kohl, "The Messiah Son of Joseph: 'Gabriel's Revelation' and the Birth of a New Messianic Model," *BAR* 34/5 (2008): 58-62, 78.

[12] For those interested in reading more concerning the temple and its aspects, the old work by the convert from Judaism, Alfred Edersheim, *The Temple: Its Ministry and Services As They Were at the Time of Jesus* (Grand Rapids: Wm. B, Eerdmans, 1958 and earlier), is still enlightening. For the report of the building see also Josephus, *Antiquities* 15.11.1–7.

family. Beginning when their child was still a mere infant, Mary and Joseph fulfilled their duty and took him to the temple for the purification rite. While there, they met the saintly Simeon and Anna, who praised God for Jesus' arrival on the stage of history (2:22–40). How often Jesus experienced the temple services thereafter is not clear, but the family brought him there when he was about twelve, probably for his Bar Mitzvah, and Jesus surprised them with his desire to remain there in theological dialogue while the rest of the family began their homeward trek (2:41–52). For Jesus the temple in Jerusalem was his "Father's House" on earth, and he was more than distressed that particularly under the watchful eye of the "godfather" Annas, the high priest, it was functioning as a profitable and not always authentic business enterprise (e.g., John 2:16; Mark 11:15–18).

b. The Construction of the Second Temple and Its Functionaries. After the destruction of the temple built by Solomon under the Babylonians, the loss of the "ark of the covenant," and the exile of many of the Jews, dreams were rekindled with a return and a rebuilding of the temple and the walls of Jerusalem under Ezra, Nehemiah, and Zerubbabel. The Second Temple was finished in 515 B.C. but was hardly as ornate as its predecessor (cf. Ezra 3:1–6:15). This situation was rectified by Herod the Great, who in 20 B.C. commissioned that the temple platform be significantly expanded and the buildings greatly enhanced. Fearing the possibility of a scheme by Herod, however, the priests not only refused Herod the right to tear down the old temple and start over but also informed him that selected Jews would do the actual construction themselves. Yet they gladly accepted his generosity in supplying support. Moreover, they insisted that the building begin by expanding the platform and then working from the outside courts toward the middle rather than the reverse. By the time Jesus was concluding his ministry (c. A.D. 27–29), the project had been in process for forty-six years (cf. John 2:20).[13] The reconstruction was still designated as the Second Temple, even though it was completely altered and was not actually finished until sometime around A.D. 64–65. It only stood in its finished form until A.D. 70, when it was destroyed by the forces of Titus.

---

[13] See the fuller discussion on chronology in chapter 9.

When the disciples marveled at the beautiful buildings, Jesus' prediction that they would soon be destroyed clearly took place in A.D. 70 with striking vividness (cf. Mark 13:1–2).

Following the first destruction by Babylonia and the loss of many priests, the twenty-four "courses" (or clans of priests) were reconstituted from the survivors in the priestly class (1 Chr 24:1–31; Ezra 2:36–39; 10:18–22; Neh 12:12–21). They prospered and multiplied so significantly that by the time of Jesus, the average priest apparently was assigned to the special ministration of the lamps and the incense offering probably once or at the most only twice in his lifetime, even though all the courses were expected to be represented at the major festivals such as Tabernacles. No special age limitations are listed for the priests. The account of Luke concerning Zechariah in the temple is an example of such a memorable ministration in the penultimate Holy Place (cf. Luke 1:8–23). Entrance to the Most Holy Place was reserved for the High Priest, and he was allowed to enter the inner sanctuary to make atonement for all the people only once a year on *Yom Kippur*.[14]

The "Levites" served as assistants and musicians in the temple (Neh 12:22–26), and they likewise increased in numbers so that the poor Jewish population in the time of Jesus supported a large number of temple functionaries. According to Numbers 4:3, the sons of Levi were authorized to do service in the tabernacle from the ages of thirty to fifty, although in the same book the ages are listed as twenty-five to fifty, and thereafter the Levites were to care for their associates but not to do tabernacle/temple service (8:24–25). David lowered the authorization age to twenty and did not specify a terminal date. He also spelled out what their new duties were to be when it was no longer a necessity for them to transport the ark and the tabernacle after the temple construction had been completed (1 Chr 23:24–32).

In the parable of the "Good Samaritan," Jesus provides the readers of Luke with an important social comparison of the privileged religious class (priests and Levites) who failed to model the loving and self-giving

---

[14] For instructions concerning the Day of Atonement and of the yearly sin offering see Lev 16:1–34.

spirit of God's *shaliach*, or agent, with a half-breed Samaritan reject who did so (Luke 10:30–37).

c. The Temple Site. The temple was built on the mountain threshing floor purchased by David (2 Sam 24:18–25) that lies immediately north of the Ophel (the earlier Jebusite town and the small city of David). To the east of the Temple Mount is the Kidron Valley and the Mount of Olives, and to the west is the Tyropean Valley (with what is today known as the Western [sometimes called the Wailing] Wall). Further to the west is the hill often today called Mount Zion (*Sion*), which in the days of Jesus embraced the Herodian/Procurator's Palace, the residences of the High Priest and his clan as well as other members of the ancient elite, both Roman and Jewish. For ease of crossing the Tyropean Valley, a bridge formerly connected the Temple Mount with this elite hill (where tradition suggests that Jesus held the last supper with his disciples, through the actual site is not certain).

d. The Festival Cycle. According to Deuteronomy 23, an annual Festival Cycle was initiated by Moses that included Passover (Unleavened Bread), First Fruits (Pentecost), Trumpets, the Day of Atonement, and Tabernacles. What readers and commentators often miss is the strategic nature of the weekly celebration of *Shabbat* (Sabbath) in the listing. Moreover, as I have indicated in my major commentary of the Gospel of John, each of the festivals was to be regarded and include a *Shabbat* to the Lord (Lev 23:7). Failure to perceive this phenomenon has often led to a misunderstanding of the role of John 5.[15]

The most significant festivals and special days celebrated by the Jews in the time of Jesus were the following:

(i) Passover (15–21 *Nisan,* our March–April, with Preparation on 14 *Nisan*) was a reminder of the escape from Egypt and God's preservation of his people;

(ii) Pentecost (or "Weeks," 49–50 days later on 6 *Sivan*) occurred at the beginning of the early harvest and was recognized as a reminder of God giving the Law on Mt. Sinai;

---

[15] For a discussion of the Festival Cycle in John, see Gerald L. Borchert, *John 1–11*, The New American Commentary (Nashville: Broadman & Holman, 1996) 224 ff., especially at 230.

(iii) The high holidays, which followed the Civic New Year (1–2 *Tishri* at the end of September) and included *Yom Kippur*/the Day of Atonement (10 *Tishri*), the holiest day of the year when the High Priest entered the Most Holy Place once a year, and Tabernacles or "Booths" (15–22 *Tishri*), which was a reminder of their pilgrimage in the desert;

(iv) Hanukkah (or Dedication, 25 *Kislev*), which usually takes place between the early and the middle part of December and was a reminder of the victory over the Syrians and the purification of the temple by Judas Maccabeus;

(v) The three days of Purim (13–15 *Adar*, which generally falls in late February or into March) was a reminder of the attempted early pogrom (extermination) of the Jews and their escape through the actions of Esther.

7. The Synagogue

Without question the vital survival of the Jewish faith after the destruction of the temple in A.D. 70 and the hostility against the Jews in the centuries thereafter has been in large part the result of great family solidarity and the development of the synagogue. The term "synagogue" is not actually used in the Old Testament, even though the word appears in the King James Version at Psalm 74:8 as a rendering of the general Hebrew word *moed* ("meeting place/s"). But when and how it began is shrouded in the mystery of the exile.

a. The Synagogue as a Community Center. What has become fairly clear, however, is that the importance of the synagogue was that it served multi-functional purposes. At the early stage, it was a kind of community center as its name would imply (a "gathering"). Among those purposes were the care of members, the education of the children in Hebrew and the Bible, a setting for the worship of God, a stimulus to the study of the Torah and the other writings, the meeting of potential couples and the negotiation of their marriages, and the friendly conducting of business. It was an institutional center that cemented the Jews into a living community. Anyone who has spent much time in the study of and attendance at synagogues will recognize that negotiation is an art that is learned and encouraged in the synagogue.

For those who think ancient synagogues were merely constructed as worship centers (in the way many of our contemporary churches and synagogues are built), a glimpse at the stone fragment that was recently uncovered at Capernaum from the ancient synagogue there should change their minds. On that stone fragment is a carved replica of an ancient ark (a box on wheels that held the scrolls). It should immediately indicate to the viewer that the synagogue hall served many functions. Accordingly, at worship time the ark would simply be rolled into the hall, and the place would be transformed for worship. In design, there were seats along the walls of the otherwise bare hall, but special seats were often added during worship, including the seat designated to represent Moses. Jesus made a point to warn his followers against adopting the patterns of the scribes and learned ones who loved to wear special religious clothing and be called by elite titles, and he particularly inveighed against those who desired to be ushered to the seats where everyone would recognize them as appearing significant while they actually lacked in integrity (cf. Mark 12:38–40; Matt 23:1–12; Luke 11:43).

b. The Composition of the Synagogue. It is imperative for readers to remember that a synagogue was and still is formed by ten Jewish men. The women were not counted in that organizational structure and are still not counted in the orthodox system today. Indeed, even in my student days, when I attended synagogue services while learning Hebrew, I was welcomed to sit among the Jewish men during their services (and actually asked for my views on prospective candidates when they were hiring a new rabbi), yet the women and children were consigned to the balcony.

The main official of the synagogue was the "ruler" (sometimes more than one) who was responsible for maintaining order in the community and integrity in the worship.[16] He was assisted by a number of other elected officers (depending on the size of the community) and often a synagogue would have a resident rabbi. The staff member was the

---

[16] Note that in Paul's mission at Corinth, Crispus, the ruler of the synagogue, became a Christian. Unless they had two rulers, if the synagogue was large, he must have been replaced by Sosthenes (Acts 18:8, 17). It is intriguing to speculate on whether this Sosthenes is the same person mentioned in 1 Cor 1:1.

school teacher (*hazzan*) who was responsible for the Hebrew education of the sons of the community. His position was not highly regarded in the community, and he often functioned also as the janitor. Sometimes a girl of high estate would become enamored with the teacher, a situation that could cause difficulty in a family and particularly for the father who was responsible for arranging her proper betrothal.

c. Synagogue Worship. The worship experience at the synagogue could have been varied, but the standard components can be recognized, and Christians have appropriated and employed many of them in adjusted forms in their services. These components would have included (i) a form of invocation and (ii) the recitation of the *Shema Israel* (Deut 6:4–5), as well as (iii) various prayers in the act of lifting up holy hands as the worshiper addressed "the Ruler of the Universe" and the "Deliverer" of his people. Among these prayers might be a recitation of all or part of the Eighteen Benedictions (to which was added in the late first century the curse on the heretics/Nazarenes in the notorious Benediction Twelve[17]). Also among the prayers would be the so-called first- or second-century (?) three-stage blessings/thanksgivings (*berakot*) to God, the ruler of the Universe, for *not* creating the worshiper "a heathen" (Gentile), "a slave," or "a woman." A form of this prayer was obviously known earlier to the Apostle Paul and is unquestionably reflected in his strategic unity statement of Galatians.[18] Another crucial component in the service was (iv) the reading of a selection from the Torah as well as a reading from the Prophets and/or the Writings, normally in Hebrew (unless the Septuagint/Greek version was used). The readings would be followed by (v) an oral interpretation or commentary in the language of the people (cf. the brief but stunning

---

[17] For the curse on the *Minim* see C. K. Barrett, ed., *N. T. Background Documents* (New York: Harper & Row, 1956) 166–67.

[18] The women in the prayer book were instructed to pray, "I thank thee…who hast made me according to thy will." These prayers are published even today in the Jewish *Daily Prayer Book: Ha-Siddur Ha-Shalem*, trans. and ed. P. Birnbaum (New York: Hebrew Publishing Company, n.d.) 15–18. When readers compare these prayers with Paul's statement in Gal 3:28, they may better understand what a radical change Paul's transformation in Christ was for him. See my comments Roger Mohrlang and Gerald L. Borchert, *Romans, Galatians*, Cornerstone Biblical Commentary (Carol Stream IL: Tyndale House Publishers, 2007) 247, 299–300.

commentary of Jesus after reading from the scroll of Isaiah in Luke 4:21). Some of these commentaries have been preserved in the *Targum*(s) of the rabbis. Other elements of the service could include (vi) the chanting of songs (probably from the Psalter) and (vii) the receiving of alms for the poor. The service would usually conclude with (viii) the Aaronic Benediction (Num 6:24–26).[19]

d. The Synagogue and Hostility to Jesus. Hostility was initiated between the synagogue and Jesus during his ministry when he preached in the Nazareth synagogue about the acceptability of Gentiles and they tried to throw him over the cliff (Luke 4:16–30). It increased further when he healed in the synagogue on the Sabbath (Luke 6:6–11). The Jews could hardly tolerate his ways, and it ultimately led to his death. Moreover, Jesus forewarned his followers that synagogues would also become their nemeses (cf. Luke 12:11; 21:12). Such was clearly evidenced in the time of the early disciples (as recorded in the early chapters of Acts) and later during the missionary visits of Paul when, for example, the Jews of one synagogue chased him through the Galatian cities from Antioch to Iconium, etc. (cf. Acts 14:19) and later the Jews from the synagogue in Thessalonica chase him through Beroea (17:13). In the context of this hostility with the synagogue, it is rather amazing that James refers to the church gathering as a synagogue (cf. Jas 2:2), but he is using the term as a general word for assembly and not as a technical reference for the Jewish institution (cf. Ps 74:8). The hostility obviously intensified in the latter part of the first century with the adoption of the curse in the Eighteen Benedictions, the exclusion of Jewish Christians from the synagogues, and the Jewish Christians' loss of protection under the rights of belonging to a *religio licita* (licenced religion). Clearly the hostility must have reached a boiling point when John in Revelation referred to the synagogue as an instrument of Satan (cf. Rev 2:9; 3:9).

That hostility was reversed later during the era after Constantine and the reprisals of Julian. The anti-Jewish sentiment then grew and has

---

[19] But the so-called "Mizpah Benediction" that some Christians use (Gen 31:49) was not employed. That statement is actually both a covenant rehearsal and a curse between Jacob and Laban as they parted from each other, not having discovered Laban's *teraphim* (the household god(s) that served as symbols of inheritance).

been present thereafter as witnessed by the villainous role assigned to the Jew, Shylock, in Shakespeare's *Merchant of Venice* (1595) and in the twentieth-century Holocaust of the Nazi period, especially in places like Poland such as in the Warsaw ghetto. Neither the activities of the Jews nor the later attitudes of the anti-Jews, however, represent the spirit of the self-giving yet forceful Jesus who called people to a different way of life.

8. The Jewish Parties in the Time of Jesus

While far more than 90 percent of the Jewish population in the time of Jesus had little time or opportunity to belong to the various parties, these parties exercised considerable influence in the political and religious life of the people. Indeed, one way in which the rabbinic leadership of the parties ultimately tried to control the people was by later declaring that the very reading (even touching) of the Scripture scrolls made a person unclean and in need of engaging in purification. In the time of Jesus, the rules were not so limiting, but, since the common people had little money to own their own scrolls and little time to engage in the involved purification rites, the Bible over that period became a source known basically through synagogue readings and commentaries of the rabbis. It was not unlike what gradually happened in the time of the Middle Ages when the church literally chained the Bible so the laity were unable to read it and thus protected its right to correct interpretation. When one understands this important phenomenon, one is closer to realizing the controlling power of the rabbis in their understanding of "binding and loosing" as it refers to the use of Scripture and the grace of God. But more important, the reader of the Gospels should recognize the authority Jesus gave to the whole church for mission and in spreading the gospel freely (cf. Matt 16:19; 18:18). To interpret the will of God both in terms of salvation and judgment for the people of the world is the mission of the entire people of God. It is not merely the role of a select few (cf. Matt 28:16–20)! And that authority is not meant to be hoarded.

a. The Pharisees. For most contemporary readers, the term "Pharisee" connotes a self-righteous or hypocritical person, but such a designation grows out of focusing on the rebukes of self-righteous Pharisees by their critics, including Jesus in Matthew 23 and elsewhere. But it is clear that not all Pharisees in the New Testament were viewed negatively. Some were like Nicodemus, who sought integrity (cf. John 3:1–9), defended Jesus (7:50–51), and finally assisted in burying his body (19:39–40). The Pharisees themselves during the Intertestamental period differentiated pious Pharisees who sought to maintain a wholesome relationship with God from other inauthentic ones and from those who grasped for power and were corrupted.

As one of my doctoral supervisors, the late Bruce Metzger, used to remind us, even the Talmud recognized the differences in Pharisees and condemned many of them such as (i) those who constantly postponed their responsibilities; (ii) those who were bruised because they closed their eyes in an attempt to avoid looking at a beautiful woman and ran into something; (iii) those who wore their righteousness on their shoulders (e.g., Luke 18:9–14); (iv) those who emphasized the weight of their humility like humped-back peasants; and (v) those who were constantly calculating their piety such as their precise tithes (e.g., Luke 11:42 and even 18:12). Of course, even the Jewish rabbis recognized that there were two more types to complete the required seven: (vi) the faithful Pharisees and (vii) Pharisees whose lives evidenced a true love of God.[20]

As Louis Finkelstein[21] reminded readers, the Pharisees were primarily city dwellers, were politically and sociologically conservative, and opposed most outside influences, including Roman dominance (but note their combining with their espoused enemies, the Herodians, in an attempt to trap Jesus at Mark 12:13–17). Yet they were theologically liberal and open to the development of their perceptions of God and the divine hand in the affairs of humanity. Moreover, they strongly asserted the concepts of freedom of the individual and of personal responsibility while at the same time advocating a moderate view of predestination as they trusted God to work out the divine will in the world. They clearly

---

[20] See *'Abot of R. Nathan*, 37.

[21] For an excellent full-scale treatment on the Pharisees, see Louis Finkelstein, *The Pharisees: The Sociological Background of Their Faith*, 3rd ed., 2 vols. (Philadelphia: The Jewish Publication Society of America, 1962) especially at 1.74–114.

espoused a view of the resurrection that is really not present in the Hebrew Scriptures, although the superintendence of God in all of life and death is certainly declared there (cf. Job 13:15 and the intriguing statement in Job 33:39). They not only asserted the concept of resurrection but also accepted the concept of two kingdoms and that the wicked would be judged while the faithful would be blessed, thus leading to the development of views of rewards and punishments. They believed in both angels and demons and affirmed that people could have spiritual experiences of the divine in their lives. Paul capitalized on these aspects of Pharisaic theology and split the council of Pharisees and Sadducees when he was brought before the Sanhedrin after he was seized in the temple (cf. Acts 23:6–10).

b. An Important Clue for Readers about Jesus from the Pharisees. There is little doubt that many Pharisees took their religious beliefs seriously, and like Saul/Paul before he became a Christian, they were often zealous in their commitments, even to the point of defending God by persecuting and killing those with whom they disagreed. They had a love for the word of God, although they generally emphasized the *word* of God whereas Jesus emphasized the word of *God*! This difference in emphasis brought the Pharisees into direct conflict with Jesus in the interpretation of the Torah. Both were committed to the words of Scripture, but the Pharisees focused on the hard exactness of the words of God while Jesus focused on the spirit and intention of the words of God for humanity. Thus, both honored the Sabbath of God, but while the Pharisees focused on the Sabbath, Jesus focused on God.

It may seem to the reader that the above distinction is like splitting thin hairs, yet those differences in perspective still exist today among religious people. They often lead to harsh treatment, unloving rejection, slandering, and even killing of other faith-oriented people so that the "spirit of God" is lost in the so-called righteous "defense of God." Such defenses often elevate personal and corporate views to the realm of the divine, thus making people the measure of God. Moreover, the focus on exactness can lead to an overemphasis on the external evidence or proof of the faith and bypass the life of the spirit. The pre-Christian Paul is an obvious example of such a Pharisee in relation to Jesus, and later he clearly articulated that difference (cf. Paul's two perspectives in Phil 3:4–

8). Understanding such a difference will greatly help the reader in recognizing the secret of Jesus and the New Testament.

c. The Sadducees. The Sadducees also arose out of a frustrating period with the Syrians and the rise of the Maccabean resisters, but in their case they emerged from the priestly class of rebels and garnered their name from Zadok, David's primary priest, the son of Ahitub, whom he selected to anoint his son Solomon as king during the early internecine struggles within Israel (1 Kgs 1:32–45). In contrast to the Pharisees, the Sadducees can be categorized primarily as the landed class; many were absentee landowners, and many were aligned with the high priestly family. They were generally politically and sociologically liberal in that they were able to cooperate with the Roman invaders if it could guarantee that their positions were fairly secure. On the other hand, as Finkelstein has also argued, they were conservative when it came to theological innovation, and they wanted to maintain the "good old customs." They rejected the developing theology of the Pharisees as revisionist and despised the individualism they sensed in Pharisaic beliefs as threatening to the corporate ideas of the theology of Moses.

Perhaps an example will help explain this difference. Many rich landowners had slaves, and if by error a neighbor's slave who was burning a field of stubble was careless and the fire spread to the Sadducee's farm and burned one of his buildings, the Sadducee naturally wanted to receive recompense, so he sought it not from the slave but from the owner of the slave. The Pharisee, however, would argue that the slave was responsible for the error and not the owner since everyone should bear his own guilt (cf. the crucial change in theology at Ezek18:19–20, and note the earlier view in Deut 24:16). The Sadducee knew that the slave had nothing and could not recompense him, so he asserted a theology of the corporate nature of the family—that all were tied together. Thus, Sadducees reaffirmed that children would be judged to the third and fourth generation for the sins of the parents (cf. the principle in Exod 20:5; 34:7; Deut 5:9). Accordingly, the fire should be the owner's responsibility.

For us in the twenty-first century with our sense of corporate responsibility, the case seems clear since we have created legal corporate entities and our laws have been designed to deal with those entities. But the Pharisee was arguing theologically for the new concept of the primacy of the individual before God, whereas the Sadducee had to counter with a corporate theological rationale using the thought pattern from the Mosaic era. It is helpful for readers to understand the importance of thought development concerning individual identity that came through Pharisees.

Likewise, for the Sadducees (who believed that when one died, one simply lived on in one's children), individual spiritual experiences, angels and devils, future rewards and punishments, and resurrection seemed to be strange new thinking that was out of kilter with both their reality and the views of the Patriarchs.[22] Based on the Sadducean views, then, Jesus just seemed to be another revisionist who lived in a dream land and was completely out of touch with the political realities of the world in which Rome was the super power and controlled life. So they tried to put Jesus in his place with a probing question. In the resurrection, they wondered to whom a woman would belong after a series of brothers had her in keeping with the Mosaic law of levirate marriage (Mark 12:18–23). Behind their question was the idea that the woman obviously could not belong to each "individual" man. Note the treatment of the woman as a possession. The brusque answer of Jesus was that the Sadducees were in error because you cannot transport earthly phenomena into the reality of heaven. Further, he even countered with a reference to the Patriarchs by indicating that God is a present reality and not merely a God of the past (12:24–27).

A concluding note needs to be mentioned at this point. Because the Sadducees were so tied to the past and to the high priesthood as well as the temple institution, after the temple was destroyed, the Sadducees ceased to exist. Thus, although readers may fail to recognize the fact, when the Gospel of John was written at the end of the first century of our era, the Sadducees were never mentioned! They were then nonexistent. In John they are simply designated by terms like "authorities." The Jews who continued after the destruction of the temple were and are today

---

[22] For his similar critical views on the Sadducees, see Josephus, *Antiquities*, 18.1.4.

basically from the Pharisaic tradition, unless they are like the medieval spiritualists (Cabalists) or are more like contemporary secularists.

d. The Essenes.[23] In trying to explain the nature of the Jewish parties to his Hellenistic readers, Josephus in the *Jewish War* likened the parties to philosophical schools with the Essenes being described as the third party after the Pharisees and the Sadducees. He also noted that they espoused a peculiar holiness in which they shunned pleasure "as a vice" and affirmed temperance "as a virtue." Rejecting personal riches, they advocated holding property in common; and even though they apparently refused to marry,[24] they readily adopted children into their communities. Becoming an accepted member of an Essene community was not done hastily. At least a two-year candidacy was a necessary prerequisite after which the initiate was required to deposit his personal wealth in the community treasury. Josephus concluded his description by indicating that in the war with the Romans, the Essenes endured torture without yielding to the conquerors' demands to renounce their faith and blaspheme or eat unlawful food.[25]

The term "Essene" was probably derived from the Aramaic *hasen*, which would equal the Hebrew *Hasidim* ("the pious ones"). Since most early references to the Essenes appear to include a theology of resurrection and a glorious afterlife, scholars usually have related them to an intense form of the Pharisees. But since their groups and documents have seemingly varied in their emphases, care should be taken not to pigeonhole the Essenes into the camp either of the Pharisees or the Sadducees. One of their special features included the rejection of the temple priesthood in the time of the Maccabees because the Maccabees/Hasmoneans were not from the official line of Zadok.

The Qumran residents have frequently been identified as Essenes, and the Dead Sea Scrolls have often been linked to Qumran. The scrolls discovered in the caves near Qumran provide further insights into a major conflict between the group's Teacher of Righteousness (the

---

[23] See also the discussions on the Dead Sea Scrolls above.

[24] Archaeologists have discovered bones of women buried at Qumran, which has led to questions concerning the idea of the celibacy of the sect.

[25] See Josephus, *Jewish Wars*, 2.8.2–13. For a brief summary see Barrett, *N. T. Background Documents*, 125–26.

covenantors' leader) and the Temple High Priest (designated as the "Wicked Priest") who actually may have been one of the later Maccabean brothers (Jonathan or Simon). Convinced that the Jerusalem Priesthood had become totally apostate, the Essenes formed their own tightly knit communities and sought refuge in the desert, where they prepared for the great eschatological battle between the sons of light and the sons of darkness. The Essenes are not mentioned in the New Testament.

e. The Fourth Party. Even though Josephus does not mention the fourth party (philosophical school) by name, it seems fairly clear that he was probably referring to groups of zealous Jews who were anxious to rid their land of the Romans and any other outside influences. These groups probably also found their kinship and origins in the period of harsh Syrian restrictions on the true worship of God and in Israel's religious heritage during the Maccabean struggle to shed Hellenizing attempts by outsiders. Later the outsiders were the Romans like Pompey and Pilate who lacked an understanding of the Jews' commitment to their heritage. The Zealots encouraged civil disobedience in the time of Jesus and later took up arms, fought, and died in the Jewish War, some making their last stand at Masada. The more radical of the Zealots were identified as the *Sicarii*, the so-called Jewish knife-men who hid their daggers (*sicae*) under their cloaks and took pleasure in stabbing the Romans or their supporters in crowds and elsewhere. These assassins caused turmoil and encouraged rebellion against Rome (cf. Acts 21:38) in the decades before the fall of Jerusalem in A.D. 70. Jesus chose his disciples from various segments of Jewish society, and one of the twelve may have been a Zealot or at least a precursor to the revolutionary party.[26]

---

[26] See Simon "the Zealot" (*zeloten*) in Luke 6:15 and Acts 1:13. He is also called Simon "the Cananaean" (*ton kananaion* in Mark 3:18; cf. Matt 10:4), which is not a geographical designation but a reference or a nickname for a "zealous person" from the Aramaic *qan'an*.

9. The Dreamers and Their Apocalyptic Expectations

a. Time and Destiny for the Jews. The Jews have lived with an expectation of destiny. They were a people who under God developed a linear concept of time. For them time had a destiny or a goal. They were unlike the Greeks, who did not even have a term for the end of time but viewed it as cyclical. So the only way the New Testament writers who penned their books in Greek could indicate this concept of the end or the fulfillment of time (and thus for eternity following time) was to use one of several forms of "unto the ages" (*eis ton aiona*) or unto the cycle of cycles.

Destiny for Israel was birthed in the call of Abraham not only to be blessed by God but also to be a blessing to the nations/all the families of the earth (Gen 12:2–3). Yet like many Christians today, the Jews generally accepted the first part of the covenant promise and conveniently overlooked or set aside their responsibility for the second part of the covenant. Thus, the theme for the people of God can easily be viewed this way: Conquer them? "Yes, if possible!" Proclaim hope to them? "No! Why should we?" But into the quagmire of Israel's history, God sent the book of Jonah as a reminder that enemies were not to be destroyed but to be saved. And what about Christians who not only seek to destroy non-Christians but even other Christians? One of the amazing phenomena of the Bible is that Jonah actually survived within the Jewish canon in the face of Jewish hostility toward their conquerors like Assyria/Nineveh (Jonah 4:11). To emphasize this fact, we must remember that—with the exception of the time of David, Solomon, and their successors as well as the brief period of the Maccabees and their Hasmonean successors—Israel has been harassed and conquered almost continuously up to the present era.

b. Death and What Comes Then in the Various Hellenistic Perspectives. Jesus came into the context of the Hellenistic world where almost no one thought much about the end or purpose of time and the hereafter but focused instead on their present state, unless they were elevated to the rank of a "god" like Alexander or Julius Caesar and their successors. The best that most people in Greece and Rome could expect at death (according to the myth of Pluto, who stole Persephone and carried her to the underworld for part of the year) was to dance in fields of flowers with Persephone in her time when she returned to the upper world, but there was also her periods of grief in the underworld with Pluto. Alternatively, they could have their souls ascend on wings as proposed by Plato if they were good enough (like a philosopher) to be absorbed into the great soul![27] Another alternative was the process of reincarnation until the person attained the necessary credits in this life to pass out of the present world and be absorbed into a general state of immortality or the immortal soul of the universe. The mystery religions may have supplied another example of thinking about the afterlife, but little is known about their actual beliefs except some ideas about their thoughts of rebirth. Yet it is not quite clear how much influence the Christian initiation of baptism had upon activities such as the *Taurobolium* (the bath in the blood of a bull) since we find early examples of rebirth "for twenty years" and then rebirth "for eternity" (*renautus in aetunum*), whatever that meant.[28] The latter example would suggest that something influenced an upgrade of the earlier ceremony. Was it Christian baptism?

Of course, there were also those like the Egyptians who expected to pass into an active afterlife and needed to be entombed as mummies with their servants, including all their possessions and equipment for a future life. But still, according to the Book of the Dead, they would have to face the judgment hall where their hearts were weighed on a balance against a feather. If their hearts were light enough and they passed the test, they could be conducted into the presence of Isis. My students have usually shown great interest in my papyrus pictorial example of the great judgment scene before the ultimate judges of life where the crocodile waited to gobble an ill-fated heart. Moreover, most of us are aware of the fact that little if any of the pharaohs' burial treasures for the future actually remained in the original tombs because of the skillful work of grave robbers, unless the place of the tomb was hidden like that of Tutankhamen under a more famous and accessible tomb. But the

---

[27] See Plato's Dialogues, especially the discussion in *Phaedrus* 246–256.

[28] See Prudentius, *Peristephanon* 10.1011–50 and Apuleius, *Metamorphosis* (*The Golden Ass*) 11, 22–26. For a convenient source, consult Barrett, *N. T. Background Documents*, 96–100.

burial process provides a commentary on how materially these ancients viewed their afterlife possibilities.

   c. The Jews and the Development of their Eschatological Views. The early Jews and the later Sadducees believed that to die was to enter the realm of Sheol (a place of dead shadows) indicated for example in Saul's attempt to bring up Samuel from the dead and gain access to his advice (1 Sam 28:11–17). But, as I have indicated above, the Pharisees and those who followed similar thought processes realized the unsatisfactory nature of such ideas of the termination of life on earth.

   Thus, the age between the Testaments was a time of development in Jewish thought. It was a period when the expectations concerning the coming of the Messianic era were stimulated by the Maccabean revolt and the emergence of the Hasmonean dynasty (even though many rejected their union of kingship and priesthood). It was also a time when the apocalypticists (the dreamers) began to express in writing their expectations of the new age, the coming of the new prophet like Moses predicted in the Torah (cf. Deut 18:15), and the arrival of the pangs of Messianic era (cf. John 16:20–24 where Jesus used of the idea of such pangs with his disciples). It was also a period when suffering Israel began to recognize that the present life could hardly be the sum total of God's intentions for this life, and the result was the coming realization that resurrection had to be God's way for his people.

   All these ideas developed together and focused on the coming of a new Messianic era. They were given verbal expression in the dreams of apocalyptic writers who used such names as Enoch, Ezra, Baruch, Abraham, and even Adam to link their presentations with the great spiritual ideas of the past.[29] The one "who was to come," they were certain, would soon come.[30] God would send his true servant (the Messiah) to rescue Israel and provide his hope for the future. These apocalyptic works had their birth heritage in the earlier prophetic books such as Joel (see his vision of hope after the tragedy of blighted crops in

---

   [29] For these important expectant texts see Charlesworth, *O. T. Pseudepigrapha*, vol. 1, 3–315, 517–603, 615–79, 681–705, 709–19, etc.

   [30] For an excellent treatment on Messianic expectations see Sigmund Mowinkle, *He That Cometh: The Messiah Concept in the Old Testament and Later Judaism* (Grand Rapids: Eerdmans, 2005).

Joel 2–3; cf. the use of Joel in Acts 2:14–21). They provide a framework for understanding the apocalyptic statements in the Gospels (cf. Mark 13; Matt 24–25; Luke 21:5–38) and in the book of Revelation.

Some scholars have attributed the development of such apocalyptic thinking to the influences of Mesopotamian dualism on the Jews while they were in exile. But beyond the great struggle between the forces of good/light (Ahurimazda) and evil/darkness (Ariman), there seems to be little basis for such a thesis. Apocalyptic thinking was Jewish at its heart, gathering up the expectations of Israel for a new David and taking seriously both the despair and hope of the Jewish people. It did not dismiss Jewish failure or the opposing power of world forces, but, growing out of the tension between despair and hope, it built a new emphasis on the ancient Jewish belief in the ultimate power of God. Expressed in symbolic terms and using strange figures like angels and demons, the literature flourished as presentations of divine answers to Israel's dilemma. The solution to the problem was not found in human strength or power but in the cosmic God who alone understood time and was able to deal with the cosmic evil that functioned behind the phenomena of the various evils in this world. Such cosmic evil could hardly be defeated by mere human means; only God who controlled history and was capable of solving human problems in the ultimate dimensions of reality could defeat it.

To dream of a future in the hands of God and of a divine realm like heaven without evil at the conclusion of time was the gift of the apocalypticists to Israel. That manner of communication was clearly used by Jesus and then employed by the church.

10. The Diaspora and Its Significance

At the time of Jesus, most Jews lived outside Palestine, and most of them spoke Greek. To give the Greek-speaking Jews a Bible they could regard as fully inspired by God, several traditions arose for the justification of the Septuagint (LXX, the Greek version of the Hebrew Scriptures). The primary ones were reported by Philo and in the *Epistle of Aristeas*, which claim that the Egyptian ruler Ptolemy Philadelphus (c. 250 B.C.) is reputed to have commissioned the High Priest to have the best translators (seventy-two, representing six from each tribe) shut into separate cells on the island of Pharos near Alexandria in order to translate the Bible from Hebrew into Greek. When they emerged after seventy-two days (!), each was said to have rendered the text identically, indicating the divine superintendence in the process and thus establishing the authority of the LXX.[31]

These Jews at the time of Jesus hailed from a wide range of places as is attested in the book of Acts (2:9–11). The brief list of Jews who heard Peter's sermon in Jerusalem at Pentecost can provide some sense of the spread of the Jewish people. They were Parthians, Medes, Elamites, Mesopotamians, and Cappadocians; others from the Roman provinces of Pontus, Asia, Phrygia, and Pamphylia and from parts of North Africa such as Egypt and Libya (Cyrene); as well as Cretans and Arabians and of course Palestinians. This list does not include most of the northern Mediterranean area encompassing the Greek territories where we know Paul visited synagogues on his missionary travels (cf. Acts 17:1–18:17). The spread was immense.

These Jews who for business or other purposes lived outside of Palestine were known as the *Diaspora* (the Dispersion), and although they honored the traditions of their forefathers, the rabbis in Jerusalem tended to regard them as second-class citizens. For them and for all Jews, however, Jerusalem was regarded as the center of religious life, and most of the Diaspora Jews contributed to the temple and expected to make pilgrimages to the holy city,[32] certainly at least once in life during a festival, much like the Muslims expect to make a pilgrimage to Mecca during their lifetime. To indicate just how central Jerusalem was to the thinking of the Jews, when they spoke of going there, they referred to it as "going up to Jerusalem" (cf. Acts 15:2). Indeed, Luke does not even need to mention the name "Jerusalem" but merely mentions that the missionaries "went up," and the reader is supposed to understand what he means (cf. 18:22). It is of course obvious that topographically Jerusalem is in the mountains, but the concept means much more than

---

[31] See Philo, *Life of Moses*, 2.26–42, and the *Epistle of Aristeas*, 301–16. See a summary in Josephus, *Antiquities* xii.11–118. For a convenient source see Barrett, *N. T. Background Documents*, 210–16.

[32] See Josephus, *Antiquities*, xiv.110–18. For convenience readers may wish to consult Barrett, *N. T. Background Documents*, 136–38.

physical direction so that for all Jews, including those of the Dispersion, Jerusalem was up in their thinking! It is only in Christian eschatology that the direction of Jerusalem gains a new dimension as the New Jerusalem is brought down out of heaven from God (Rev 21:2).

But there was one important exception to the primacy of Jerusalem among the Dispersion—Babylon. Many of the exiles preferred to remain in Mesopotamia and not return to Palestine when they were given permission by Cyrus to return and rebuild the temple in Jerusalem (cf. Isa 44:24–45:13; Ezra 5:13–6:12). As a result, a strong rabbinic tradition developed in Mesopotamia. From that community of scholars emerged the Babylonian Talmud, which is generally regarded as more authoritative than the Jerusalem (Palestinian) Talmud.

In order to maintain the unity of the Jews in a time when communications were primitive, a system of lighting fires that had been developed much earlier was expanded so that at the initiation of the festivals and at the beginning of Shabbat (Sabbath), bonfires were lit in Jerusalem and the signal was passed on by the successive lighting of fires from one station to another. Since Sabbath and the festivals were so important to Jewish life, this system where fire signals were possible enabled Jews to be informed of the time when the official ceremonies should begin and to sense a community spirit in spite of isolation. Of course, with the development of accurate timepieces and new communications patterns, the old system became unnecessary. But those who have lived in Israel know that *The Jerusalem Post* currently publishes the official time when Sabbath starts so that Jews today know the exact time for the cessation of work. This time is important so that buses, taxis, and trucks that use the streets regularly in places like the *Mea She'arim* (the orthodox district) in Jerusalem will avoid using them at the beginning of the Sabbath. The possibility of being stoned by the residents for breaking Shabbat is very real.

The presence of the Jewish Diaspora was recognized during the ministry of Jesus when he said he was going away and the people could not follow him. Their reaction was to ask him if he was going to the Diaspora to teach the Greeks (cf. John 7:35). The concept of a Dispersion was also used in early Christianity. As the result of persecution, Christians were scattered away from Jerusalem (Acts 8:1b) so that when the first letter of Peter was written, Christians in Asia were described as a Diaspora (*diaporas*; 1 Pet 1:1).

I turn now to examine the Gospels themselves as witnesses to Jesus. My hope is that these background studies will provide a sufficient introduction to help readers understand more clearly the significance of Jesus' arrival on the world scene and the strategic importance of the Gospel testimonies.

Recommended for Further Study

The Apocrypha of the Old Testament: Revised Standard Version. New York: Nelson & Sons, 1957.

Barrett, C. K., editor. *N. T. Background Documents*. New York: Harper & Row, 1956.

Cartlidge, D. R., and D. L. Dungan. *Documents for the Study of the Gospels*. Minneapolis: Fortress, 1980.

Charlesworth, J. H. *O. T. Pseudepigrapha*. 2 volumes. Garden City NY: Doubleday, 1983.

Danby, H., editor. *The Mishnah*. London: Oxford Univeristy Press, 1933.

Flusser, D. *Judaism of the Second Temple Period*. Volume 1 of *Qumran and Apocalypticism*. Grand Rapids MI/Jerusalem: Eerdmans/Hebrew University Magnes Press, 2007.

Martyinez, F. G. *The Dead Sea Scrolls Translated: The Qumran Texts in English*. Leiden Netherlands/Grand Rapids MI: Brill/Eerdmans, 1992.

Nickelsburg, G. W. E. *Jewish Literature Between the Bible and the Mishnah*. Philadelphia: Fortress, 1981.

Vermes, G. *The Dead Sea Scrolls in English*. London: Penguin Books, 1995.

Whiston, W. *The Works of Josephus*, complete and unabridged, new updated edition. Peabody MA: Hendrickson, 1987. For a scholarly Greek and English translation of Josephus, consult the Loeb Classical Library in thirteen volumes published by Harvard University Press.

PART II

UNDERSTANDING THE GOSPELS AS TESTIMONIES

The New Testament opens with four Gospels. Each is unique, and yet each presents a portrait of Jesus that is clearly related to the others. In this chapter I will first review the nature of a gospel in the context of other literary genres. Then I will discuss each book separately and indicate some of the significant features of each work. Finally, I will close with a brief introduction to some of the non-canonical portraits of Jesus and suggest reasons why those works were not accepted by the church.

The Gospels and the Genre Question[1]

The term "gospel" in English is from the Old English word "God's spell," which means "good news," but what does it mean when applied to the first four books of the New Testament? Scholars have long wrestled with the issue of identifying a gospel as a certain kind of literature. At the beginning of the twentieth century, C. W. Votaw argued that the Gospels were similar to ancient biographies, but shortly thereafter Karl L. Schmidt countered with a strong response that the Gospels were a unique type or category of literature within the ancient world. That thesis ruled the day until scholars brought together the results of form and literary studies in the last two-thirds of the century.

---

[1] For a discussion on the nature of a Gospel, see G. L. Borchert, *John 1–11*, NAC (Nashville: Broadman & Holman, 1996) 24–30.

Yet in spite of recent research, it is difficult in this new century to identify the exact genre to which the Gospels most belong.

When one compares the Gospels with other works, one is left with the conclusion that they do not fit neatly into one category. For example, they are not merely histories, even though they record historical data. They are not simply biographies, yet they do contain biographical elements. They cannot be categorized just as memoirs, although they include remembrances. They are not merely good news statements like proclamations of victory in war, despite the fact that they do proclaim good news (*euangelia*). They are not simply chronicles about a heroic figure called Jesus, but it would be hard to suggest that he was not heroic. And, to pinpoint where some of the arguments have been, they are not just theological treatises, though one would scarcely suggest they were not theological.

One is forced to conclude that the Gospels are a combination of all these genres and maybe more. This reflection leads me to suggest that the Gospels are "testimonies" that contain the above elements, and their goal is not merely to engender belief in the verity of the factual statements that have been made but also to bring about a commitment to the one who is the focus of the statements, resulting in a new dynamic of life for the reader (cf. John 20:31).

As I have indicated elsewhere,[2] these testimonies provide pictures of Jesus, but they are not like photographs. They are like portraits where the personality of the artist is contained in the picture. My long-standing illustration of this idea is that when I was in Thailand, I asked a superb portrait artist to paint a portrait of my wife that now hangs in my study. I gave him a small photograph of her as a basis, and he produced a fine portrait. But as I have frequently pointed out to visitors, when you look at it, you can tell by the eyes that it was painted by an Oriental. He painted what he understood a person was like. Someone else would have painted the portrait differently. The same applies to the evangelists

---

[2] See my discussion on the Gospels in G. L. Borchert, *Worship in the New Testament: Divine Mystery and Human Response* (St. Louis: Chalice Press, 2008) 9–11.

in the New Testament. Each is slightly different, but each is an authentic portrait (or testimony) of Jesus.

Moreover, each Gospel has been recognized by the church as a standard (a canonical measure) for judging the authenticity of other portraits of Jesus Christ. Many portraits of Jesus have since been written, and some have been faithful to the standard while others have not. Recognizing and understanding the canonical models is crucial for the faithful follower of Jesus.

Furthermore, it is imperative not to confuse the four models by so amalgamating them that their uniqueness is lost. Such an approach occurred in the second century with Tatian in his *Diatessaron*. Fearing that some critics would find errors or variations in the Gospels, Tatian brought all four of them together in an attempt to create one unified historical harmony of the life of Jesus. In doing so, he deleted any variations in their messages, and when he found slightly different reports he often duplicated them at different times in the life of Jesus. The early Christians, however, were quite aware of the slight differences in the testimonies, and since they were from a Semitic heritage (not western), those differences did not trouble them. But Tatian was a Semite, he became a logical, calculating Greek, and differences were intolerable for him, especially since he was a Hellenistic apologist intent on defending Christianity against its critics. Unfortunately, Tatian's methodology has been congenial to many in the western world and especially in recent years. The result is that many have a harmonized picture of Jesus that may not represent any single Gospel. In addition, since we read the Gospels in short snippets and preachers often fail to provide adequate contextual frameworks for their teaching and preaching, we tend to shove our fragmented readings of Gospel pericopes into our preconceived harmonized pictures of Jesus.

Such an approach may be attractive to many readers, but often what is lost in this style of reading is the focus of a Gospel story in the overall presentation of a particular Gospel. What the student of the Gospels needs to learn is why a pericope appears where it does in a particular Gospel.

A similar problem occurs in the use of red-letter Bibles. Why do we have red letters in Bibles? Are those words more significant than the black words? To be more precise, should John 3:16 actually be in red letters or in black letters? These words are not distinguishable in the original Greek, so the red letters are some recent editor's idea of which words are directly from Jesus and which words are the evangelist's interpretation of Jesus' thoughts. In the case of John 3:16, we cannot be sure if Jesus actually said them, no matter what a modern editor might suggest! But the question remains: Does it really matter whether one can tell if they are the actual words of Jesus or a recollection concerning the sense of what Jesus' coming meant?

Perhaps the study of the four Gospels can provide answers to these and other similar questions that may have arisen in your mind as a reader. I begin with the witness of Mark because it was probably the first one to be written. It provided the format of Jesus' life and work that both Matthew and Luke used and expanded. The reason Matthew was placed first is not because it was written first or for any historical purpose but for theological and organizational purposes. It is the only Gospel that mentions the "church" by name (Matt 16:18), and it provides both significant directions for church life in the Sermon on the Mount (chs. 5–7) and warnings of false piety in the woes against the Pharisees (ch. 23). Similarly, Romans was not the first of the Pauline letters to be written, but it was placed first because it is an excellent summation of Pauline thinking on salvation. So Matthew serves as an excellent introduction to the implications of the coming of Jesus, whereas the Gospel of John functions as the encapsulating conclusion to the acceptable portraits of Jesus. With these comments in mind, I turn now to the analysis of each of these Gospel testimonies. As you read my comments, please remember my earlier advice that you keep your New Testaments open and available for comparison and confirmation of the ideas expressed in this study.

THE WITNESS OF MARK TO JESUS: WHO IS HE?

My favorite reflections concerning the portrait of Jesus in Mark revolve around the question of who Jesus is. He seems to be treated as someone who took people by surprise, making them wonder at his ways. He did not fit into their conceptions of who he should be, and he seemed to act spontaneously. One only needs to read the first chapter of this work that is called a Gospel[1] to note how often the word "immediately" (*euthys*) occurs. Moreover, it does not take the reader long to discover how stunned the people were at his actions and words (cf. 1:27; 2:12; etc). He did not fit well into any human perceptions of who he should be. Indeed, even his disciples did not really understand him. Who was this person, they wondered, who could say "shut up" (*siopa*) to a storm and watch as it obeyed him? Jesus was strange, awesome, and, yes, one might even say he was from another world (4:39)!

Since the early disciples were primarily oral people, they must have thrilled to tell the stories of this person named Jesus and watch the responses. Those responses must have sometimes been strangely mixed themselves. Some people probably stared at the disciples in total disbelief. Indeed, their witnessing concerning Jesus often engendered hostility. The stories in Acts 2–4 confirm such reactions. People at that time preferred oral witnessing because they could check the integrity of the witnesses. When I served in Africa, I learned how people could read eyes and reactions of people in the process of negotiating prices. Writing was a secondary form of confirmation in the first century, while personal

---

[1] Note the two uses of the term "gospel" (*euangelium*) in Mark 1:1 and 1:15 that suggest a connection between the proclamation of the good news and the written witness.

encounter was the primary form. Yet as the witnesses began to die, it was necessary not merely to "tell" the stories of Jesus orally but also to record them for posterity. In the transition, this Gospel of Mark provided a new type of written witnessing concerning the stories of Jesus, and it was from the pen of the person who has come to be known as John Mark.[2]

I normally suggest to my students that they read the beginning and the end of a Gospel to discover the key to its focus, but in the case of Mark, in spite of many arguments to the contrary, I am convinced that both the beginning and end are missing as though the outside folio pages were lost early in its existence.[3] One cannot simply argue with some scholars that the ending was ripped off because of some heretical opposition to the resurrection since the idea of Jesus' resurrection is actually declared four times before the end (cf. 8:31; 9:9, 31; and 10:34). But in spite of the missing beginning and end of the book, some intriguing clues are present. One key and strange feature of the Gospel was noted by Wilhelm Wrede early in the twentieth century. He called the concept the "Messianic Secret." He used this idea to dissuade other scholars from thinking Mark was merely a history book that was so primitive as to have no theological framework.[4]

There is no doubt that the "secret" idea is important to Mark because Jesus refused to allow the evil and unclean spirits to speak openly about him, even though they knew who he was and feared him (cf. 1:25, 34, etc.). The demons obeyed him because they had no option, but when he told humans who had been given a free will to do the same, they really did not understand who he was and therefore they did not obey (cf. 1:43–45, etc.). The portrait became quite clear at Caesarea

---

[2] Tradition dating back to the second century and Papias, a disciple of John of Zebedee, seems to have linked the John Mark mentioned in Acts (13:5–13; 15:37–39), in the Pauline letters (Col 4:10; Phlm 24; 2 Tim 4:11), and in 1 Pet 5:13 with the writer of this Gospel, but the records in Eusebius, the early church historian, are not totally conclusive. See *Historia Ecclesiastica* 3.39.4 and 15.

[3] Prior to his death, I shared this idea of the lost beginning and end of Mark with C. F. D. Moule, the stellar Cambridge New Testament scholar, and he indicated that he also had grown in his conviction that such was the case.

[4] His work was finally translated into English as *The Messianic Secret* (London: James Clarke, 1971) decades after it appeared in German.

Philippi when Peter was able to confess Jesus as the long-expected Messiah (Christ, the anointed one) and the disciples were again told not to reveal him (8:29–30). But when Jesus then tried to explain his necessary role as the dying and rising Messiah, it was the same Peter, the confessor, who rebuked Jesus for such a shocking idea of a dying Savior. His reaction again revealed that he had no understanding of what he had confessed and that he was pathetically little more than a foolish human being who acted like Satan (8:31–33).

The question of course is this: Since demons were not allowed to witness concerning Jesus, when would his followers be allowed to do so? The answer comes after the Transfiguration, when the disciples witnessed the amazing conversation of Jesus with Elijah and Moses. Peter again showed that he completely misunderstood Jesus and the significance of this crucial event in the preparation for Jesus' Messianic role. He excitedly suggested that Jesus was equal to the two great figures in Israel's history (9:5–8), but he was immediately rebuffed by the voice of God. Yet that exchange was not the end of the encounter. As they were descending from the mountain, Jesus provided them with the crucial key for understanding the situation. They would be free to witness concerning him but *not* "until the time when the Son of Man had risen out [of the tombs] of the dead" (*nekron*; 9:9)! The answer was that most humans would never understand Jesus until they had experienced the reality of the resurrection. Then, and only then, would they be able to witness appropriately concerning him.

With this key in mind, join me for a brief excursion through this Gospel. It is important because it served as the foundational document for both Matthew and Luke. For ease of treatment, the Gospel can be divided as follows: (1) introduction (1:1–13); (2) ministry in South Galilee (1:14–7:23); (3) ministry in the north (7:24–9:50); and (4) events in Judea (10:1–16:8).

1. The Introduction: Mark 1:1–13

In Mark's introduction as we now have it, the witness to Jesus begins with a brief reference to the baptizer, John, and the baptism of Jesus. At this initial stage he was identified clearly by a divine voice as the "beloved Son" of God (1:11)! Note how this first confession coordinates perfectly with the Roman officer's confession concerning the dying Jesus as the Son of God at the cross near the conclusion of the Gospel (15:39). But the introduction here does not end without identifying the opposition to Jesus.

The wilderness (desert) is the site of the opponent's attack. But the enemy of Jesus was and is not merely human agents, but Satan himself (1:13). Yet Jesus was not abandoned by God in the persistent conflict between good and evil because angels ministered to him even in the harsh wilderness of the world (1:13). This statement is crucial for interpreting the often misunderstood cry of dereliction from the cross by Jesus later in the Gospel (15:34).

2. The Southern Galilean Ministry: Mark 1:14–7:23

The southern Galilean ministry of Jesus opened immediately without fanfare as Jesus began to collect his followers (1:16–20) and proceeded to confront the forces of evil in the context of the synagogue at Nazareth. The result was that the people were not only awestruck but appropriately raised the question of his authority. What kind of a person can confront the spirit world and win (1:21–27)?

After healing several people and silencing the spirits but failing to deter humans in announcing his miraculous acts, the next stage was reached. This time faithful friends brought a paralytic to be healed. But instead of merely healing him, Jesus transformed him by announcing that his "sins [were] forgiven!" The challenge was given to the religious leaders with their legalistic formulas and religious constructs. They judged Jesus' words to be blasphemous because only God could forgive sins. Who was this fellow, they wondered, who claimed such authority? Jesus responded with another question: Which is easier, healing or forgiving sins (2:1–11)? The loaded question revealed the depth of the inevitable conflict with the religious leaders: Was the holy God primarily concerned with religious rules or with people? The people responded with awe or amazement, but the religious leaders would soon reveal their understandings about God and religious rules.

The stage was set to describe the next several encounters on the issue of religious practices, but first Mark continued Jesus' selection of disciples: this time Jesus had the audacity to choose a despised tax collector (2:13–17)! That event was followed by a "religious" question: Why do your disciples not fast like every other respectable religious group? Jesus answered that something new was taking place, and it was time to celebrate (2:18–22). Why should they fast? A confrontation about Sabbath obedience quickly followed. His disciples had grabbed some grain and eaten it while walking through a field, breaking several Sabbath rules of reaping, threshing, and winnowing all at one time. The "religious" must have thought Jesus was totally irreligious, but he compounded the situation by making the astonishing claim that the Sabbath was made for humanity and not the reverse. Moreover, he added that he was the "Lord of the Sabbath" (2:23–28). Clearly everyone was given a signal that Jesus was trouble! The religious leaders were sure he was a rebel and so they watched him for a chance to indict him on punishable charges. He actually acquiesced by healing someone in the synagogue on the Sabbath. After witnessing the event, the religious Pharisees even joined forces with their traditional opponents (the Herodian stooges) to plot Jesus' destruction (3:1–6). We are barely into the Gospel and the end of the story is already in view. To make the point more evident, Mark then gives us the insight that Jesus' ways were so captivating that huge crowds followed him from the north and the south. Many other healings were done, and even the spirits cried out that he was "the Son of God" as they lost their battles with him. But he quickly shut down their unacceptable screams and acknowledgments of him (3:7–12).

The next stage was initiated with the appointment of Jesus' complete band of twelve (reflecting the select number of the people of Israel), and he gave them a ministry that derived from his own preaching and his having authority over the spirit world (3:13–19). This move was countered by his friends trying to protect him from himself (3:20–21) and the scribal authorities circulating an illogical charge that he had been conquering demons by the power of Beelzebul, the prince of demons (3:22–27). At this point Mark inserted one of the most telling statements of Jesus dealing with the unforgivable sin, namely, blaspheming the good Holy Spirit's work or in this case designating the good as bad (3:28–30). Blaming God for evil is actually high treason or blasphemy itself. With the temperature of the conflict having risen, the earthly family of Jesus sought to intercept him for his own protection, but Jesus countered them by announcing that his true family was composed of people who did "the will of God" (3:31–35).

At chapter 4, Mark includes a few parables as examples of Jesus' thinking and teaching. Matthew and Luke have many more parables disbursed throughout their Gospels, but Mark has only a few. The parables here represent clues into the "kingdom of God." Jesus used this method of teaching to challenge his listeners to search beyond the outward aspects of religion. While he did not explain the implications to everyone, he made them clear to his disciples (4:10–12, 33–34). People, he said, are like various types of soil that respond to the communication of the gospel in different ways (4:1–20): (a) some are as hard as cement and can not receive it; (b) some are as thin as a minimum coating of top soil, and even though they seem to be enthusiastic in receiving the gospel, they have no depth to sustain them; (c) others are so busy and involved that their reception of the gospel is choked like thorns choke grain;(d) but some actually respond to God's ways and are productive in the kingdom. Moreover, true people of the kingdom do not hide who they are because they are like illuminating candles (4:21–25). Also, although their integrity may not be obvious immediately, followers of Jesus continue to develop (4:26–29), and even though their faith begins small, they mature into stalwart models of authenticity (4:30–32).

Having provided insights into the kingdom, Mark returned to the reality of events that were taking place in the ministry of Jesus. The Gospel writer set the next part of his testimony in the context of two powerful sea stories (4:35–41 and 6:45–52). The first story describes how the disciples were out in a boat with Jesus when a great storm arose on the Sea of Galilee (see my references to the topography of Israel). But Jesus was peacefully asleep on a pillow. In terror the disciples woke him and questioned whether or not he cared about their safety. In response Jesus turned to the stormy sea and sharply told it to "shut up" (be muzzled)! Immediately a great calm returned to the entire lake (4:39). The second story reveals that Jesus had retreated to the hills in solitude, where he saw the disciples in a distressing storm in their boat. Jesus calmly came out like he was taking a stroll in the middle of the night, walking on the water! Indeed, he was about to pass them by when they screamed, thinking he was a ghost (6:48–49). He tried to calm their electrified imaginations and spoke to them using the historic Old Testament words addressed to Moses, "I am!" (*ego eimi*), and adding the familiar reassuring words from theophanies (divine visitations), "Do not fear!" (6:50).

Before I leave these stories, I want to point out the hook in both accounts. The disciples' reactions are significant. In the first story their response is "Who is this fellow that can control a storm?" and in the second story they are stunned by the water-walker who did not sink and who could stop the terrifying wind (4:41 and 6:51). The disciples might have been his companions, but they did not understand this person called Jesus. He was spooky!

Sandwiched between these two stories, Mark has set significant pericopes that provide further insights into Jesus. In the first one, Jesus confronted an uncontrollable demon-possessed man. The demonic spirits recognized Jesus immediately and, after crying that Jesus was the "Son of the Most High God," they begged him not to disturb them. When the spirits realized that they would no longer be allowed to reside in the man, they bargained with Jesus to be sent into a huge group of pigs rather than consigned to a "no-man's land." Jesus granted their request, but as soon as the spirits entered the pigs, the herd became so confused that they stampeded and ran off the cliff into the sea (5:1–13). The result was that the spirits actually perished in the watery *tahom* (the ancient concept of the formless depth of Gen 1:2).

My students do not generally like this story because they (probably like the ancient Romans who liked pork) are concerned about the poor pigs and regard the result as a great loss of bacon and ham. The Jews of Jesus' day, however, would hardly have worried about the pigs. They probably would have cheered because the pigs were unclean animals and should not be eaten. For the Jews, the evil spirits and the pigs belonged in the same category of rejects. Still, the point of the story is not the pigs; it is the rescuing of a man who is precious in God's eyes. When he was sane again, this man was given a commission by Jesus to return to the frightened Gentile villagers of the Decapolis and explain about the transforming power of God in Jesus (5:14–20). A Gentile human instructed to proclaim Jesus? It is indeed intriguing, but it is no less surprising than the fact that a Gentile Roman centurion issued the climactic confession concerning Jesus in the Gospel (15:34). Gentiles do count!

The next two stories provide a fine example of Mark's use of literary "sandwiches" or envelope stories (one story placed within another that gives focus to both). In the outside story, we read that Jairus, one of the rulers of the synagogue, asked for Jesus to come and heal his daughter, but while they were on their way, the events of the inside story took place. A poor sick woman pushed through the crowd, believing that if she could only touch a fringe of Jesus' cloak, she would be healed. In response, she was instantly healed, and Jesus immediately asked, "Who touched my clothing?" The press of the crowd, however, made his question seem foolish. Yet the woman acknowledged her act and Jesus replied that her faith had been instrumental in the healing (5:25–34). But notice the second part of the outside story. A report arrived for Jairus that his daughter had died. Jesus assured the synagogue leader not to worry, but "only believe!" When they arrived at Jairus's house, as one might expect, the weeping and mourning was well under way. When Jesus tried to suggest that the daughter was not in danger, the leader's household and friends simply laughed at him. Nevertheless, Jesus summoned the girl, and she immediately she came back to life, stunning everyone there. The contrast is evident, and Jesus required silence from this "religious" family who did not believe (5:35–43).

The point of the above "sandwich" illustrated for Mark the differences in believing patterns: the one who was likely expected to have faith (the religious) hardly turned out to be the model, whereas the poor woman hardly needed to be told to have faith. This issue is highlighted next in the context of the synagogue near Jesus' home. While his neighbors received reports about his amazing feats, they could not believe the reports because he was just a neighbor and they knew his family! The result was that those closest to him, his own neighbors, could not experience his power for themselves because of their unbelief (6:1–6). But to his disciples Jesus gave the authority to represent him in preaching, in having power over the spirits, and in healing (6:12–13).

Rejection of God's servants is nothing new. It was true of the prophets of old, it was true of the faithful in the days of Jesus, and it is true of believers today. John the Baptist had clearly called for integrity, and he forcefully condemned immoral patterns of life, even challenging the integrity of those in authority—including the powerful offspring of Herod the Great (cf. Matt 3:7–10). Because of John's forthrightness concerning Herodias (and her inauthentic life, including her manipulative divorce and quest for power; cf. Mark 6:19), this scheming wife of Herod Antipas made John pay for challenging her integrity by demanding his head (6:16–29).

The remaining stories in this section give us further insights into the two sides of Jesus. The feeding of the five thousand (6:30–44) highlights Jesus' compassion and sense of caring for those who needed a shepherd (6:34), even if the crowd was huge.[5] By way of contrast, instead of focusing on Jesus' care for the people, Mark next highlighted Jesus' condemnation of the Pharisees for their lack of integrity in concentrating their attention on external matters and overlooking the real issues of authentic life (7:1–13). The purity of pots and hands could hardly

---

[5] While I am not given to the study of numbers, one cannot read the book of Revelation, reflect on some of the Gospel stories, and study the ancient Semitic world without giving some attention to this matter. The numbers involved in the feeding stories appear to have been significant for the early Christians. The five loaves and two fish in the feeding of the five thousand add up to the perfect number of seven (three plus four). The twelve (three times four) baskets of leftovers also were important as a motif. In the feeding of the four thousand (Mark 8:1–9), there are seven loaves but the fish are not counted because the number seven had already been achieved and seven baskets are left. In the ancient world the number three was used to represent the divine whereas the number four represented the world, which was viewed from such a perspective as being flat and having four sides. The numbers seven and twelve were thus seen as combinations of the divine and the created or human order. These combinations gave the sense of perfection (unity or wholeness in the case of seven) and a special God-selected community (in the case of twelve, especially for the Hebrews). Beyond Israel and the church, consider the pyramids of Egypt, which are triangles (threes) on the base of a square (four), identifying the person (a pharaoh) buried in such a man-made mountain as the combination of the divine and the human. While much more could be added here, this brief introduction should stimulate further reflection on such numbers as five and its multiples (as human completeness), especially forty as the equivalent of "many" and six as "incomplete" (or deficient), etc. But great care must be taken not to use numbers to speculate in a predictive manner as though secrets are hidden in biblical numbers.

compare to genuineness of life or, as Isaiah had written, "Words from the lips are no substitute for obedient hearts" (Mark 7:6; cf. Isa 29:13).

Jesus forcefully denounced hypocrisy as he cited an illustration of a familiar ploy used by the Jewish elite to avoid caring for parents. If children declared their property to be "temporarily" assigned as *Corban* (dedicated to the temple or another Jewish institutional cause), then it could *not* be used to support one's elderly relatives, thus sloughing off responsibility for honoring parents in keeping with the Decalogue (Exod 20:12). Of course, after the parents had died, that temporary status could later be removed, and the property would revert to the original owner. Mark concluded this segment by stipulating that Jesus reminded the Jews that the defilement question focused *not on what was outside* persons *but on what was inside* and came out (7:14–23).

3. The Ministry of Jesus in the North: Mark 7:24–9:50

At this point in his testimony Mark indicated that Jesus left Galilee and went north to the area of Tyre and Sidon (modern Lebanon) where a Gentile woman (a Syrophoenician) came to him and begged to have her sick daughter healed of a demon. Jesus' response often troubles readers; he told her that it was not appropriate to "cast the children's food to the dogs." But the reader must remember that Jews often referred to Gentiles as "dogs." That she would come to a Jew meant she had understood that designation and was willing to use it of herself. Yet she still approached this Jewish teacher/healer for help. The caring Jesus assuredly answered her crying heart (7:27–30).

From Lebanon, the wonder-working Jesus went back to the Decapolis (the ten Greek cities in the north, all east of the Sea of Galilee and the Jordan except Beth Shean/Scythopolis). There he healed a deaf mute but charged him to maintain the secret (7:31–37). Then he fed the four thousand near the Sea of Galilee (see my comment on numbers in footnote 72). But his opponents were also nearby, and they came ready for an argument, wanting him to prove that his miraculous ability was genuine and not like the acts of some magician or performer. Instead, he left them by the boat in disgust (8:11–13). As they departed, the disciples began to bemoan the fact that they forgot to bring food. Do you have the feeling that Jesus would have shaken his head in exasperation at the short memories of the disciples (8:14–21)? Then at Bethsaida he healed a blind man (8:22–26). This last story of blindness seems to serve as Mark's sad capstone on the above accounts of Jesus and as an introduction to the strategic stories at Caesarea Philippi.

In the introduction to Mark's witness, I have already commented on the importance of these accounts for understanding the Gospel. Here I will merely highlight the main points. First, in light of the disciples' short memories and misunderstandings, the questions of Jesus—"Who do people say that I am?" and "Who do you say that I am?"—seem fitting. Second, on the surface, the confession of Peter that Jesus was the Messiah may seem appropriate until we realize the lack of understanding that accompanied Peter's response (8:27–30). Third, when Jesus began to inform them that he would be a suffering and dying Messiah (cf. Isa 52:13–53:12), Peter launched into a castigation of Jesus for such an idea. Jesus' well-known response was to identify Peter's reaction with the way of Satan; it was totally foreign to the divine way (8:31–33). Fourth, having thus identified clearly the way of the Messiah, Jesus indicated that the pattern of the faithful disciple would also have to be the way of the cross. To reject this way would also mean to be rejected by the "Son of Man." But Jesus was confident that his disciples would experience the power of his coming kingdom (8:34–9:1).

With these statements as a framework, Mark then introduced the crucial Transfiguration story with its implications. First, the encounter of Jesus with Elijah and Moses (the two stellar figures in Israel's history[6]) was patently viewed as a communication from God that conveyed an affirmation of Jesus' role in fulfilling God's intentions in history and also helped the disciples understand the significance of Jesus in those intentions (9:2–4). Second, not only did the experience of divine mystery (*mysterium tremendum*) frighten the disciples but Peter completely misinterpreted the event and needed to be shocked into a correct perspective that Jesus was in fact the Son of God (9:5–8). Third, Jesus had

---

[6] Moses and Elijah (as well as the shadowy figure of Enoch), were never buried by the Jews, and therefore they were assumed to be in the presence of God. As a result, their names were used to present various apocalyptic prophecies concerning the future.

to inform them that they could be his witnesses in the future but not "until" they had experienced his resurrection (9:9). Fourth, the preliminary predictions for the expected arrival of the Messiah had been fulfilled, including the coming of a new Elijah in John the Baptist. The time of the Messiah had clearly begun (9:10–13).

When those on the mountain came down, they were confronted with another failure on the part of the disciples. Those who had been left below had sought to represent Jesus by trying to confront an evil spirit that rendered a young boy helpless,[7] yet they were unsuccessful. When Jesus arrived on the scene, he had no difficulty dealing with the situation, but he chastened the disciples for a more serious failure of not spending time in prayer (9:14–29).

These two stories must be interpreted together: (a) the ones on the mountain were criticized for misunderstanding the significance of Jesus in their experience of spiritual retreat, and although they wanted to remain in the mountaintop experience, Jesus took them back down to the valley of life; and (b) the ones in the valley misunderstood their task of ministry because they had not spent time in spiritual retreat. Both retreat and action are necessary for Christian spiritual vitality and service, but both must be correctly related to the perspectives of Jesus.

This section closes with Jesus' return to Galilee. It contains a restatement of Jesus' messianic mission to suffer, die, and be raised from the dead, and it provides another indication of the disciples' misunderstanding of that mission (9:30–32). It concludes with a special consideration of humility in which Jesus illustrated for his followers the true model of servanthood, choosing a child as an example to emphasize the fact that his followers should be concerned for those who are helpless (9:33–37). Moreover, he clearly indicated that his followers did not all have to belong to the same party (9:38–40), but in a series of brief examples he called them both to authentic service and to complete personal integrity with God so that they would not experience the fire of Gehenna, the state designated in later second temple Jewish thinking as the place of torment and judgment for disobedience, frequently rendered today as Hell (9:41–50).

---

[7] Apparently similar to a person suffering from an epileptic fit.

4. Conflict and Conclusion in Judea: Mark 10:1–16:8

As Jesus moved into Judea, the intensity of the conflict increased. While the people continued to follow him (10:1), the hostility of his opponents mushroomed. Employing a major point of dissension among the rabbis, the Pharisees sought to test Jesus concerning his view of divorce and the legitimacy of the Mosaic options. Jesus' response pointed his questioners not to a legal prescription but to the original intention of God for marriage and the fact that in the process, men (who usually put women out) were not freer from adultery than women (10:2–12).[8] Then employing another set of "sandwich" texts, Mark set the so-called story of the rich questioner (10:17–23) in the context of two pericopes about children (10:13–16 and 24–31). Although the disciples rejected the people who brought children to Jesus, he severely censured them and indicated that children were the kinds of people who belonged to the kingdom of God (10:15). Then the rich legalist asked him what he needed to do to inherit eternal life. When the man confirmed that he had kept all the commandments, including the second ledger of the Decalogue, Jesus lovingly told him to sell all his possessions and give the proceeds to the poor (10:21). Such a demand was too much for the rich man. The disciples were stunned at the response (10:24), so Jesus addressed them as children and declared how difficult it was for the rich to enter the kingdom. This text has troubled some Christians, but Jesus did not pander either to the rich or the poor. Instead, he identified the aspects of people's lives that were "substitute gods" for them (see Exod 20:3), and he emphasized that those who appear to be primary in the world's eyes would likely be last in God's kingdom. But those who have given much for the gospel would be overwhelmingly rewarded (Mark 10:29–31).

Next, Mark inserted into his witness the third passion prediction of Jesus (10:32–34) before focusing on the disciples' failures in understanding his thinking. Not perceiving the force of the previous

---

[8] For a discussion on the confusion in translations of the words for divorce and putting women out of the house, see Gerald L. Borchert, "1 Corinthians 7:15 and the Church's Historic Misunderstanding of Divorce and Remarriage," *R&E* 96/1 (1999): 125–29.

dialogue, the sons of Zebedee requested the chief places of recognition and authority next to Jesus in the kingdom (glory). They were typical self-seeking humans and had no idea what they were requesting. The rest of the Twelve probably would have hoped for the same positions but were disgusted with the two who had the audacity to ask first. That Jesus had his hands full with his "followers" is not an exaggeration. But he did not give up on them and reminded them that his way was not the world's way. Indeed, his purpose was not to seek power over others but to serve them and be their redeeming sacrifice. Likewise, the role of the disciples was not to be rulers but servants (10:35–45). In the next few verses, the pericope of blind Bartimaeus reminds us that change can take place, and even unaware disciples can be given the clarity needed for understanding (10:46–52).

The Gospel testimony then moves to its climax with the so-called "triumphal entry" into Jerusalem (11:1–11). Another set of "sandwich" texts gives focus to that entry. It may seem on first glance that the entry was a victorious event, but the cursing of the fig tree (11:12–14) points in another direction. It is employed by Mark to introduce the cleansing of the temple (11:15–19). When Jesus and the disciples returned the next day, they saw that the fig tree was dead (11:20–21). My students are sometimes troubled that Jesus cursed a helpless fig tree, which the text indicates should not have had fruit on it at that time of the year. But Mark does not use the fig tree story as a commentary on horticulture. It is a commentary on the state of the temple administration: it was dead and useless. The disciples received an example of what faith could do because they were called to the world not to kill people (who already could be judged as dead) but to proclaim life and forgiveness (11:22–25).

Of course, the Jewish establishment was not going to let the events of the entry and the cleansing of the temple go unchallenged. They confronted Jesus on the matter of his authority. When they refused to answer his question on the authority of John the Baptist, he also refused to answer them (11:27–33). Then he told them a parable about wicked tenants occupying a vineyard, mistreating the owner's servants, and actually killing the son when he came for a reckoning (12:1–11). The religious leaders had no difficulty recognizing that they were implicated; they knew the prophets had frequently identified Israel as God's vineyard (e.g., Isa 5:1–7; 27:2–6), and they recognized Jesus' reference to the rejection of the corner stone (cf. Ps 118:22–23). They were the wicked tenants! They could not get Jesus at that point, but they would do so later (Mark 12:12).

The showdown began in earnest. The Pharisees and their Herodian conspirators sought to trap Jesus on the issue of taxes, but he shocked them by telling them to render to Caesar what was his due but, more important, not to forget to render to God what belonged to God (12:13–17). Then it was the Sadducees' turn. They tried to confuse him by positing a question about levirate marriage (cf. Deut 25:5–10; Ruth 4:1–11), wondering whose wife a man would have in the resurrection after seven brothers had "had her" on earth. Jesus countered their attempt to snare him in a theological conundrum by indicating that they had tried to transport worldly realities to heaven, which would not work (12:18–27). Finally, one of the scribal teachers took his turn and asked the crucial question of rabbinic debate concerning the primary law for Israel. Jesus answered by giving him the twofold law of love—love God and love neighbor (12: 28–33; cf. Deut 6:4 and Lev 19:18)—that surpassed all the temple ceremonies. With these encounters, Mark indicated, the interrogations of Jesus ceased (12:34).

But then it was Jesus' turn for a rebuttal. He asked, "How could David in Psalm 110:1 say 'the Lord said to my Lord'? How could his son be his Lord?" (12:35–37). They refused to answer that question, and so Jesus condemned the scribal leaders who publicly paraded their religion but cheated widows and were inauthentic (12:38–40). To confirm this point, Mark indicated that Jesus employed an illustration of a poor widow whose meager gift to the temple surpassed all the great gifts of the rich (12:41–44).

Scarcely, however, did the disciples understand this condemnation of show. In the next pericope, they called Jesus' attention to the magnificent buildings of the temple.[9] The response of Jesus was the

---

[9] The magnificent rebuilding of the second temple that started in 20/19 B.C. under the sponsorship of Herod the Great was still in process during the lifetime of Jesus. In fact, it would not be completed for another thirty years, and then it only stood in its finished state for about five years before its destruction (see the discussion on the temple above).

stunning announcement that all the buildings would be destroyed (13:1–2). Naturally, many questions followed concerning this destruction and how it related to the end of time. Accordingly, the stage was set for the eschatological instructions of Jesus. Several important points can be highlighted briefly here. First, many theories of the end would be proposed, but Jesus' followers are warned that "apocalyptic proclaimers" would lead people astray. They should not be heeded (13:5–8, 21–22). Second, Christians would suffer persecution and be betrayed by friends and family, but the call was for endurance in the face of suffering (13:9, 12–13). Third, the gospel had to be preached throughout the world prior to the end, and the Holy Spirit would empower Christians for that task (13:10–11). Fourth, the temple and Jerusalem would be destroyed, and believers were warned to flee from the destruction (13:14–18).[10] Fifth, the return of Jesus and the end of time would be a cataclysmic period of cosmic destruction (13:19–20, 24–27). Sixth, Christians should be alert and on their guard not to miss the signs of the times (13:28–29, 33–37). Significantly, seventh, while the end is certain, no one knows the time of the end. It was even hidden from Jesus (13:30–32)! Therefore, Christians are forewarned not to trust apocalyptic predictors—even today!

From the stringent words concerning the end, Mark moved to the conclusion of Jesus' ministry on earth, employing yet another set of "sandwich" texts to frame this part of the testimony. The Passover was near and a plot was necessary for Jesus' death, but it had to be done without arousing the crowd (14:1–2). Judas Iscariot supplied the basis for the plot (14:10–11). Between the two segments of the plot, Mark placed the strategic anointing of Jesus. In Mark, the woman who anointed Jesus remained unnamed although in John we learn that her name was Mary (cf. John 12:3). The large value of the ointment (300 denarii) suggests that it could have been a part of a bride price (dowry). Some who witnessed her act gasped at the waste, but Jesus recognized it as an important symbol of his forthcoming death and indicated that she would be remembered wherever the gospel was preached (Mark 14:3–9).

---

[10] Jewish Christians in Israel took this warning seriously in the days prior to the fall of Jerusalem and fled to the Decapolis city of Pella.

The next events moved like the incessant drumbeat of a death march. The day of sacrificing the Passover lambs had arrived along with the time when Jesus would eat the Last Supper with his disciples (14:12–16). Then traitorous Judas was unmasked while reclining next to Jesus at supper, using the same bowl for dipping as Jesus (14:17–21).[11] The meal initiated the "Lord's Supper" with the promise that Jesus would not drink the fruit of the vine until the coming of the kingdom (14:22–25). After the dinner, in typical Jewish tradition, they sang a hymn and left for the Mount of Olives. Jesus announced that all of them would abandon him. Dear Peter once again thought he knew better and pledged his total commitment to Jesus. But this unique teacher was hardly impressed and instead informed Peter that he would deny Jesus three times that very night (14:26–31).

The Gethsemane story follows, and the poor disciples hardly perceived what was about to happen as their eyes were too heavy with sleep for them to stay awake and pray (14:32–40). All, however, was not tranquil. The traitor arrived with armed forces from the chief priests and the Sanhedrin, and in an act that symbolized ultimate hypocrisy, Judas called Jesus "Rabbi" (my Master) and kissed him not as a sign of friendship but as an identification to his enemies (14:41–45). As the band arrested Jesus, one of the disciples took matters into his own hands and sliced off the ear of the high priest's servant (undoubtedly Peter; cf. John 18:10). But then they all gave up and abandoned Jesus. Mark here added a unique reference to a young man who followed but lost his linen cloak and then escaped when the arresting band tried to seize him. This note may reflect a personal experience of the writer (Mark 14:51–52), but it also could be symbolic of the state of the nakedness or being bereft of hope on the part of the writer and of all the disciples.

---

[11] One should understand the formation of a "U-shaped" triclinium table arrangement where service is done from inside the "U." Those eating a meal would normally lie leaning on their left elbows with feet outstretched, using their right hands to eat the food in front of them and dip the bread, etc. in the sauces. Such an arrangement would basically put one person on each side of Jesus for sharing a dipping bowl. Since the beloved disciple ("John") was said to have been lying in the bosom of Jesus (in front of him; cf. John 13:23), it would mean that Judas was likely at the back of Jesus.

The armed band marched Jesus directly to the late night council, and while Jesus was being falsely charged, Peter stealthily followed and entered the courtyard of the high priest. By contrast, the frustrated high priest openly asked Jesus if he was "the Christ, the Son of the blessed one." Jesus responded affirmatively, adding that they would soon discover him sitting at the right hand of omnipotent power. Then, employing the symbolism of judgment, Jesus indicated that he would come on the clouds (14:62; cf. Dan 7:13). The high priest needed no further testimony to condemn Jesus as a blasphemer (Mark 14:64). While the Jews pronounced their judgment on Jesus (14:65), in the courtyard another part of the contrast took place (14:66–71). Peter was confronted three times with the charge of being a follower of Jesus, which he stoutly denied. The last time, he even took an oath against himself. Then the cock crowed! Peter was shaken to the core of his being (14:72).

Confirming the judgment against Jesus, in the morning the Jewish Sanhedrin agreed to deliver him to Pilate for the administration of death, but in this case they charged him *not* with blasphemy (which would have been inconsequential to the Romans) but with treason (*maiestas*). When Pilate asked Jesus if he were the king of the Jews, Jesus merely acknowledged the charge. He did not seek to defend himself, which was clearly shocking to Pilate (15:1–5). But sensing that the high priests were jealous of Jesus, Pilate tried a ploy. He used the recent Passover tradition of releasing a prisoner at the feast and offered the Jews what seemed to be a clear choice: namely to release either the hardened murderer and insurrectionist Barabbas or the popular Jesus. The religious leaders, however, had programmed the crowd, who chose Barabbas (15:6–11). Then Pilate faced a problem. What was he to do with Jesus? The Jews were ready with an answer: "Crucify him!" "Why?" Pilate demanded. "What wrong has he committed?" But when he could gain no answer, he finally acquiesced, granting the requests of the Jews and beginning the typical flogging of Jesus in preparation for his death (15:12–15).

The Roman soldiers then played their torture games with him, and when they were finished, he was led out to be crucified (15:16–20). As they were en route to Skull Hill (*Golgotha*), the soldiers commandeered the back and shoulders of a visitor (Simon from Cyrene in North Africa) to haul the horizontal crosspiece (*patibulum*) for the victim (15:21–22).

Usually condemned criminals were attached to the crossbar, and people would jab them along the way to the site of their death. Why that pattern was not followed here is not clear.

On Skull Hill Jesus rejected the drugged wine and was crucified between two thieves at the third hour of the day (9:00 A.M.). According to Mark, passersby and even those crucified with Jesus scoffed at him (15:23–32). Then darkness descended on the area from noon until 3:00 in the afternoon, and Jesus in his pain uttered his well-known cry of abandonment before he breathed his last breath. Mark indicates that when he did so, the temple veil separating the Holy Place from the Most Holy Place was shredded from top to bottom as an obvious response from God at the crucifixion of his Son (15:33–38).[12] Finally, at the cross, neither a Jew nor a disciple but a Gentile Roman centurion uttered the crucial confession of Mark's Gospel. That confession was virtually none other than a repetition of what has been preserved as the opening statement of the Gospel: Jesus was indeed "the Son of God" (15:39; cf. 1:1)!

Readers are advised to take seriously the fact that Jesus actually died on the cross, and it was the faithful women who witnessed his death there (15:40–41). But since it was still the Day of Preparation (the day on which the lambs were slain for Passover) and before the start of Passover, Joseph of Arimathea, a faithful member of the Sanhedrin, approached Pilate for the body. Shunning any obvious criticisms that were sure to be leveled at him, Joseph honored the body by wrapping it in a linen shroud, burying it in his new tomb, and closing it with a typical heavy rolling stone while the women followed him in their vigil to the tomb (15:42–47). Jesus was dead and buried. For most people,

---

[12] As I indicated in connection with the temptation statements in Mark 1:12–13, even though Jesus had to suffer temptation in the wilderness, God's angels then ministered to him there. Here at the cross, the suffering of Jesus was so intense that he truly felt alone as he went through the valley of death. But the idea that God actually abandoned Jesus is clearly an incorrect interpretation of the event. Instead, it is better to understand that God was there suffering with his Son when Jesus died on the cross. The ripping of the temple veil, then, was recognized by the early Christians as the presence of God in the event and the clear judgment of God upon the Jewish practices of religion.

including the disciples and the women, those facts should have marked the end of the story, except of course for the final treatment of the body with spices to cover the anticipated smell. But it was *not* the end of this story. It was the *beginning* of a new era!

When the women returned after the Sabbath early on the first day of the week, they were intent on finishing their task of anointing the body. But they were in for another surprise. They found the stone rolled away and a white-robed angelic figure sitting there (16:1–5). They were addressed directly by this figure and told to put away their amazement because Jesus was no longer dead! He had kept his promise and had risen from death. They were invited to look at the same place where they had earlier seen him laid. Then they were given an important commission: to tell the disciples and especially the mourning Peter that Jesus would meet them in Galilee as he foretold them he would (16:6–7).

What would you do if you had an experience like these women had? Would you be shaken and tremble? Would you have expected a resurrection and an encounter with an angelic figure? Your immediate reaction no doubt would have been shock and numbness! Such a statement is precisely the way the Gospel ends (16:8). But was it the way the Gospel originally ended? It seems unlikely, even though one of my former doctoral students proposed in his dissertation that it did so, and it is the way some scholars have recently argued. The early transmitters of the Gospel hardly thought it ended this way, and they added a couple of possible endings, neither of which is original. But for an entire Gospel to end with a Greek post-positive *gar* ("for") seems highly unlikely. I assume there were some resurrection appearances in Galilee, but I cannot speculate on their content. About all I can do is affirm that Jesus was raised from the dead and that Mark clearly believed it to be the case as is evident in his earlier predictions concerning both Jesus' death and his powerful resurrection (8:31; 9:9, 31; 10:34).

This Jesus is *not* now dead. And the question for Mark is clearly answered. "Jesus Christ, the Son of God," is alive, and he calls us "to repent and believe the good news" (1:1, 15)!

Recommended for Further Study

Garland, D. E. *Mark.* NIV Application Commentary. Grand Rapids MI: Zondervan, 1996.

Hengel, M. *Studies in the Gospel of Mark.* Philadelphia: Fortress, 1985.

Rhodes, D., and D. Michie. *Mark as Story: An Introduction to the Narrative of a Gospel.* Philadelphia: Fortress, 1982.

Witherington III, B. *The Gospel of Mark: A Socio-Rhetorical Commentary.* Grand Rapids MI: Eerdmans, 2001.

Guelich, R. *Mark 1:1–8:26.* WBC. Dallas: Word, 1989.

Evans, C. A. *Mark 8:27–16:20.* WBC. Nashville: Thomas Nelson, 2001.

The Witness of Matthew to Jesus as Emmanuel ("God with Us") and the Fulfillment of Old Testament Prophecies

The Gospel of Matthew has often been designated by Christians as the Gospel for the Jews. Indeed, Irenaeus (a second-century writer against heresies) argued that this Gospel was published for "the Hebrews in their own dialect."[1] Unfortunately, we now know that he made some errors concerning the biblical books, including the fact that Matthew was written in Hebrew (see below). But his thesis that the book was written to the Jews has also created some misunderstandings among Christians. There is no doubt that Matthew had Jews in mind as he wrote, but his goal was to help the Jews understand that God's intentions in Jesus went far beyond the Jews as a national entity. Indeed, Jesus came to expand Jewish understandings of God and to fulfill God's intention in blessing Abraham so that the blessing would extend to the Gentiles and thus to the whole world (Gen 12:2–3 and Matt 28:19–20).

The focus of the Gospel is therefore on Jesus as the fulfillment of Old Testament prophecies. More than any other Gospel, Matthew repeatedly states that Jesus fulfilled what the Lord had promised through one of the prophets (e.g., 1:22; 2:5, 15, 17, 23; 3:3; etc.). For Matthew Jesus was the Messiah and did what the Messiah was destined to do. Thus, almost immediately after the genealogy, Matthew gives the first fulfillment statement and sets the stage for understanding the role of Jesus. Jesus is epitomized in Matthew as "Emmanuel," the true God who is "with us" (1:23). Moreover, Matthew concluded his inspired work

---

[1] The Greek is *en tois Hebraiois te idia auton dialecto*. See *Against Heresies* 3.1.1–2.

with the promise that Jesus would be with his followers "until the end of time" (28:20)! The beginning and the end of Matthew are thus in harmony and form what interpreters call a powerful *inclusio* (enclosure). The parameters of the Gospel claim that the personal presence of God was and is in Jesus (cf. 18:20 concerning Jesus among his followers/the church).

Our knowledge of the authorship of this Gospel depends, like the other Gospels, on early reports of which there are not many. The work is designated as *kata Maththaion* ("according to Matthew"). This Gospel does mention a tax collector by that name (9:9), although Mark 2:14 and Luke 5:27 apparently refer to him as Levi, but all of the Synoptic writers do agree that Matthew is one of the twelve called by Jesus.[2]

The evangelist's interest in Jewish patterns within the Gospel would clearly argue that he was a Jew. But, as I have frequently pointed out, Matthew's statement at the entry into Jerusalem that Jesus rode on two donkeys ("on them;" *epano auton*) at 21:7 would argue that he did not know Hebrew or Hebrew poetic parallelism. The reader should ask which is more likely. Did Jesus sit and ride on two donkeys, or did Matthew in his fulfillment quotation of Zechariah 9:9 misunderstand that reference? Instead of using the Hebrew Bible, it seems more plausible that Matthew (as a business man collecting taxes) spoke Greek and read from the Greek Old Testament (Septuagint–LXX).

1. Introduction of Emmanuel—Fulfillment through the Coming of the Messianic King: Matthew 1:1–2:23

The task for Matthew was to present Jesus as both "God with us" and the fulfillment of the Old Testament expectations for the coming of the messianic king. Although many today (with our changing political structures) prefer not to think of Jesus in terms of a being a king or a monarch, that image was among the most honoring that would come to Matthew's mind. Jesus for him was God's chosen king who fulfilled God's intended purposes for humanity. To accomplish this task, in contrast to Mark, Matthew began with a genealogy that went back to

---

[2] See the lists of the twelve in the Synoptic Gospels where one of the followers of Jesus is "Matthew" (Matt 10:3; Mark 3:18; Luke 6:15; cf. Acts 1:13).

Abraham and linked Jesus with the father of the Jewish faith. He also included four women in the process, which provides a clear hint concerning his overall goal. Those women in the royal genealogy indicate that God was not particular in having an absolutely pure line. The line up to David and Solomon was riddled with outsiders/Gentiles: Tamar the outsider who had married into the clan; Rahab, whoever she was, but whose name was forever associated with the Gentiles at Jericho; Ruth the Moabite outsider and great-grandmother of King David; and finally the mother of King Solomon who had been married to a Hittite before being seduced by David (Matt 1:3, 5, and 6).

If such an introduction were not enough of a hint, the next question involves the identity of the people in Matthew who came to honor the newborn king, Jesus. Were they Jews? No! They were Gentile stargazers from Mesopotamia (2:1–2, 9). Did the Jews know where the king would be born? Yes (2:4–6). But Herod, the Idumean pretender, probably hid the coming of the stargazers and the probable birth of a royal baby from them. Also the religious leaders apparently were not interested in stars. When the Gentiles came to Bethlehem, they entered a "house" (2:11), which should help correct the faulty translation of "inn" at Luke 2:7. Then the Jews suffered what could be reckoned as the beginning of the so-called birth pangs of the Messiah with their dead children in Bethlehem. Jesus had to escape from the treachery of Herod to the land of Egypt from whence God would again call his Son as he did with the children of Israel many years before (2:13–18). Matthew's infancy narrative ends with the death of Herod, yet Jesus did not move back to Judea. The family went north to Nazareth, so the move fulfilled, according to Matthew, the prediction that Jesus would be called a Nazarene (someone from Nazareth), a term that Matthew may have thought sounded like Nazarite and that has led countless artists to portray Jesus with long hair (2:19–23).

2. The Preparation of Jesus, the King, for Ministry: Matthew 3:1–4:11

At this point Matthew (also Luke) basically reused Mark's account of John the Baptist's call to repent because the kingdom was near, enhancing it slightly from Mark by pointing to John's theological conflict with the Pharisees and Sadducees (Matt 3:7–10; cf. Luke 3:7–9). Then he reported the story of Jesus' baptism with the important notation that John at first refused to baptize Jesus, but when Jesus insisted that such an act was necessary "to fulfill all righteousness" *(plerosai pasan dikaiosunen;* Matt 3:14–15), he acquiesced.

Highlighting this section is the temptation of Jesus. Obviously employing another source than Mark, Matthew (also Luke) expanded greatly the brief temptation account in Mark. The encounter between the devil and Jesus is presented as a fascinating face-off between two strong wills, and a spirited exchange ensued using quotations from the Bible as a foundation for the two opposing arguments (4:1–11). The intriguing approach of the devil should give notice to humans that to take on the devil is risky business. The enemy skillfully confronted Jesus with (1) a human physical need, (2) a desire for acceptance and acclamation, and (3) a peaceful negotiation and the suggestion for Jesus to achieve God's purposes of establishing the kingdom by acquiescence to the devil. Notice, however, that in contrast to the Lucan account (Luke 4:1–13), the Matthean report ends with the encounter on a mountain and the temptation by the devil to give Jesus, God's chosen king, the kingdoms of the world! But the devil does not own these kingdoms. He is a usurper.

The confrontation on the mountain as the climax to the temptations in Matthew 4:8 is a reminder of the importance of mountains to the Jews (e.g., Abraham's potential sacrifice of Isaac was on a mountain in Moriah [which has traditionally been identified with Jerusalem's temple mount]; the Law was given to Moses on Mt. Sinai; Elijah proved the superiority of Yahweh on Mt. Carmel; and the temple was built on the mountain threshing floor of Jerusalem). Similarly, Matthew has given particular attention to mountains in his Gospel. The initial teaching section in this Gospel following the temptation account is usually called the Sermon on the "Mount" (Matt 5–7). Healing, which was also significant in the ministry of Jesus, is reported to have occurred when Jesus ascended the cliffs near the Sea of Galilee and unlike most medical doctors did not merely dispense a prescription for medicine but actually gave on-the-spot healing to the people (15:29–31). Then, as Jesus prepared for his coming passion, he retreated with his disciples to a high mountain (probably Mt. Hermon) near Caesarea Philippi and met with Moses and

Elijah (the two earlier mountain men) in the astonishing Transfiguration event (17:1–8). Later, he delivered the fifth and final teaching session in Matthew, the Discourse on the Future, from the Mount of Olives (see 24:3). The Gospel then is brought to a powerful conclusion with the appearance of the resurrected Jesus on a mountain in Galilee where he gave the disciples his closing commission (28:16). Do not overlook the significance of mountains for a Jewish audience.

3. Introduction to Jesus' Teaching Ministry of the Kingdom: Matthew 4:12–7:29

This section begins with a brief announcement of the imprisonment of John and the initiation of Jesus' ministry in "Galilee of the Gentiles" as a fulfillment of prophecy (cf. Isa 9:1) together with his heralding of the necessity for repentance as a basis for the kingdom of heaven (Matt 4:12–17). After describing how Jesus chose his first four disciples and embarked on his ministry of preaching the kingdom and healing all sorts of illnesses throughout the entire country (4:18–25), Matthew focused on detailing Jesus' first teaching section.

As I have suggested above, Jesus delivered five focused teaching sections in Matthew. Each is specifically identified by its closing statement in which Matthew noted that Jesus "finished" teaching at that point (7:28; 11:1; 13:53; 19:1; and 26:1). The fact that there are five teaching sections in Matthew could hardly have been a chance happening for a Jew who was taught from childhood that God gave the Torah to Moses in five books (the Pentateuch). The intention therefore seems obvious that the evangelist intended Jesus' teaching to supersede the teachings of Moses. This view is highlighted in the first teaching section known as the Sermon on the Mount (5:1–7:29).[3] It is regarded by many interpreters as one of most strategic texts in the Bible and therefore necessitates special attention.

---

[3] For further study of this section of Matthew see Robert A. Guelich, *The Sermon on the Mount: A Foundation for Understanding* (Waco: Word Books, 1982) or the more popular work of John Stott, *Christian Counter-Culture: The Message of the Sermon on the Mount* (Downers Grove IL: InterVarsity Press, 1978).

Jesus began this sermon by sitting down on the mountain like a mighty sovereign dispensing his grace and wisdom (5:1–2; cf. 15:29; 24:3) and then enunciated the *Beatitudes*, the ideal characteristics for those who would gain entrance into the kingdom of heaven (5:3–12). These ideals emphasized God's acceptance of those who in this life have little status, those whom the Jews would have designated as the *anawim*, the poor and dispossessed. They were the ones who had little comfort in mourning and were meek and frequently hungry. They were often the ones who displayed the most mercy and were not inauthentic in worship. They sought genuine peace but were unable to escape persecution. After hearing many sermons and reading books on the Beatitudes, I still remain amazed at how many interpreters miss the *inclusio*, since the first and the eighth both promise the "kingdom of heaven" (5:3, 10). That phenomenon alone should alert the reader to the fact that these Beatitudes should not be divided into separate ideas or characteristics but should be treated as a unit that Jesus expected from all his followers. Finally, to cap his message, Jesus ended with the concluding ninth beatitude by changing the focus from general third person statements to the second person: "Blessed are you!" which drove home his point in a way that should sting every Christian into a new understanding of authentic life. These words carry the promise of a joyful linking of the believer with all the faithful who have belonged to God's great realm (5:11–12).

After concluding this compilation of Christian characteristics, Jesus illustrated the nature of the true citizen in the kingdom by referring to the purposes of salt and light (5:13–16). Then he indicated that his kingdom teaching did not violate or alter the intentions of God for humanity. Indeed, authentic obedience would have to exceed the rule-type patterns of the scribes and Pharisees (5:17–20).

To clarify what Jesus meant, Matthew detailed what have since become known as the *Six Antitheses* in Jesus' sermon (Matt 5:21–48). They involve a forceful critique of the various expanded legalistic formulations propounded by the rabbis. Instead of adopting the rabbinic pattern of constantly developing new interpretations of the Torah and exceptions to the statements in the Bible, Jesus mandated a return to the original intentions of God for the Law. When briefly reviewing these important alternatives, it is obvious that the first antithesis is related to the sixth command of the Decalogue (cf. Exod 20:13), but Jesus was concerned with more than physical killing. He called for citizens not merely to eschew murder but also to eliminate anger, insult, and the derogation of others (Matt 5:21–26). The second alternative involved the seventh command (cf. Exod 20:14), and Jesus demanded not simply avoiding adultery but also eschewing all forms of lust in the mind (Matt 5:27–30). The third antithesis confronted the Deuteronomic Code and the gracious Mosaic permission for granting of a divorce decree to help women who had been unceremoniously put out of the house (cf. Deut 24:1–4).[4] In this case Jesus reminded men in particular of God's original intentions for marriage (Matt 5:31–32; but note that even the disciples attempted to avoid the plain meaning of Jesus' teaching in 19:10). The fourth involved the Levitical rules for guaranteeing truthfulness (cf. Lev 19:12 and Num 30:2), and Jesus summoned followers to the plain practice of truth without the need for the common rabbinic manipulation of oaths (Matt 5:33–37). The fifth counter-pattern involved the rules of retaliation and the formulations of when revenge is satisfied (cf. Exod 21:23–25; Lev 24:19–20, etc.). Instead of following the old ways, Jesus proposed the startling idea of "no revenge," even encouraging a willful and gracious response to the hated Roman rules of forced service (*angareia*; Matt 5:38–42). Finally, the sixth antithesis actually provided the key to all the rest. It was commonly believed by the Jews that they should "love the people of God" (Lev 19:18). But the rabbis had argued that, if they were commanded to love, the practical opposite was to hate their enemies, although the Bible nowhere makes such a statement. Jesus countered them with the idea of also loving their enemies because it represented the way of God. After all, God's people were called to be like God (Matt 5:43–48).

In chapter 6, Matthew included Jesus' advice on proper worship,[5] which is foundational to authentic Christian life. Jesus perceptively

---

[4] See my comments on this concern in Gerald Borchert, "1 Corinthians 7:15 and the Church's Historic Misunderstanding of Divorce and Remarriage" in *R&E* 96/1 (1999): 125–29.

[5] I have detailed the New Testament perspectives on worship in Gerald L. Borchert, *Worship in the New Testament* (St. Louis: Chalice Press, 2008).

understood the human desire for recognition, but he emphasized that genuine piety did not emerge from either public display of offerings (beneficence) or out of loquacious prayers in clever rhetoric before God (6:1–7). Instead, he gave humans a model of a direct, simple, and receptive prayer to God (the so-called *Lord's Prayer*) with a forewarning that praying such a prayer implied forgiving others if one expected to be forgiven by God (6:8–15). Moreover, he did not negate the value of fasting but insisted that it should be a private and personal activity and should not be for public observation (6:16–18).

Then he made clear the reality of the two different ways of life. True treasure does not consist in hoarding the "stuff" of the world. What one treasures reflects the focus of one's heart. The same applies to where one's eyes and mind are focused. It all comes down to who or what one serves in life. Is the pivot point of one's life God or the things of this world, including money (6:19–24)? If it is the latter, then life will be marked by worry. Accordingly, humans are forewarned by Jesus that worry can do little to change people's basic orientation; they need to focus on the kingdom and the ways of integrity and justice rather than on the world and its anxieties (6:25–34).

The reader is also reminded that patterns of judgment can be problematic because humans often do not recognize their own weaknesses. Certainly there is a place for authentic analysis of those whom we trust. But rather than seeking our basic support from the world, we ought to seek it from our caring God who treats his followers like his own children and expects them to treat others as they would like to be treated (the so-called Golden Rule). From the perspective of Jesus, such a pattern would truly represent the original intentions of God in the Law and the Prophets (7:1–12).

The section is brought to a forceful conclusion with several vivid illustrations about life and religious practice: (a) There are two patterns among people like two gates that lead to two paths—the wide one ends in destruction, and the narrow and hard one results in genuine life (7:13–14). (b) These two types are like two kinds of fruit trees—the bad ones are the result of the work of false prophets, and their fruit is rotten to the core but good fruit is produced from sound trees (7:15–20). (c) The two are also like people who talk about God—some are authentic but not all are genuine; some are like a house built on a solid foundation and are sustained in the storms, while others are built on a shifting, sandy foundation and are destroyed during those storms. Some people practice what they hear from God, but others do not (7:21–29). The sermon therefore is a call to integrity.

4. The Kingdom, Jesus' Miraculous Mission, and His Commission to His Followers: Matthew 8:1–11:1

a. The Kingdom and Jesus' Miraculous Mission: 8:1–9:38. In his Gospel, Matthew revealed a fascinating ability to combine stories and organize them into congenial groupings. This subsection is an excellent example of his method as he took the stories of Mark and pericopes from elsewhere and combined them for a striking witness to the miraculous mission of Jesus. The order is hardly chronological; it is organizational, and its effect is to emphasize the presence of divine power in the midst of humanity. Stop and read this subsection as a unit and ponder its impact upon a small group of struggling Christians. Their reaction must have been, "Wow, what a powerful Jesus we serve!"

As Jesus descended from teaching on the mountain, he was confronted by an untouchable leper who begged to be cleansed. When Jesus actually touched him, the man was immediately healed (8:1–4). Then a Roman officer begged him to heal his servant at a distance! Matthew was so impressed that in his writing, he made sure his readers recognized Jesus' assessment of the Roman. Nowhere among the Jews had Jesus found such faith (8:5–13). The officer was not a Jew! Then Matthew used the healing of Peter's mother-in-law from Mark, but he added another fulfillment text about taking away our diseases (8:14–17; cf. Isa 53:3). To bring the issue to a head, he followed these healings with critiques of those who apparently desired to follow Jesus (e.g., a Jewish scribe and a potential disciple who first had to take care of a long burial process). Current readers may be tempted to become critical of Jesus' responses here (concerning foxes and the burial of the dead), but Matthew was stressing the presence of inauthentic disciples in contrast to earlier evidences of faith (Matt 8:18–22).

Matthew then returned to detailing the miraculous work of Jesus as he briefly reused the Marcan accounts of the stilling of the storm, the healing of the demoniac as the spirits sought refuge in the pigs, and the healing of the paralytic (8:23–9:8; cf. Mark 4:36–41, 51–20; and 2:1–12). In the second story, to indicate that Jesus healed many such demoniacs, Matthew simply doubled the number treated earlier. Readers who are used to western precision may be troubled by such a pattern of writing. The Gospel, however, is an eastern book, and inspiration must be understood in the context of a Semitic writer's purpose rather than based on western logic of what inspiration ought to be.

To make his point and before continuing with Jesus' miracles, Matthew turned to the call of tax collectors (including Matthew/Levi) as an indication of Jesus' openness to the rejects. Jesus indicated to the critical Pharisees that authentic faith was not a matter of performing religious sacrifices but of showing mercy. Moreover, the Jews needed to realize that the coming of the kingdom was something new in their midst and not merely a continuation of their old Jewish religious practices such as fasting (Matt 9:9–17). The evangelist then employed a brief retelling of the longer Marcan "sandwich" text involving the healing of both the synagogue ruler's (Jairus's) daughter and the woman with the issue of blood (9:18–26; cf. Mark 5:21–43). He followed it with the healings of two blind men (another doublet) and of a demoniac (Matt 9:27–34). He brought this subsection on miracles to a climax by perceptively linking Jesus' preaching of the kingdom and his miraculous ministry with a picture of Jesus as a compassionate shepherd who was concerned about the helpless sheep of the world. This shepherd delivered a mandate to his disciples (then and thereafter) to pray for laborers who would gather the harvest for the kingdom (9:35–38). The call also serves as an introduction to Jesus' second discourse.

b. Jesus' Commission to His Followers: 10:1–11:1. Having concluded his special emphasis on the miraculous nature of the kingdom, Matthew next included the second major teaching section—the commissioning of Jesus' missionary followers. To do so, he first introduced the calling of the twelve and described how Jesus bestowed on them authority over the spirit world (10:1–4). Then, in contrast to the concluding commission after the resurrection, Jesus instructed them to go not to the whole world (not to the Gentiles or even the Samaritans) but only to the sheep of Israel at this preliminary stage (10:5; contrast 28:19). Their task would not be easy because they too would be like sheep in the midst of wolves, and like their Master, Jesus, they would be subjected to harassment and worse. Their authority over the spirit world did not mean they would escape great hostility, but their calling was to endure because they could be assured of divine support in the face of persecution (10:16–23). As servants of Jesus, they were not to consider themselves more privileged than their master. Their enemies were not to be feared because God was in charge of the battle, and they needed to understand that they were in the crucial war of the world. To follow Christ to the cross was the cost of discipleship, but they would be rewarded for their faithfulness of service (10:24–42). With this stark message for his disciples, the initial commission of Jesus to his missionary followers was brought to a conclusion (11:1).

5. Hostility, the Parables, and the Mystery of the Kingdom: Matthew 11:2–13:53

This section of the Gospel opens with a key question from the imprisoned John the Baptist: "Are you the one who is coming?" (11:2). Jesus did not answer that question directly but sent back a report of what he had been doing so that John could make the decision for himself. When the messengers from John had departed, Jesus asked the crowd a question: "Who did you go out into the wilderness to see?" For Matthew, the answer of course was found in another fulfillment statement (cf. Mal 3:1; 4:1). John was the great preparatory messenger for the Messiah. If they would accept what he had done, they would realize he was the promised Elijah! Were the Jews ready for such a mysterious fulfillment? Or were they just like immature children playing games (Matt 11:16–17)? If they did not accept the hermit-like John, would they accept the gregarious Jesus? Wisdom dictated that the answer would be negative (11:18–19).

So the conflict erupted in earnest. Jesus began by identifying the cities of Galilee that had witnessed his miraculous acts as more worthy of condemnation than the Gentile cities of Lebanon or of ancient Sodom that was destroyed by God. Yet to helpless people he offered his soothing comfort for life (11:20–30). In this context Matthew used the Sabbath attacks of the Pharisees from Mark 2:23–3:6 to introduce another fulfillment statement proclaiming hope for the Gentiles (Matt 12:1–21; cf. Isa 42:1–4). Still, the healings of Jesus only engendered more conflict with the Pharisees since they labeled him as an agent of Beelzebul (another name for Satan or the devil meaning "lord of flies" or of garbage). When Jesus countered their illogical name calling, they demanded a divine sign that brought a harsh judgment from Jesus that they were obviously an evil and adulterous generation and had no right to another sign. Yet those who truly did the will of God were welcomed as his kin in the faith (Matt 12:22-50; cf. Mark 3:20–35). Matthew then concluded this section with the third of Jesus' teaching segments involving parables that in part were drawn from Mark 4:1–32 and through which Jesus sought to define the mysterious and hidden nature of the kingdom and its citizens (Matt 13:1–52). Before Jesus again "finished" this teaching segment (Matt 13:53), however, Matthew added another fulfillment statement confirming in his mind the role of the Messiah in parabolic teaching (13:35; cf. Ps 78:2).

6. Revealing the Nature of the Kingdom: Matthew 13:54–19:2

This section opens with the crucial question in the Nazareth synagogue: Where did Jesus get his wisdom and his great power (13:54)? When Jesus did not answer the question, the Jews concluded that he had become "too big for his breeches." Like a window or a fateful precursor of what was to happen to Jesus, Matthew inserted from Mark the murder of John the Baptist (14:1–12). Then he returned to his plan and briefly included the two miracle stories of the feeding of the five thousand and the walking on water from Mark along with using the Isaiah fulfillment text in condemning the Pharisees and scribes concerning their hypocritical worship (Matt 14:13–15:20; cf. Mark 6:30–7:23 and Isa 29:13). These pericopes were followed by several healing stories including the Canaanite woman's daughter and the feeding of the four thousand as well as another demand by the Pharisees and Sadducees for a sign from heaven—all from Mark. But when the disciples bemoaned the fact that they forgot to bring enough bread for their journey, Jesus must have shaken his head at their failure to learn from his miraculous acts (Matt 15:21–16:12; cf. Mark 7:24–37; 8:1–21). Accordingly, the stage was set for the crucial revelatory pericopes that followed.

Mark had earlier indicated the importance of Caesarea Philippi, but Matthew added strategic features to these stories that beg for interpretation. The first comes in the context of Peter's revelatory answer of "You are Christ, the Son of the Living God" to Jesus' probing question concerning his identity. What follows relates to Peter and the "rock" on which Christ would build his church. These words have become the source of a significant debate among Christians (Matt 16:13–18). Is Peter the foundational rock, or is the confession about Jesus the foundation? To help clarify the issue, I usually refer to Peter here by the nickname "Rocky"; the answer seems to be given in 1 Peter 2:4–8 where Peter reminded his readers that Jesus is the great living stone who suffered rejection. Followers of Jesus are not the stone but are called to be replicas of that stone and represent him as living stones themselves ("Rockies"). Confessing the uniqueness of great stone is clearly the basis for overcoming the powers of Hades ("death"; Matt 16:18). Jesus' gift of the "keys of the kingdom" thus must be understood as the privilege of communicating (opening the door to) the gospel of salvation for others.

Moreover, as I have already discussed under the work of the rabbis, Matthew (a Jew) uses the Jewish concept of "binding and loosing" to identify the process of communicating the will of God to his readers or listeners. Failure to use the "keys" for the extension of the gospel can only mean that people will be not be properly bound to God's purposes for their lives and will fail to be loosed from the chains of sin and death (16:19; cf. the same responsibility that is given to all the disciples in 18:18). At that point in the discussion, the disciples and particularly Peter unfortunately failed to comprehend the role of Jesus as the suffering and dying Messiah. Thus they misinterpreted their own task. Accordingly, in the next statement Jesus was forced to condemn Peter as representing Satan (representing self-centered humanity). The task of the disciples, like that of Jesus, was to "take up" their crosses and follow him (16:21–28).

Then, after a brief retelling of Mark's accounts of the Transfiguration and the healing of the epileptic lad (17:1–21; cf. Mark 9:2–29), and after displaying his own interest in Jesus paying his taxes (17:24–27; miraculously from the mouth of a fish!), Matthew introduced the fourth discourse of Jesus (18:1–19:1). In this teaching subsection,

Jesus focused on matters of the Christian model and church discipline. In response to the disciples' query about greatness in the kingdom of heaven, Jesus placed a model in their midst (a child) and charged the disciples to adopt such a pattern of humility while warning them sternly to avoid temptations to sin.

Then, returning to the issue of children, he advised them that children were precious to the heavenly Father who searches for all his lost ones (18:1–14). Believers, therefore, should also help rescue brothers or sisters who are bound in sin, and they should not harshly discipline others without seeking their restoration first. In this context, Jesus enunciated his understanding of the church, which contrasted with the rabbinic view of the synagogue. Whereas it took "ten men" to form a synagogue, Jesus reminded the disciples that when two or three (not merely men) were "gathered in my name," he would be present as Emmanuel in their midst (18:15–20).

As an answer to Peter's question concerning forgiveness, Jesus next responded with an illustration of a servant who had been forgiven a huge debt but refused to forgive a colleague a small debt. The result was severe judgment on the servant (18:21–34). After applying the illustration to forgiveness, Matthew noted that Jesus "finished" this fourth segment of his teaching (18:35–19:1a).

7. The Climax to the Kingdom Ministry of Jesus in Judea: Matthew 19:1b–26:1

After Jesus completed his Galilean ministry, he moved south to Judea, and many followed him. The Pharisees, who were never far away, confronted him on the divorce laws, but when Jesus reaffirmed the original intention of God for marriage, as discussed earlier, even his disciples questioned his approach (19:1–12). While male privilege was the disciples' idea, such was hardly the perspective of Jesus.

Moreover, following Mark's lead, Matthew returned to Jesus' model by reaffirming the acceptability of children in the kingdom and comparing them to the rich man who sought the kingdom but sadly departed when told to give away his riches and follow Jesus (19:13–30; cf. Mark 10:17–31). To emphasize the gratitude humans should have for God's gift, Matthew added a new parable of Jesus concerning unhappy day workers who were distressed that the owner paid them all the same amount despite the differences in the amount of work they had done (20:1–16). The point of course is that what ultimately counts is not our effort but God's gift. But the disciples continued in dense fog as James and John sought priority of position in the kingdom. In good Jewish fashion, however, Matthew had them commandeer their mother to seek the places of preferment for her sons. Jesus recognized the ploy and addressed them directly concerning their misconception of the kingdom (20:20–28).

What follows next is a series of brief but focused pericopes. The entry into Jerusalem via a donkey ride was identified as a fulfillment of an earlier prophecy (Matt 21:4–5; cf. Zech 9:9), but as I indicated in the introduction to this Gospel, Matthew apparently misunderstood the Hebrew poetic parallelism. He reports Jesus coming in on two donkeys ("them," *auton*; Matt 21:6). In the cleansing of the temple that followed, although the authorities were distressed at the children shouting "*Hosanna*" ("save now"), Matthew indicated that Jesus confirmed their action was a fulfillment of Psalm 8:2 in which praise is said to come from the mouths of babes (Matt 21:16). Here Matthew does not follow the strategic Marcan "sandwich" format in the cursing of the fig tree. Did he understand it? Probably not! But he does follow Mark's lead in noting the challenge of the high priests thereafter (21:23–27; cf. Mark 11:27–33).

Three parables are added next: (1) the two sons, one of whom did the will of the father; (2) the wicked tenants who refused to acknowledge the owner and killed his son; and (3) the disrupted marriage feast. All are commentaries on the failure of the Jews to do God's will and recognize God's messenger in Jesus (Matt 21:28–22:14). Indeed, the rejection of Jesus is highlighted by another fulfillment text concerning the rejected corner stone (Matt 21:42; cf. Ps 118:22–23; also Isa 8:14; 28:16). But equally significant for understanding the parables is the fact that unfaithful Israel was pictured in the Old Testament as a fruitless vineyard (e.g., Isa 5:1–7).

Before Matthew reported Jesus' caustic condemnation of the Pharisees, he reused the three probing challenges to Jesus (on taxes, resurrection, and the primary commandment, 22:15–40) and Jesus' unanswerable challenge to the Jews concerning David's twofold use of

"Lord" from Mark (Matt 22:41–46; cf. Mark 1:13–37). Then Jesus unleashed one of the most stinging verbal attacks in the Bible on the pseudo-religious practices of the Pharisees. The attack could hardly be viewed as anything less than a climactic move on the part of Jesus to call the Jews to account (Matt 23:1–36). But the Jewish leaders had hardly been in a mood to respond to calls for repentance issued by John the Baptist, and it was not different with Jesus. What follows is the well-known lament of Jesus over Jerusalem as he recalled that Jerusalem had often killed prophets from God, and it was destined to bear judgment until the people would recognize the coming of Emmanuel (23:37–39).

This section is brought to a conclusion with the final teaching segment in Matthew. This fifth segment has often been designated as the Olivet Discourse in which Jesus again sat down, indicating his supreme authority. At this time as he was looking over Jerusalem he detailed his perspectives on the future, expanded greatly from the account presented in Mark 13. In this teaching Jesus clearly specified that the gospel would have to be preached throughout the world before the end (Matt 24:13); that great desolation would be experienced before the return of the Son of Man (24:29–31); and that watchfulness was mandated for believers. Then, in the two intense parables of the ten virgins and the distribution of talents, Matthew laid bare the fact that the Lord would certainly return unexpectedly and demand an accounting (25:1–30). Finally, the section ends with a great judgment scene in which the Son of Man would sit on his magnificent throne and the people from the entire world would be gathered to witness the divine decision when he would divide humanity into two groups: sheep at his right hand and goats on his left (the two symbolic apocalyptic sides representing good and evil). All would be judged by what they had done (cf. Rev 20:12). Those on the left would be consigned to eternal punishment and those on the right to eternal life (Matt 25:31–46). This fifth and final discourse in Matthew is once again closed with the note that Jesus "finished" his teaching (26:1).

8. The Death and Resurrection of the King: Matthew 26:2–28:20

The concluding section of Matthew begins with the stark announcement by Jesus that in two days Passover would arrive and he would be "handed over to be crucified" (26:2). It continues with a series of vivid contrasts: (a) Caiaphas and the council plotting the secret capture and death of Jesus; (b) a caring woman anointing the head of Jesus; (c) distressed disciples judging the act as a waste of money and Jesus censuring them; (d) Jesus affirming the woman's conduct as a memorable preparation for his burial; and (e) Judas's conspiracy to betray him (26:3–16).

Matthew then focused on the fact that at the Passover dinner as they were leaning on their elbows in the Semitic fashion eating around a triclinium (U-shaped) table, Jesus identified the betrayer as the one who dipped with him in the bowl. During that time Jesus also instituted the "Lord's Supper" and effectively memorialized the elements by identifying them with his broken body and spilled blood, and he promised not to drink again of the fruit of the vine until they would participate together in the kingdom (26:17–29).

After dinner and before they left for Gethsemane, Jesus predicted his abandonment by the disciples and the denials of Peter. Then they went together to face the painful time of prayer and the traitorous kiss of Judas. When one of the disciples sought to defend Jesus by slicing off the ear of one of his captors, Jesus (as the Jewish apocalyptic Messiah) emphasized that he would hardly engaged in a puny battle of human swords and clubs because he had at his disposal legions of angels, which Matthew stressed was a fulfillment of Scripture (26:30–56)!

When Jesus yielded to the arrest, all the disciples fled. He was brought before Caiaphas, and after a series of conflicting testimonies, the frustrated high priest demanded under a Jewish oath that Jesus declare if he were the Son of God. Jesus not only responded to that demand but also testified that he would be seated at the right hand of God and would be seen coming as the eschatological cloud-rider of the apocalyptic writers. After such a confession, Matthew reported that the high priest ceremonially ripped his priestly robe as a signal of heresy, and the council condemned Jesus to death (26:57–68). During this time, Peter was outside and denied Jesus three times, and true to Jesus' prediction it was before the signal of morning with the crowing of the cock (26:69–75; cf. 26:34). Then Peter "wept bitterly."

The rest of the Matthean passion and death accounts contain some features that are quite particular to this Gospel. Not only did Peter weep over his denials but Judas was also singled out for his regret over his traitorous betrayal. Even though he sought to reverse the decision by returning the money, the high priests and the Sanhedrin were unmoved. They had their prize. When Judas committed suicide, the council refused to keep the "tainted" blood money and bought a "blood" field for the burial of those who were outsiders and rejects to their society (27:3–10).

Pilate focused on the charge against Jesus as the "King of the Jews," but when Jesus made no response to the charge and Pilate's wife warned him that her dreams revealed that Jesus was not a criminal but a "just" (*dikaio*) man, he faced a dilemma with the programmed Jewish mob. Earlier in his dealings with the Jews, he had backed down to a Jewish mob when he brought Roman ensigns (pagan military symbols of authority) into Jerusalem (see the earlier comments on Pilate in chapter 1, section 3c). At this point he again capitulated, but not before he sought to claim his innocence by washing his hands in the presence of the mob who accepted the blood curse for their actions (27:11–26).

The crucifixion segment generally follows the Marcan account except that the mob taunted Jesus with his claim that he was "the Son of God." But the centurion made that statement in all seriousness. Matthew indicated that when the temple veil was ripped, that the earth responded with violent shaking and bodies were said to emerge from tombs (27:43, 51–53). Matthew also reported the concern of the council. So they set their guard to protect the tomb of Jesus for fear his followers would claim that he had risen after three days (27:62–66).

Indeed, Matthew must have been delighted to indicate after the Sabbath that the Jewish fear actually came to pass and the puny human guards were hardly able to deal with the divine power in the resurrection. Instead, they melted in fear and were immobilized during the earthquake and the opening of the tomb by the angel of God. Faced with this reversal of events, however, Matthew declared that the council bribed the guards to report that Jesus' disciples had stolen the body, confirming the fact that lying and corruption are not total strangers to religious leaders and their institutions (28:4, 11–15).

But Jesus was certainly raised from the dead as he had predicted (16:21; 17:23; and 20:19). And even though his enemies apparently took seriously the possibility of an empty tomb and the possibility of the disciples' stealing the body, his disciples in fact had fearfully abandoned him (26:56), except for the women (27:55)! Accordingly, he was buried by Joseph, a hitherto unmentioned follower of Jesus (27:57–60).

Hopelessness for the disciples, however, was not in God's plan. The angel instructed the women to have the disciples assemble in Galilee to meet the risen Jesus, and Jesus actually met some women en route to share their message and confirmed their earlier instructions to the tell the disciples the good news and to meet him in Galilee (28:7–10). As a good Jew might expect, that meeting in Galilee took place on a mountain.

There Jesus proclaimed his omnipotent authority and issued his new commission for the disciples. They were mandated to go to "all the nations" (*panta ta ethne*) for the purpose of evangelization (making disciples), the development of the church and worship (baptizing), and the establishment of catechetical instruction (teaching) in the name or nature of the Triune God. With that enduring commission ringing down through the corridors of time, Matthew concluded his witness with Jesus issuing his perpetual promise that Emmanuel would be with them "every day" (*pasas tas hemeras*) of their lives "until the end of time" (*heos sunteleias tou aionos*; 28:16–20)!

Recommended for Further Study

Blomberg, C. L. *Matthew*. NAC. Nashville: Broadman, 1992.

Boring, M. E. "Matthew." *NIB*. Nashville: Abingdon, 1995.

Davies, W. D., and D Allison. *Matthew*. International Critical Commentary. Edinburgh: T. & T. Clark, 1988.

Guelich, R. A. *The Sermon on the Mount: A Foundation for Understanding*. Waco TX: Word, 1982.

Gundry, R. H. *Matthew: A Commentary on his Literary and Theological Art*. Grand Rapids MI: Eerdmans, 1981.

Hagner, D. A. *Matthew 1–13* and *Matthew 14–28*. WBC. Dallas: Word, 1993, 1995.

Harrington, D. *The Gospel of Matthew*. Sacra Pagina. Collegeville MN: Liturgical Press, 1991.

Stagg, F. "Matthew." Volume 6 of *BBC*. Nashville: Broadman,1972.

Witherington III, B. *Matthew*. Smyth & Helwys Bible Commentary. Macon GA: Smyth & Helwys, 2006).

The Witness of Luke to the Jesus who Cares for the Hurting and Dispossessed

As an evangelist, Luke ranks as one of the most vivid writers in the New Testament. Moreover, he is surpassed by no one in communicating Jesus' storytelling techniques to readers. I have often told my students that once you hear or read Luke's stories, you are not likely to forget them. They quickly become embedded in your memory. Consider for example "the prodigal son," "the good Samaritan," "the little Zacchaeus," "the rich man and Lazarus," "the boy Jesus in the temple," "the Pharisee and the publican," "the shepherds and the baby Jesus," "the widow and the judge," and the encapsulating "Emmaus journey." Each story is found only in Luke! Each provides a marvelous glimpse into the heart of the caring God, and most are focused on people who were often regarded by the Jewish elite as being at the bottom of the religious ladder. One can hardly miss the conclusion that if Jesus cared for such people, he clearly must care for me.

To understand the Gospel of Luke, it is important to remember that the evangelist also wrote the captivating book called the "Acts of Apostles." I should quickly add that Acts only concerns a few of the apostles, and the term "acts" (*praxeis*) that was later attached to that book may not be the most appropriate title. *Praxeis* appears only once in Acts 19:18, where it means "magical practices," an idea Luke would hardly consider worthy of a title for his work.

In Acts 1:1, Luke refers to his Gospel as the "first word" or treatise (*proton logon*) that records what Jesus "began" (*erxato*) "to do and teach" (*poiein kai didaskein*), implying that Acts records what Jesus was *continuing to do and teach* among the early Christians. But whether Luke intended to write more than these two books is an open question. That the Gospel of Luke and Acts are related, however, is beyond question. While there is no textual evidence that they were ever joined in circulation, there are many parallel ideas in them. Among the similarities are the miraculous birth of Jesus and the miraculous birth of the church; the dying forgiveness of Jesus and the dying forgiveness of Stephen; the determination of Jesus to go to Jerusalem in the face of death and the refusal of Paul to be deterred in his goal of going to Jerusalem; the fact that the central part of the Gospel is a travel narrative and that most of Acts is a travel narrative; and the consistent declaration of the innocence of Jesus in the crucifixion (Luke 23:4, 14, 22, 41, 47) and the later repeated declarations of the innocence of Christians (e.g., Acts 16:35–39; 18:14–17; 19:37; 23:9; 26:32).

Both works are directed to "Theophilus" (Luke 1:3; Acts 1:1), who at this stage is unknown and may have been a rich and honored sponsor (*kratiste*, "noble") for Luke or perhaps, since it means "lover of God," simply the surrogate name for any respected Christian. As far as the author is concerned, the name "Luke" was assigned to these works by the early church.[1] He was well known as a respected physician and coworker of Paul (cf. Col 4:14; 2 Tim 4:11; Phlm 24). Both books were probably written in the late seventies or early eighties following the fall of Jerusalem in A.D. 70 since Luke interpreted Mark's "desolating sacrilege" as "Jerusalem surrounded by armies" (Luke 21:20; cf. Mark 13:14).

Concerning other introductory matters, I need to mention briefly that the Lucan Gospel is intriguing in that its composite nature can be determined by careful examination. Yet Luke was an astute editor in joining together sections from (a) "M" = Mark or an earlier form of Mark of about 320 verses; (b) a "Sayings Source" (often called "Q" from the German word *Quelle*) of about 250 verses, which was probably known to Matthew as well; and (c) "L" = Luke's own information of about 579 verses. Luke has enfolded them together in a genuinely beautiful

---

[1] See Irenaeus, *Adv. Haer.* 3.1.1–2; cf. Eusebius *H.E.* 5.8.2. See also the introduction to Jerome's *Commentary on Matthew* in Daniel J. Theron, *Evidence of Tradition* (Grand Rapids MI: Baker, 1958) 52–53.

synthesis. Roughly (a) 1:2–2:52 is from L; (b) 3:1–4:4 is a composite from M and L; (c) 5:1–11 is from L (cf. John 21); (d) 5:12–6:16 is from M; (e) 6:17–8:3 is from Q with some perspectives from L; (f) 8:4–9:56 [or perhaps 9:50] is from M; (g) 9:57–18:14 is from L with some additions from Q and M; (h) 18:15–43 is from M; (i) 19:1–27 is from L; (j) 19:28–36 is from M; (k) 19:37–44 is from L; (l) 19:45–22:71 is from M; and (m) 23:1–24:53 is from L with some basic materials from M. While one can identify these elements rather easily in the Gospel, the new combination has become truly a Lucan masterpiece.

As one might expect, scholars have debated most matters of introduction during the last century and a half. The historical issue, however, has been primary in these debates. F. C. Baur, who in the eighteenth century was attracted to the dialectical thinking of Hegel, considered Luke and Acts to be politically motivated works. He argued that Acts in particular sought to unite old-style Jewish (Petrine) views with Gentile "revisionist" (Pauline) thinking in a new synthesis (Old Catholic theology), and therefore Luke's works were not to be considered legitimate history. W. K. Hobbart (1892) sought to counter the skepticism by arguing that Luke could be trusted because his technical use of language revealed that he was clearly a physician. He was followed by H. J. Cadbury (1920, 1927), who demonstrated decisively that the most one could prove from language analysis was that Luke was an educated person. William Ramsay (1904), who began his work as a follower of Baur, however, retraced the travels of the Apostle Paul and concluded that geographically Luke was a reliable historian. For its time, his work was regarded as conclusive, and in response to it Ramsay was knighted by the English crown. In the middle of the twentieth century, however, Hans Conzelmann (1953 German, 1960 English) once again argued that Luke was not a reliable historian but basically a theologian. Since that time, scholars like I. H. Marshall (1970, 1989) have countered with arguments for the legitimacy of Luke as a historian.[2] Today the best consensus is that Luke was both a legitimate

---

[2] For a review of these matters, see for example John Noland, *Luke 1–9:20*, WBC (Dallas: Word Books, 1989) xxxvii–xl; Howard Marshall, *Luke: Historian and Theologian* (Exeter: Paternoster, 1970).

historian but also an articulate theologian. I would argue that the Gospel writers were not merely writing histories. They were writing testimonies and using legitimate historical data as their means for communicating their goal of witnessing. With these brief remarks concerning introductory matters in mind, I turn now to the content of the Gospel of Luke.

1. Introduction: The Coming of God's Caring Messenger: Luke 1:5–2:52

After the introduction to Theophilus, Luke commenced his vivid testimony by placing the story of Jesus in its historical framework. Having stated clearly that the setting was in the time of Herod the Great, he opened with an account of an old priest, Zechariah, and added a strategic note that the experience took place in the Temple of Jerusalem (Luke 1:9). The evangelist not only provided the priest's name but in good historical writing he also supplied the name of the "course" or division to which the priest belonged (1:5, namely, Abijah, the eighth course of the twenty-four priestly clans; cf. 1 Chr 24:10).

As I indicated in connection with the other Gospels, it is also important in Luke to relate the beginning to the end of this testimony. Luke ends his work after the resurrection and ascension of Jesus with the disciples waiting in Jerusalem for the promised "power" and worshiping God in the temple (Luke 24:52). This linking of the Jerusalem temple in Luke should signal to the reader that the temple was significant for the author.

To confirm this point, do not forget that in their first act after his birth and circumcision, the parents of Jesus brought the baby to the temple for his initial sacrifice and the purification of his mother (2:22–27, only in Luke); that the first pericope involving Jesus' assertion as a committed young lad in Luke took place in the temple (2:41–52, only in Luke); and that Satan's crucial last of the three temptations in Luke does not take place on a mountain (as in Matthew) but on the high point of the temple (Luke 4:9). The temple and its stones were and continue to be of crucial significance to the Jews (even today). Accordingly, during Jesus' fateful entry into Jerusalem and in response to the Pharisees' criticism of the people's praises, Jesus countered that if the people were silent, the hallowed "stones would cry out!" (19:40, only in Luke). And in his judgment of the Jewish rejection, Jesus proclaimed that "the stone which the builders rejected has become the [marking or] corner stone" (Luke 20:17, only in Luke's Gospel; cf. Ps 118:22–24 and 1 Pet 2:6). Jerusalem and the temple were constantly present in the mind of Luke. To confirm this fact, remember that Paul returned to Jerusalem frequently on his journeys, but Luke did not even have to mention the name "Jerusalem." He merely could say "he went up" (Acts 18:22), and that expression meant Paul went up to Jerusalem. Luke, a Gentile, had learned from Paul and others that Jerusalem was central to their religious perspectives!

In returning to the beginning of the Gospel, one notes that there were two miraculous visitations from Gabriel (the messenger angel of God). The first was to Zechariah, who was informed in the temple setting that his prayers and those of his wife Elizabeth would be answered, and they would have a baby who should be called John (Luke 1:13; cf. the births of Isaac and Samuel in Gen 17 and 1 Sam 1). Unfortunately, like the early Christians who prayed for the release of Peter from prison and did not actually believe it was possible (cf. Acts 12:5–15), the old priest hardly believed his own prayers. Therefore, he was judged by the angel, who struck him dumb until the event took place and he publicly acknowledged the angelic instructions (Luke 1:20, 63–66). In clear contrast to the first visitation, Gabriel announced to the young maiden Mary that she too would have a baby. While her initial response might seem to parallel that of the priest, Mary had clearly not prayed or anticipated a baby at that stage in her life, and her question was quite legitimate. How was such possible? Although she was formally promised, she did not yet have a husband (1:26–34). The angel did not judge her but carefully explained the nature of the coming miraculous birth. Mary's response was then one of humble submission (1:38). Protestants, especially, need to thank God for the willingness of Mary to accept God's purpose for her in bringing Jesus into the world.

One learns quickly when reading Luke that he often pairs men and women in stories with the obvious impact that his writing actually becomes revolutionary for his time (e.g., 2:29–40; 7:36–50; 10:25–42; 13:10–17; 15:8–32; 18:1–14; 20:45–21:4; 24:22–27; cf. also Acts 9:32–42). Unfortunately, writers who pursue either women's rights or are bent on affirming the superiority of men often fail in evaluating Luke (also Paul) to recognize the overall significance of his writing in the cultural context.

These two angelic visitations are accompanied by two magnificent canticles or hymns of praise. The first (the Magnificat of Mary) magnifies the Lord for his mercy to the faithful and his elevating of the poor and humble while judging the rich and proud (Luke 1:46–55). The second beautiful canticle (the Benedictus of Zachariah, 1:68–79, in which he praised God after the birth of his son, John) reminds one of the many Jewish synagogue benedictions or blessings that are offered to God. It ends with a prayer for peace (*shalom/eirene*), one of Luke's clear themes.

In the context of this chapter I should point out a significant fact in Luke's writing (for those who may have thought, according to Acts, that the Holy Spirit came only at Pentecost) that both Elizabeth and Zechariah are "filled with the Holy Spirit" (1:41, 67), that John would be filled with the Holy Spirit in the womb (1:15), and that the Holy Spirit led Simeon (2:25–27). Western readers need to understand that in the New Testament, basically only Luke uses the expression "filled with." He uses it for many emotions such as fear, awe, madness, indignation, envy, wine, etc. (cf. Acts 2:4; 4:8, 31; 9:17, etc., but note also Eph 5:18, which may suggest that Luke was involved in the writing of Ephesians).

With Luke's concern for historical precision, he placed the birth story of Jesus in its historical context by reference to both Augustus and Quirinius (2:1–2). Moreover, his emphasis in this story falls on the lowliness of the birth of the Savior, with the visitors being lowly shepherds (the *am haeretz*) who had little position among the religious and political elite (Luke 2:8). Contrast Matthew's testimony where the visitors to the baby Jesus were Gentile stargazers from Mesopotamia who brought royal gifts (cf. Matt 2:1–2, 11). Yet the shepherds, like Zechariah and Mary before them, received an angelic visitation that filled them with fear, but they heard crucial words of acceptance in such a divine visitation (an angelophany or theophany, "an appearance of an angel or of God"). The words here were "Fear not!" (cf. Judg 6:22–23; Isa 6:5–7; Mark 6:49–50). Accordingly, they were blessed to receive God's good news of the Savior and instructed to see for themselves the baby who was born in the hometown of King David—even though it was in a lowly crib or manger! Moreover, they were given the unique privilege of hearing the heavenly choir chant the strategic announcement of God's glory on earth and the proclamation of "peace" for the world to humans who *please God*. Note that this proclamation in the KJV translation and some messages on Christmas cards is not quite accurately rendered; peace was not promised to everyone but only to those who "please God" (2:14).

We must pause briefly concerning translations of Luke 2:7, 12, and 16 with respect to renderings of "inn" and "manger." These words have now taken on a life of their own in terms of our Christmas stories, nativity crèches, and church pageants so that a scholar must take care in any contrary comments. But *kataluma* is best rendered "guest room" rather than "inn" (cf. Luke 22:11), whereas *pandocheion* is used in Luke for "inn" (cf. 10:34). Thus, Luke was probably referring to a "guest room" in a family home of a relative of Joseph that was already occupied. Such an idea would agree with Matthew 2:11 concerning "house." Note also that no "innkeeper" is mentioned, and Bethlehem was probably a small village at that time. Although no "animals" such as sheep and cows are mentioned in the texts of Luke or Matthew, small family homes at the time probably had some sheep. *Phatne* certainly might suggest their presence, but the Greek meaning is not totally clear. It can be a manger, a stall, a feeding trough, or a storage crib, and it can be inside or outside the house. The presence of animals in Christmas traditions probably can be linked to the humble life and teaching of Francis of Assisi.

The presentation of the baby Jesus in the temple by his parents is highlighted by what must have been one of Luke's favorite texts from the Old Testament (Isa 4:6) in which the promise was given by God for the coming of new "light to the Gentiles and glory to...Israel" (Luke 2:32, cf. Acts 13:47). But in this event Simeon, the old sage who met them, predicted that the wonderful child would not only bring "joy" to the world (cf. Luke 2:10) but also initiate division and render judgment (2:34–35). Yet Simeon had seen the new light and issued what has since become known as the *Nunc Dimittis*, the death statement of God's faithful: "Lord, let your servant depart in peace!" (2:29). The elderly, righteous Anna then added her thanksgiving for the coming redemption in the baby (2:28).

This section is brought to a stirring conclusion with the appearance of the boy Jesus again in the temple, probably the time of his *bar mitzvah* (the acceptance ceremony of passing from childhood, which today is repeated countless times by Jews at the Western Wall [of the destroyed temple in Jerusalem] and in synagogues throughout the world). Thinking that Jesus was with the company of the other boys in their trek back to Galilee, Mary and Joseph began the journey home. When they discovered he was missing, they hastily returned to the great city and found him three days later in the temple, obviously discussing the law and the Jewish traditions with the elders there (2:46–47). Shocked, Mary told him she and his father had been anxiously looking for him. It was at this point that Jesus set the record straight: he had to be in "his Father's [place/work]" (2:49). Although Mary and Joseph did not understand the implications of what Jesus had said, Luke indicated that Mary continued to reflect on its meaning. This text serves for Luke the way the twist in the first Cana sign served for John when Mary reversed her attempt at instructing Jesus and told the servants to obey him (John 2:5). The pericope ends with a statement that the boy Jesus obeyed his human "parents" and that he matured in relationship to both God and humanity (Luke 2:51–52).

2. The Preparation of Jesus for Ministry: Luke 3:1–4:13

This section begins where the extant text of Mark now starts—with John the Baptist—but (as one might expect) Luke sets this part of his testimony in its historical context. The time was the fifteenth year of Tiberius. The problem for deciding the exact time is that Tiberius was established by Augustus as emperor in the provinces (including Syria) in 764 A.U.C. (A.D. 11), but he became emperor fully at the death of Augustus in 766 A.U.C. (A.D. 13). Accordingly, the above date is either A.D. 26 or 28 (for a further discussion on dates related to Jesus, see my discussion in the introduction to chapter 9). Luke also adds more historical information to the effect that Pontius Pilate was then the procurator/praefect of Judea, Herod Antipas and Herod Philip were both tetrarchs of the central and northern regions respectively, and the Roman Lysanias was in charge of Abilene (a mountainous region north of Damascus that was later incorporated into the territory of Herod

Agrippa I). In addition, Luke indicates that Annas and Caiaphas were high priests. Technically there should have been only one high priest at a time, but since Annas (a godfather type) was deposed by the Romans for his scheming, he never gave up the title among the Jews, even though his son-in-law actually occupied the position (Luke 3:1–3).

The introductory story of John the Baptist basically follows the Marcan text with the exception that Luke adds the call for repentance (3:7–9; also in Matt 3:7–10) and lists a series of questions asked by the people, including tax collectors and soldiers, to which John responded with a Lucan thematic concern of caring for the weak and not cheating them in their dealings (Luke 3:10–14). Then the story moves to a foreshadowing[3] of the imprisonment of John by Herod Antipas because of Herodias (3:19–20), and the account concludes with a brief mention of the baptism of Jesus (3:21–22). Of particular note is that (a) Luke added one of his thematic ideas in this event concerning Jesus "praying" when the Holy Spirit descended; and (b) the heavenly voice that announced that Jesus was God's "beloved Son" served to introduce Luke's version of the genealogy (3:23–38). In it Luke negates any idea that Jesus was Joseph's son and carries the line back to Adam, the created son of God. The vivid contrast reminds the reader of the carefully articulated Pauline comparisons between Christ and Adam (cf. Rom 5:12–21; 1 Cor 15:20–28).

This section that prepares for the introduction of Jesus' ministry concludes by summarizing the temptations of Jesus as outlined in Matthew, but they are altered (physical sustenance, compromising with evil, and gaining followers through show) to conclude with the temple, one of Luke's emphases (Luke 4:1–13; cf. Matt 4:1–11). The important point in these temptation accounts is that the temptations are actually an indication of the kind of person Jesus was. They are hardly temptations for mere humans because we do not possess the capability of doing what Jesus was tempted to do. But when they are reduced to our level of ability, the nature of the temptations Jesus faced can certainly test the

---

[3] Luke's style is to provide windows into future events. For example, in Acts 11:19–26 Luke introduces Barnabas before he comes on the scene, and Luke outlines Paul's future plans while he remains in Ephesus (19:21–22).

resistance of all Christians (see my comments in chapter 9). The need for divine resources, including the use of the Bible, to counteract the wiles of the devil is clearly evident. It takes more than biblical information, however, to deal with Satan and temptation because even the devil is able to quote Scripture (4:10–11). Jesus understood the seriousness of temptation, and he did not play games with the devil. He knew he would face temptation continually (4:13) even at the end of his life, and temptations would continue to confront his disciples as well (e.g., 24:42–45).

3. The Beginning of the Caring Ministry of Jesus: Luke 4:14–7:17

In a brief linking text, Luke tells us that Jesus moved in the power of the Spirit from the wild hostile dessert to the fruitful plains of Lower Galilee. There he began his ministry in his hometown synagogue of Nazareth,[4] where he read from the scroll of Isaiah that was a much-loved text for Jews concerning the coming great celebration of Jubilee, the time when the poor and helpless would find welcomed relief (Isa 61:1–2). In Luke, the Isaiah text is like a divine summons for Jesus to declare his mission, and Jesus gave his own brief commentary (or Jewish midrash) on the text by declaring to his listeners that the great day had arrived (Luke 4:21)! To say the congregation was stunned is an obvious understatement because the people began immediately to challenge his integrity since they thought he was merely a son of Joseph. Even though the Lucan text omits the reference in Isaiah to Jubilee as a day of vengeance, the hostile actions of the people also signaled the inevitable coming of God's judgment. Jesus countered by charging the people that their response was typical of treatment given to earlier prophets. Thus, Elijah and Elisha focused their ministries not on Jews but on the hurting foreigners—Gentiles! At the mention of blessings being visited on the hated *goyim* (Gentiles), the townspeople were filled with anger and

---

[4] Nazareth was a small village in the time of Jesus, and it is not mentioned in either the Old Testament or Josephus. Today it is a large city with a mixed population of Christians and Muslims in the old town, and the Jews live in the new outskirts. An early Nazareth home has recently been excavated, and visitors to the city can gain a sense of old village life in the recently constructed model of a first-century village home and farm.

sought (but failed) to punish him by throwing him over the high precipice outside Nazareth (4:24–30).

Then, to illustrate that Jesus brought the healing and relief predicted in Isaiah, Luke used a series of healing miracles from Mark (4:31–5:26) along with the call of a despised tax collector, Levi (5:27–32). He also inserted an initial call to the early disciples in the context of a miraculous catch of fish (5:1–11), a pericope that is not found in the other Synoptic Gospels.[5] Next follows a series of accounts from Mark 2 and 3 involving worship issues such as fasting, and questions about Jesus' relation to the Sabbath (Luke 5:33–6:11). The question of whether Jesus was actually Lord of the Sabbath and could heal on the Sabbath was unquestionably viewed by Luke as an indication that Jubilee had arrived. He also included the story of choosing the twelve disciples (Luke 6:12–16) before turning to the matter of Jesus' teaching. Intriguing in this choosing episode is the fact that Luke once again added that before the selection, Jesus spent the night in prayer. Repeating the theme of prayer suggests that Luke was concerned with communicating that Jesus offered people a dominical model for spiritual formation.

When turning to the teaching segment that follows, those familiar with the Sermon on the Mount (Matt 5:1ff.) should notice, according to Luke, that Jesus delivered his message on a flat or level plain (Luke 6:17). In this context of healing and casting out evil spirits, Luke pictured Jesus as delivering a truncated version of the Beatitudes along with exhortations on the nature of love and admonitions about judging and forgiving (6:17–45). Luke finished this digest of Jesus' teaching with a warning that words of commitment to the Lord are not enough. One's actions are also crucial. Jesus then likened people to two types of foundations for two houses—one survived the flood surge while the other collapsed (6:46–49; cf. Matt 7:24–27).

To conclude the importance of Jubilee, Luke identified two special healing events. In the first he focused on Jesus' evaluation of a Gentile Roman centurion when Jesus declared that he had not found a

---

[5] This story of the miraculous catch of fish is somewhat similar to the later post-resurrection account in John 21:4–8 and is viewed by some scholars as a rewritten version of the same event.

comparable faith in Israel (Luke 7:9). Then Luke concluded the section with the amazing feat of Jesus raising the dead son of a poor widow from Nain wherein the people realized that divine mystery had "visited" them (7:16; cf. 1:68). This amazing miracle led the entire region to recognize that the miraculous grace of God was in their midst (7:17).

4. *Ministry and the Winds of Hostility Begin to Blow: Luke 7:18–9:55*

In the earlier preparation section, Luke indicated that Herod Antipas had imprisoned John the Baptizer (3:18–20), a fact that is assumed as this section begins. This forerunner of the Messiah sent messengers to inquire whether Jesus was actually "the coming one." Instead of answering that question directly, Jesus told them to report to John that he was doing what was expected when the time of Jubilee would arrive (Luke 7:18–23; Isa 35:5–6). But after the messengers departed, Jesus referred the crowd to the texts from Malachi 3:1 and 4:5 confirming that John was indeed the forerunner of the messianic period. But he also pointedly noted that as John was rejected by the Jewish authorities, Jesus would likewise not be accepted (Luke 7:28–35).

As an illustration of what was to come, Luke employed a special pericope involving a dinner given at a Pharisee's home in honor of Jesus. To the host's dismay, a sinful woman arrived, and in gratitude to Jesus she broke an alabaster flask of precious ointment over Jesus' feet, kissed them, and wiped his feet with her hair—each element indicating her reverence for him and her sense of humility before him (7:37–38). When Simon, the Pharisee, objected, Jesus told the story about two debtors and compared the "thankful" woman to a debtor that could never repay the debt. Then he blessed the woman for her faith and dismissed her in "peace" (7:49)!

Before moving to the next teaching section on parables, Luke indicated that Jesus was accompanied not only by the disciples but also by a number of women (8:1–3). In this instructional account, Luke provided only a brief summary of the parable of the soils and closed by comparing faithful followers to a bright, shining candle (8:4–18).

Then Luke returned to detailing the miraculous acts of Jesus and focused his testimony on fear and faith. When Jesus calmed the storm, he asked his fearful disciples, "Where is your faith?" (8:25). Next in the

Decapolis, he healed the Gerasene demoniac by sending the evil spirits into pigs. The inhabitants there were so overwhelmed with fear that they asked him to leave their region. In contrast to the fearful inhabitants, the healed man begged to join Jesus, but the Lord ordered him to stay and gave him the task of witnessing to his fearful Gentile neighbors (8:26–39). The following stories provided another contrast. Jesus praised a poor, ill woman who touched the edge of his cloak and was healed because of her faith. Typical of Luke, Jesus blessed her with "peace" (8:48) but challenged Jairus, the leader of the synagogue, to have faith when the ruler came begging Jesus to heal his dying/dead daughter (8:50). Then Luke tied these segments together by indicating that Jesus gave the disciples the gift of exorcizing demons and healing the sick as he sent them out to proclaim the kingdom of God. But Jesus warned them that not everyone would accept their ministry (9:1–6). To emphasize the coming hostility, Luke noted that John the Baptizer was now dead and Herod Antipas, his murderer, was inquiring about Jesus (9:7–9).

The feeding of the five thousand that Luke here used from Mark 6:30–44 serves as a kind of introduction to his crucial subsequent stories—the final group of pericopes in this section. In the process, Jesus gave witness to Jubilee through the healing of the sick, a declaration of the kingdom of God (Luke 9:11), and the feeding of the multitude.

Then, signaling its presence and significance, Luke employed Peter's confession and the Transfiguration from Mark 8:27–9:13, but he bathed them in the praying of Jesus (Luke 9:18, 28, 29). Instead of highlighting the consequent condemnation of Peter as Satan that is indicated in both Mark and Matthew and the binding and loosing addition in Matthew, Luke concentrated on the fact that the Son of Man would be rejected by the Jewish leadership and be killed, yet would subsequently be raised (9:22). Jesus' death therefore implied that his followers were also duty bound to take up the cross in order for them to experience Jubilee and the kingdom of God (9:23–27).

Luke focuses the Transfiguration story through the reference in 9:31 to the "exodus" (*exodon*) of Jesus. This use of this term should immediately raise for readers the memory of God's great deliverance from Egypt. In other words, this event in Luke marks Jesus' preparation for the new exodus of God's people—their freeing from bondage!

Unfortunately, many English translations merely render the term as "departure" or something similar and fail to identify the "exodus" as a strategic picture of what was about to take place in Jesus' death and resurrection.

Not only did Peter and disciples on the mountain misunderstand the significance of that event, but the disciples who sought to heal the epileptic boy in the valley were no better off because Jesus designated them all as a "faithless and distorted generation" (9:41). To make plain the point of the coming hostility and the disciples' misunderstanding, Luke (9:43–56) used the second passion prediction and the discourse on humility from Mark 9:30–37. A child was the model of what a disciple ought to be like, and disciples were not to be concerned about building personal resumes or initiating movements or condemning others. They needed a new perspective!

This section of Luke concludes with the note that Jesus set his face like an arrow to go to his rendezvous in Jerusalem for his terminal "lifting up" (9:51). The commitment to go to Jerusalem in spite of the certainty of death became a model that Luke later used in his portrayal of Paul (cf. Acts 20:22–24; 21:11–14). On the way from the north to his destiny, Jesus passed through Samaria, but the Samaritans did not welcome him. As a result, the disciples wanted to call down God's judgment upon them like some of today's preachers who view their task as one of condemning others with whom they do not agree. But the disciples had to learn that this type of judgment is God's role. It is not theirs! Jesus had to reprimand them (9:51–55) since his followers seem(ed) to have a hard time "following" the model of their Lord.

5. Jesus' Ministry of Caring on the Long Way to Jerusalem: Luke 9:56– 19:27

As Jesus began his protracted, final trek to Jerusalem, a number of people indicated that they desired to join him. Jesus recognized their lack of seriousness and their actual wish to postpone their immediate response to him. His judgment of such people was that commitment to the kingdom implied no turning back (9:57–62). He knew what was coming, and he expanded the number of two-person teams he commissioned to ministry. But he warned them that in their work they would be like lambs in the midst of wolves. Although their task was difficult, as they returned rejoicing in their ministry successes, Jesus interpreted the events eschatologically as Satan being dethroned from his power. Nevertheless, he wanted the disciples to focus not on their achievements but on the fact of their own acceptance by God and their destinies with him in heaven. Moreover, he thanked God that it was not to the wise and powerful in the world but to mere novices that God had revealed the ways of the divine will (10:1–24).

Then in a brilliant move, Luke exemplified the above eucharistic prayer of Jesus by employing the vivid story of the "good Samaritan" to answer the cross-examination of a probing lawyer. In this defining account, Luke illustrated one who demonstrated the nature of God by contrasting the hardheartedness of the Jewish religious leaders (a priest and a Levite) with the caring spirit of a despised Samaritan reject. Each of the three came upon the helpless victim while traveling between Jerusalem and Jericho, but only the Samaritan was willing to be supportive and care for the injured person. The lawyer had his answer about God's expectations of humans, and Jesus challenged him to act accordingly (10:25–37).

But lest the reader would think that eternal life was merely a matter of activity and ethical behavior, Luke added another special pericope—the story of Mary and Martha. According to Jewish custom, women were expected to care for household duties, and men were supposed to concentrate on matters of religious importance. But in this case Mary did not join her sister in doing housework. She spent her time listening attentively to Jesus while Martha became angry with her for neglecting her "womanly duties." Therefore, Martha complained to Jesus. But instead of censuring Mary, Jesus challenged Martha to remember that the measure of a person's life (even a woman's) is not to be evaluated simply in terms of activity with pots and pans (10:38–42). These two stories illustrate Luke's amazing ability to balance perspectives in his testimony. They provide a genuine model for interpreting Christian integrity.

Prayer becomes the next concern for Luke, and he summarized the teaching of Matthew (or the Q source) on this subject (Luke 11:1–13; cf. Matt 6:5–15; 7:7–11). The point is that prayer should be both direct and simple. Followers of Jesus should be confident that God hears his children's prayers and will give the Holy Spirit to those who ask.

But the opposition to Jesus had hardly evaporated en route to Jerusalem, and when Jesus cast out demons, he was charged with being in league with Beelzebul and Satan. When he countered the charge logically, a woman cried out and blessed the womb and breasts that birthed and nourished him. Unwilling to accept the woman's categorization of childbirth as the epitome of a woman's purpose in life, Luke's Jesus responded that a woman's purpose should be identified with receiving and obeying the word of God (11:14–28).

Hardly, however, were Jesus' opponents willing to cease their critical questioning. They wanted signs of his authority, but they were given only the warnings that one greater than Solomon or Jonah had come (11:29–32). The Pharisees next wanted him to perform the ritual washing before eating. Jesus responded that they were filthy inside, and their tithing was meaningless compared to their neglect of justice. These legal experts were in fact no different than their predecessors who killed and persecuted the earlier prophets. The blood guilt of all the righteous in the Old Testament from Abel (in Genesis) to Zechariah (in Chronicles) was upon their heads[6] So as Jesus departed from there, the Pharisees plotted how they could snare him (11:53–54).

The Lucan pericopes that follow focus on Jesus' integrity, his critiques of his opponents, and their hostility and lack of integrity. Their hypocrisy was compared to *hametz* (fermented grain or leaven that infected everything surrounding it), the equivalent of yeast for the Jews, which was symbolic of what had to be removed from the house prior to Passover. Moreover, Jesus warned his listeners against blaspheming the Holy Spirit (designating the good as evil). Indeed, Luke clarified for Christian readers the fact that hypocrisy was completely outside the nature and work of God. Instead, the Holy Spirit would be the protector and teacher of Christians when they were being intimidated by both political and Jewish religious authorities (12:1–12).

To carry the issue further, Luke drew attention to the difference between trust and anxiety and introduced the topic with one of Jesus'

---

[6] Note that the Hebrew canon runs from Genesis to Chronicles, not Malachi.

special parables concerning a foolish rich farmer who thought he was in control of his life. Instead of focusing on God, the farmer filled his newly constructed large barns with supplies and told himself he was set for life. But God was in control and demanded the farmer's life that very day. The man's trust was misdirected (12:13–21). Then Jesus reminded his listeners that if God cared for birds and lilies, humans should take a lesson from them concerning God's kingdom (12:22–34; cf. Matt 6:25–34). Because the kingdom was so crucial for Luke, he emphasized that we should be prepared for the return of the Son of Man (Luke 1:35–40). Peter asked if Jesus' warning applied to the disciples. The answer should have been obvious. The wise servant of the Lord should always be ready for his master's return (12:41–48).

The astute follower of Luke's testimony of Jesus, however, should recognize that the Lord's coming did not bring a fairy tale ending in the present world. We might think peace should have resulted, but actually Jesus' coming brought fundamental divisions between humans. Heeding this reality is essential for Christians (12:49–59)!

Next, employing an illustration from Pilate's hostility toward the Jews, Jesus asked his listeners if they thought the Galileans who died at the hands of Pilate's soldiers were worse sinners than other Galileans. And, he added, were the people who died when the Siloam tower collapsed worse sinners than other Jerusalemites? The answer of course is that all people actually deserve such an end without repentance (13:1–5). So Luke added a parable about an unproductive fig tree. When the owner suggested that it should be cut down, the gardener asked that it be given one more chance to survive (13:6–9). Although the end of the story is not supplied, the implication seems obvious. God looks for repentance and is slow to bring judgment, but without the fruit of repentance, condemnation is certain.

With such an answer in mind, Luke added another fascinating story. This one is about a physically contorted woman whom Jesus healed on the Sabbath. The synagogue leader was disgusted that Jesus did not wait until the holy day had passed. Jesus' response was to call such religious people vile "hypocrites." For the woman, the caring spirit of Jesus wrapped her in the incredible designation as "a daughter of Abraham" (13:10–17)! To recognize Jesus' use of such a title for a woman in that context must have been astounding to the observers, and Luke makes it clear that the people rejoiced in the glorious events that were occurring.

Luke then used a couple of parables that stress the secret nature of the kingdom. As Jesus continued on his way, he indicated that many would be shut out. Indeed, as Jesus thought about Jerusalem, he wept, feeling like a mother hen who could not gather her little chicks under her protective wings until they acknowledged him as the *"one who was coming"* (13:18–35).

A series of other parables followed, most of which are found only in Luke. In them, Jesus laid out more particulars concerning God's kingdom. Places of honor were assigned by the host and not gained by personal choice. The poor, lame, and blind would be heartily welcomed because the privileged who were normally expected to be present were too involved with other matters to accept the invitation. Reckoning the cost of taking up the cross was also essential because, like a leader preparing for battle or a person constructing a building, failure to make adequate preparation would soon become evident. Failure to prepare would be like worthless salt that had lost its salty characteristics (14:1–35). But in this group of parables, the best known are the trilogy of the so-called lost sheep, lost coin, and lost (or prodigal) son (15:3–32). Each of these stories emphasizes the concern for something/someone precious that strayed or became lost from the caring searcher. The story of the prodigal son, however, is a much more developed parable and illustrates the father's care for two sons: (a) one was selfish, demanded his inheritance, and strayed far from the ways of God while he was away from home; (b) the other was unforgiving and strayed from the ways of God while at home. The concern of the father in both cases is like the care of God for his children.

The evangelist next added an intriguing parable that some of my students have found a bit difficult to accept—that of the unjust steward (16:1–13). Why did Jesus highlight someone who cheated his boss in order to prepare for his own future when he was being terminated? To make matters worse, why did the master commend the steward? The point, however, is that the people in the world who are concerned about this life and money usually know how to take care of themselves, even if they are unscrupulous. So the real question is: Do the people of God know how to prepare for the kingdom? Loving money and loving God are of course two different realms. You cannot focus your life on both! This idea is then brought to a climax with Luke's story of the rich man and Lazarus (16:19–31). Actions in this life have eternal consequences. Although someone might mysteriously return from the dead and speak of the hereafter and the consequences of this life, unconcerned people will not accept such a witness—even from the risen Jesus!

The important concepts of forgiveness and faith are next highlighted as Jesus proceeded on his way to Jerusalem (17:11). He first called attention to the continuing presence of temptation in human life with the necessity of repentance and increased faith by servants of God (17:1–10). Then, as Jesus entered a village, he was entreated to heal ten lepers. Only the foreigner, a Samaritan, was sufficiently grateful to return, acknowledge the healing, and express his thanks (17:11–19). Jubilee had indeed come! The kingdom was in their midst. But who would recognize its coming (17:20–21)? The answer was not much different than it was during the days of Noah when God sent the flood or in the time of Lot and his wife when God destroyed both Sodom and Gomorrah (17:22–27; cf. Gen 7 and 18–19).

As they moved closer to Jerusalem, Jesus' parables and messages became more intense. He described a widow who continually bothered a judge in order to receive satisfaction. Then Jesus asked, "Will not God respond to the constant pleas of his people" (18:1–8)? As we read the Gospel, who were those who really listened to Jesus? Were they the Pharisees who usually informed God of their "righteous" acts, or were they humble tax collectors and others who cried out for God to have mercy on them as sinners? The answer is obvious (18:9–14). To emphasize his point, Luke used several texts from Mark. First, Jesus welcomed children because to enter the kingdom one must have faith like a child (18:15–17; cf. Mark 10:13–16). Second, a rich leader sought assurance of his place in the kingdom, but he quickly learned that riches were "his stumbling block" to eternal life (Luke 18:18–30; cf. Mark 10:17–31). Third, even at this stage of his ministry, the disciples still did not understand, so Jesus reminded them that the time was near that Scripture would be fulfilled: he would be treated horribly and killed, yet on the third day he would be raised (Luke 18:31–34; cf. Mark 10:32–34). Fourth and finally, Luke used the story of the blind man who received his sight near Jericho as a symbol of the coming of Jesus when his followers would be able to understand (Luke 18:35–43; cf. Mark 10:46–52).

To draw this entire journey section to a conclusion, Luke added two striking pericopes. The first is one of Luke's special stories—the transformation of Zacchaeus (Luke 19:1–10). This story highlights the fact that genuine transformation can take place in a person who was regarded by the Jews as completely unscrupulous. Zacchaeus in fact admitted as much in that he promised Jesus he would repay fourfold those whom he had cheated (19:8). In response, Jesus called him an authentic son of Abraham. As you reflect on this story and others, you may find it fascinating that Luke's Jesus actually countered the Jews' earlier pompous reply to John the Baptist when they said, "We have Abraham for our father." Clearly, in Jesus, "God is able from these stones to raise children to Abraham" (Luke 3:8). Accordingly, Jesus used that honored designation of a child of Abraham for a physically contorted woman and a hated tax collector (13:16; 19:9), both of whom were regarded as rejects in Jewish society.

The second pericope involves Luke's use of the parable of three "*mina*" (large accounts[7]) that a nobleman put on loan to three of his servants to see what they could do with the money (19:11–27; cf. the somewhat similar story in Matt 25:14–30) while he went off to obtain his royal power. The point of the parable is clear. Servants of the Lord are responsible for the gifts they have been given in the absence of Jesus, and they are expected to use their talents and opportunities for the kingdom. Moreover, they are warned against misapplying these gifts or burying them. The story also reflects the activity of Archelaus, one of the sons of Herod the Great who traveled to Rome for a kingdom (cf. Luke 19:27; note Luke's concern for historical relevance here).[8] With these two

---

[7] Each *mina* would be the equivalent of approximately three months' wages for a day worker.

[8] After the death of Herod the Great, Archelaus went to Rome to have Herod's will probated and receive the kingdom, but while he was there, citizens from Judea and Samaria also journeyed to Rome to plead that he not be given

significant pericopes, the long central journey section of Luke is brought to a forceful conclusion.

6. *The Entry into Jerusalem and the Death of Jesus: Luke 19:28–23:56*

As indicated earlier, the unique aspect of the Lucan entry story involves shouts of praise that are raised by the people. In response to the Pharisees' criticism, Jesus announced that the hallowed stones would cry out if the people did not honor him (19:40). But a careful review of the people's acclamation may be even more revealing; in contrast to the angels' praises at the birth of Jesus that promised highest glory to God and peace on earth (2:14), now the highest glory is repeated but the peace is declared *in heaven* (19:38). Is this change just a chance happening, or is Luke indicating that a significant transition was taking place? One can merely hypothesize at this point, but the fact that Luke added a second weeping of Jesus over Jerusalem (19:41–44) after he had been greeted in the city (13:34–35) is certainly worth pondering. Moreover, a brief statement on the cleansing of the temple and the plot to kill Jesus is noted immediately (19:45–48). It is trite to add at this point that the end was now clear.

All that remained was for the death march to begin. It started in earnest with a series of face-offs between the Jewish leadership and Jesus, the stories of which are drawn from Mark 11:27–12:40. The three-point challenge to Jesus involved his authority and his view on both taxes and the resurrection. Jesus countered point for point with his barbed parable of the wicked tenants, his question concerning David's son, and his condemnation of the ostentatious actions of the Jewish leadership and their scandalous cheating of widows (Luke 20:1–47). Luke brought this segment to a classic climax with his special story concerning the offering of the poor widow whom Jesus said in reality gave more than all the wealthy donors (21:1–4).

---

such authority. When Archelaus returned with only a small territory and only the title of ethnarch, he executed many of his enemies. His cruelty was the beginning of great turmoil in that part of the kingdom and ultimately resulted in Archelaus being sent into exile. (For further information see my comments in chapter 1, section 3.c.)

While the death of Jesus was now in sight, so was the destruction of the temple! Editing slightly the message from Mark 13 for his own purposes, Luke in chapter 21 reported that the temple stones would soon be torn down, that wars and famines were coming, and that persecution of Christians was on the horizon. Then, providing a clue that he knew what had already happened, Luke interpreted the desolating sacrilege of Mark 13:14 as the terrible Roman siege of Jerusalem in A.D. 70 in which there was no food or water and people actually ate their children (Luke 21:20). Early Christians, however, took the eschatological warnings of Jesus seriously and fled Judea, believing the fall of Jerusalem was imminent (21:21–24). When the Romans were on the march to Jerusalem, Christians fled to places like Pella in the Decapolis (A.D. 69). Luke wanted his readers to understand the historical implications of these predictions.

Luke was also able to distinguish between the two aspects of eschatology: (a) the immediate time associated with the traumatic fall of Jerusalem and (b) the cataclysmic end of the world order with the coming of the Son of Man (21:25–27). Moreover, with respect to prediction and eschatology (both the "already" and the "not yet"), Luke clearly enunciated Jesus' perspective so that his followers should not be taken off guard but instead should heed the strategic signs (such as lessons from nature, like the fig tree) preceding significant events. Then, in typical Lucan fashion, he noted that Christ's followers should watch in prayer (21:36).

With these ideas in mind, Luke turned to the plot to kill Jesus and the agreement between the traitorous Judas and the scheming Jewish leadership (22:1–6). Jesus conducted the Passover (22:8) meal with his disciples and instituted the Lord's Supper in which he began the ceremony with thanksgiving for the cup (22:17). The Greek verb for "giving thanks" is *eucharistein*, which provides the basis for the word "Eucharist," the term used for the Lord's Supper in a number of churches. Then Jesus gave thanks for the bread (22:19). Western readers are sometimes troubled by the order of the elements in the Synoptic Gospels, but they should remember that the cup of wine is imbibed four times in a Jewish Passover Seder service. The important point is that the elements represent the life of Jesus that was laid down for humanity. The disciples, however, hardly understood the self-giving act because, using an earlier saying of Mark at this crucial time, Luke indicates that the disciples were more concerned with their status than the humble model of Jesus. This text is pertinent when we reflect on the "elevated" status many churches give those who serve the Lord's Supper, especially in the light of the "serving" that is enunciated by Jesus at this point in Luke (22:24–27). Interestingly, Luke follows this text with a comment on the disciples' role in judging the tribes of Israel (22:28–30), but care must be taken in applying it to the church. In concluding the meal, Jesus made it clear that the disciples should be prepared for major trouble and that Peter would deny him three times (22:31–38).

When turning to Luke's pivotal story of Gethsemane, one must note the crucial nature of prayer (22:39–46). Five times in eight verses Luke mentions prayer! To miss this fact would be unconscionable; for Luke as for Jesus, prayer was the means for resisting evil and temptation. It prepared Jesus for the traitorous kiss (22:48) and for the hostile Sanhedrin and their stooges (22:63–66), and he refused to back down when asked if he was "the Son of God" (22:67–71). But the sleepy disciples were hardly ready for confronting vile darkness and easily succumbed to the use of force just like the rest of the world (22:49–53). Moreover, Peter yielded to lying in an attempt to escape detection until his motives were uncovered by a shrill rooster (22:54–62).

According to Luke, the series of trials that followed only proved that Jesus was "innocent" of any criminal charges and should be freed (23:4, 24, 22), but Pilate yielded to expediency and sentenced him to die in place of the rebellious insurrectionist, Barabbas (23:18–19, 25). On his way to the crucifixion, women wailed for him, but Jesus warned them to be concerned for themselves and their Jerusalemite offspring. Then, in an explicit contrast to the blessing that a woman had earlier uttered concerning the woman's birthing role (cf. 11:27), Jesus announced that such a role would be a blight because of the coming tragedy to the great city (23:28–31).

At Skull Hill they crucified Jesus, but he eschewed any bitterness and petitioned God to forgive those who crucified him because they had no idea of what they were doing (23:34; cf. Stephen at Acts 7:60). Confirming Jesus' prediction that he would radically separate people, one criminal denounced him while the other asserted Jesus' "innocence" and begged for acceptance into Jesus' kingly realm (23:39–43; cf. 2:34; 12:8–9). So Jesus died, committing his spirit into the care of his "Father." The Roman officer at the cross also declared Jesus' "innocence" (23:44–49). Then Joseph of Arimathea buried his body in a new rock tomb, and since it was the preparation for Sabbath, the women prepared the burial spices and everyone rested (23:50–56).

7. The Startling Resurrection Stories and Waiting for the Promised Gift: Luke 24:1–53

Yes, Jesus was dead, truly dead! None of his followers expected otherwise. All that remained was for the women to put spices on the body so that as it deteriorated it would not smell too badly in the heat of Israel. Afterward, they could put his precious bones in a white ossuary box for storage. But as the women approached the tomb on that morning after Sabbath, something was strangely different. The stone that closed the tomb had been rolled away, and two uncanny figures stood there and asked why the women were looking for a living person among the dead (24:1–5). Luke was at his best in writing this chapter, and if the reader spends a little time pondering the series of questions that are presented, Luke's storytelling ability soon becomes evident. The angels reminded the women of Jesus' prediction, and the women reported the event to the male followers of Jesus. But just like men who needed more proof, they judged the women's report to be nothing more than a fabricated dream (24:6–11).

Then it was the men's turn as Luke unfolded his crowning Emmaus story of two despondent men on their "journey" from Jerusalem. They were met by a stranger who was filled with questions concerning their conversation about the recent tragic events in Jerusalem. Finally, the stranger chided them for their lack of understanding and instructed them in the Scriptures (24:13–27). When they reached their destination, the stranger seemed intent on continuing, but they invited him to join them for the evening. At the table in the breaking of bread, the men (along with the reader) discovered that it was Jesus. And then he vanished! That liturgically significant encounter in the breaking of bread, however, reinvigorated the men, and they immediately returned to

Jerusalem, asking themselves the reflective question about their burning hearts as Jesus "exegeted" or uncovered (*dienoigen*) the Scriptures for them on the way (24:28–33).

When the men returned, they discovered that others were excited about reports of seeing Jesus, including Simon. But the surprises were not yet finished. Jesus was about to supply his followers (and also the logician Luke) with unforgettable proof that he was alive and clearly not a ghostly apparition. He not only showed them his hands and his feet but ate some fish before them (24:36–42). They had the answer to their multiple questions and troubled hearts. Ghosts do not have bones and do not eat food!

Jesus' physical presence would not remain long with them. After reminding them of his earlier words to them and his fulfillment of Scripture, he commissioned them to witness to "all nations" the message of "repentance and the forgiveness of sins." He promised them that if they waited on God, they would be endued with power (24:44–49). Then he led them to Bethany and the Mount of Olives and was separated from them. Luke concluded his testimony with the joy of the disciples as they obediently waited in Jerusalem, worshiping the Lord in the temple (24:50–53). Still, the story of Jesus was not finished because, although the Gospel treats the events of his work before he was received into heaven (cf. Acts 1–2), the living Jesus continues to work among his followers and calls them to be witnesses throughout the world (Acts 1:8). His commission continues for us today!

Recommended for Further Study

Block, D. L. *Luke*. NIV Application Commentary. Grand Rapids MI: Zondervan, 1996.

Bovon, F. *Luke the Theologian*. Second edition. Waco TX: Baylor University Press, 2006.

Culpepper, R. A. "Luke." *NIB*. Nashville: Abingdon,1996.

Conzelmann, H. *The Theology of St. Luke*. New York: Harper & Brothers, 1960.

Craddock, F. *Luke*. Atlanta: John Knox, 1990.

Fitzmyer, J. A. *The Gospel According to Luke I–IX*; *The Gospel According to Luke X–XXIV*. AB. Garden City NY: Doubleday, 1981, 1985.

Marshall, I. H. *The Gospel of Luke: A Commentary on the Greek Text*. Grand Rapids MI: Eerdmans, 1979.

Noland, J. *Luke 1–9:20*; *Luke 9:21–18:34*; *Luke 18:35–24:53*. WBC. Dallas: Word Books, 1989–1993.

Parsons, M. *Luke: Storyteller, Interpreter, Evangelist*. Peabody MA: Hedrickson, 2007.

THE WITNESS OF JOHN TO THE
DIVINE WORD WHO BECAME FLESH

The Gospel of John has been in my thoughts and heart for most of my life. My journey with this guidebook began while I was confined to an isolation hospital when I was in grade school. I had no television, no telephone, and was unable to see my parents or anyone else I knew for nearly a month. During that time, in my loneliness I put to memory most of this marvelous testimony about Jesus, and since that time I have penned scores of articles and two commentaries on this book.[1] I have also taught it on television and in countless places around the world. It is a living reality in my life, and perhaps it has served me somewhat like Galatians served Luther when he called that book his Katarina, after his wife. This precious book of John was my nearest companion until God gave me my dear wife, Doris (his gift), and it continues to be a foundation for my life. My prayer, of course, is that it would serve my readers similarly.

The early patristic scholar Clement of Alexandria in his *Hypotyposes* designated this witness to Jesus as a "Spiritual Gospel." In our Bibles, it stands at the end of the four canonical testimonies as the pinnacle of the Gospels about our Lord, and for me at least it literally breathes the Spirit of the mysterious yet revealed God in Christ Jesus. As the text itself indicates, it was written to engender believing in Jesus as "the Christ, the Son of God" in order that the believer might actually gain "life in [or

---

[1] See Gerald L. Borchert, "John," *MCB* (Macon GA: Mercer University Press, 1995) and also *John 1–11* and *John 12–21*, NAC (Nashville: Broadman and Holman, 1996, 2002).

through] his name" (John 20:30–31). Nothing less than a new life in Christ is the stated purpose of the inspired evangelist!

To set the stage for a brief review of this Gospel, it is necessary to consider a few matters of introduction. During much of the twentieth century, debate concerning this Gospel swirled around many matters, including authorship and dating. Rudolph Bultmann and others argued that the theology was too highly developed for a Palestinian fisherman to write the book. They proposed that it must have been written by some unknown person well into the second century, in spite of tradition that indicated otherwise. The discovery from Egypt of the Roberts Fragment (P52) of the Gospel (now in John Rylands Library) that can be dated early in the second century and the Egerton Papyrus #2 a little later (in the British Museum) have necessitated a rethinking of such speculative dating. In my larger commentary, I have indicated that I am still prepared to accept the traditional authorship of John and that he lived into the nineties of the first Christian century when he wrote this book, even though many scholars staunchly argue that the Gospel and the Epistles of John were written by some other unknown elder by the name of John and that linking the name to the son of Zebedee is a construct of the early church.[2] Although these matters are important, I do not concentrate on such matters unless they greatly affect the interpretation of the content of the Gospels. Too many scholars have unfortunately majored on these issues and have failed to get to the content of the works. Such has not been my approach; I am concerned with what is written therein as the canonical texts now stand. So with these brief comments in mind, I turn now to the witness of John.

The finely tuned nature of this Gospel necessitates that I provide a brief overview of the testimony. This work begins with an eighteen-verse, complex Prologue that was most likely written as a theological

---

[2] For the perspectives of Bultmann, see his *The Gospel of John* (Philadelphia: Westminster, 1971) 11–12. For later discussions, see R. Alan Culpepper, *John, Son of Zebedee: The Life of a Legend* (Columbia: University of South Carolina Press, 1994). See also the arguments of Raymond Brown in *The Community of the Beloved Disciple* (New York: Paulist Press, 1979) 25–91 and his altered view in *The Epistles of John*, AB (New York: Doubleday, 1982) 30–35. Please see my arguments in Borchert, *John 1–11*, 42–50 and 80–94.

summation after the rest of the Gospel was finished. The remainder of chapter 1 is then composed of a fairly long pericope on John the Baptist and three cameos (beautiful tiny pericopes/stories) that give witness concerning Jesus. Chapters 2 through 4 form the first major section, which I have designated as the "Cana Cycle" and which deals with believing in Jesus. The next section involves chapters 5 through 11, which I have called the "Festival Cycle," and they witness to the fact that Jesus replaced the Jewish worship calendar. Then chapter 12 begins the second half of John and serves as an introduction to the death and resurrection of Jesus. It is followed by the third major section, which I have titled the "Farewell Cycle" and which starts with the dominical example of foot-washing (ch. 13) and ends with Jesus' magisterial prayer (ch. 17). It is not simply a series of Farewell Discourses as some scholars have suggested. The Gospel then moves to the "Death Story" (chs. 18–19) and the concluding Resurrection Accounts (chs. 20–21). The final chapter (21) was no doubt written after the manuscript was first completed because it gives the appearance of being an appendix although, like the Prologue, there is no textual evidence that the Gospel ever circulated without both attachments.

The magnificent portrait of Jesus presented by John is clearly one in which the divine agent of God is also the Lamb of God who died on the cross to take away "the sin of the world" (1:29). As a result, Passover is the overarching image that enwraps the entire testimony so that each section except the resurrection stories mentions the Passover or the dying Lamb. After the resurrection, however, there is no longer a need for the Passover. The new era has begun! This feature of John has led to an unfortunate misunderstanding in the church concerning the length of Jesus' ministry as lasting three years. Sadly, most readers do not understand that John moves his stories around not chronologically but theologically for his own purposes, such as the cleansing of the temple (2:13–25) and the anointing of Jesus for death (12:1–8). Moreover, if they would examine the Synoptic stories of Jesus closely, they would discover that about all the Jewish leadership could tolerate of Jesus was one year of his life and work. Instead, as western logicians, readers today generally follow the pattern of Tatian. In their harmonization attempts, they usually read the Synoptic stories into the construction of John, when they should understand that John is a sophisticated writer and thinker rather than a mere chronologist of the life of Jesus. Furthermore, John was so capable in developing his theological themes throughout the Gospel that I have enjoyed watching my students present their research papers on selected themes (such as believing, truth, life, light, love, judgment, and many others) and frequently telling the rest of the class that their theme was the most important in the Gospel. In addition, as I have indicated elsewhere, almost every person in the Gospel is treated not merely as a historical figure but also as a representative of a certain type of individual before God.[3] Such writing, therefore, is the work of an inspired genius.

This fact leads to a further comment. The Greek text is rather simple and not difficult to read, but the thought process behind the writing is incredibly complex. To give a new believer the text of John is a practice among many Christians because of well-known passages like John 1:12; 3:16; and 14:6. One should remember, however, that the Gospel also has passages that are not easy for new Christians to understand, such as 6:53 and 14:17, which have often been interpreted poorly. But now without further introduction, I turn to a brief contextual summary of the Johannine testimony. A full examination of the text would take many more pages such as in my two-volume commentary.

1. The Prologue to the Witness of John: John 1:1–18

The Gospel opens with a profound statement concerning the beginning that reminds one of the introduction to Genesis, as it starts with God acting (Gen 1:1). Unlike other early Near Eastern literature, there is no discussion either in Genesis or in John concerning the creation of God. God was assumed to be from the beginning, and in this Gospel "the Word" is also assumed to have existed from the beginning and was instrumental in the creation of everything, including all derivative life and light (John 1:1–4, 9). The major problem in the world according to John is that human creatures, especially God's chosen Jewish people, refuse to acknowledge the lordship of "the Word" in the world. Instead, people falsely suppose that acceptance by God depends on human

---

[3] See Borchert, *John 12–21*, 369–80.

physical relationships, human desires, or human efforts. But becoming God's children depends instead on receiving or believing in God's agent in the world (1:11–13).

This agent/the Word of God actually became a human and was present among mortals like the tent/tabernacle that represented God's presence in ancient Israel. Moreover, even though no one has ever really seen God, humans were able to witness God's magnificent glory in God's one and only Son who provided a far greater insight into God's overwhelming graciousness than anyone had/has ever done either previously or thereafter, including Moses, who had provided a sense of God's will through delivering God's gift of the Law to humans (1:14–18).

2. John the Baptist and Three Cameos of Witness: John 1:19–51

John the Baptist had already been briefly introduced in the Prologue as not being the light but a witness to that light (1:6–8). In this section, the evangelist made the distinction between John and Jesus absolutely clear in several pericopes. The investigating committee of the Jewish leadership cross-examined John as to whether he was any of the long-expected messianic figures like Christ, Elijah, or the Prophet, who were anticipated by the Jews. His repeated answer of *ouk eimi* ("I am not"— 1:20, 21) functions here in stark contrast to Jesus' later repeated self-affirmations of *ego eimi* ("I am"). In frustration, John's questioners finally demanded to know who he was and why he was calling the nation to a new water lustration, or baptism, in making a way (preparation) for the Lord. His answer was that he was a mere voice calling the people to "prepare" for the "worthy" one (1:23). The rabbis recognized his imagery of not touching feet because they knew they could call their students to menial servitude, but they were not allowed to require the students to touch their feet. In contrast, John, as a witness here, enunciated his extremely menial role with respect to "the coming one"—a traditional designation for the Messiah (1:26–27).[4] Moreover, readers should also not

---

[4] This statement and the concern of John's disciples in 3:26 is reflected in the evangelist's knowledge that after the death of both John and Jesus, the disciples of John continued to vie with the early Christians for followers. While the later Mandeans claimed their prophet to be John the Baptist in order to fulfill the Muslim requirement for a prophet preceding Mohammed in order to be allowed

overlook the fact that before his death, Jesus the Messiah actually took the role of such a menial servant himself by washing the feet of his disciples and was rebuked by Peter for assuming this demeaning role (cf. 13:5–8).

The three cameos of witness that follow are meant to be treated as a unit because of the repeated expression "the next day" (1:29, 35, 43), and they are significant because they begin to unveil some of the various roles of Jesus. He is the Lamb of God who takes away the sin of the world (1:29, 35), the one who is not really known (1:31), the one who baptizes with the Holy Spirit (1:33), the Son of God (1:34, 49), the teacher or rabbi (1:38, 49), the Messiah or Christ (1:41), the one who names people like God does (1:42), the fulfillment of the Law and the Prophets (1:45), the King of Israel (1:49), the embodiment of the new Israel/Jacob (1:51), and the Son of Man (1:51). There are others, including the decisive "my Lord and my God" (20:28), but if readers went no further, this early testimony concerning Jesus would already be decisive.

The first cameo portrayed John in the humble spirit of a true witness who testified to what he had experienced. The second cameo bore witness to the fact that John was not concerned that Jesus would "steal his sheep," but it also indicates that the disciples were focused on their new leader's outward adornments such as where he lived (1:38). Yet in the play on the word "found" (*euriskein*), the evangelist reveals that the disciples thought they were the ones doing the finding (1:41 [2x], also 1:45 [2x]). The third and final cameo indicates that it was not Philip who actually found Nathaniel; Jesus already knew before their meeting that he was not only faithful and studious but, more important, an eschatologically expectant Israelite (i.e., "under the fig tree" is a designation for such a one, 1:48–50). The concluding image of the "angels of God ascending and descending" on Jesus indicates that the evangelist pictured Jesus as the new Bethel (house of God, cf. Gen 28:12).

---

religious existence in countries dominated by Islam, a direct historical connection between the Mandeans and John the Baptist is not proven, in spite of Bultmann and others.

3. The Cana Cycle and the Importance of Believing: John 2:1–4:54

To know or to believe in Jesus is one of the most crucial ideas in this Gospel. Instead of using nouns such as "belief" (*pistis*) or "knowledge" (*gnosis*) like Paul, John uses only verbs (*pisteuein*, *ginoskein* and *oida*). By the time John wrote his Gospel, Christians apparently were misunderstanding Paul and others. John clearly wanted readers to understand that he was not talking about "information" but about a "relationship." It is *not* "what you know" *but* "whom you know" and "in whom you believe" that is crucial. For example, the meaning of "knowing" in Genesis comes to mind. When reading that Adam "knew" his wife and she gave birth to a son, no one considers such knowing to be merely intellectual. It was relational at a deep sexual level. Similarly, for John, to know and believe in Jesus is not merely an intellectual or a sexual experience. It is a knowing at the deepest relational level. The stories in this section force readers to examine their understanding of believing and knowing in relation to God.

The first story involving the wedding feast at Cana is not primarily about marriage (even though the church often uses this text to justify Christian marriage). It is about Jesus' relationship with his Jewish "mama." Mary had to learn that she could not use her motherly role to command him (2:4–5). It is also not about Jesus making non-alcoholic wine (as I have heard it proposed). It does suggest that people often got drunk at wedding celebrations (2:10). Further, it clearly indicates that this marriage took place on the third day (Tuesday, 2:1), which was quite typical and is so even in Israel today because God declared twice that what he created on that day was "good" (Gen 1:10, 12). If Jewish couples are married on that day, they hope for a double blessing. Besides indicating Jesus' independence from his mother as well as his dependence on God's timing ("hour," John 2:4), the story asserts that this beginning (*archen*) of signs led the disciples to believe in him (2:11). To what extent they believed, however, is not yet clear.

The second pericope moves to Jerusalem and involves the cleansing of the temple. It carries the message of believing further. In this story, after Jesus condemned the Jewish leadership for turning the temple (*hieron*) into a place of business, he gave the Jews a predictive "sign" that if they destroyed his sanctuary (*naos*), he would raise it in three days. The play on the words for "temple" by John was both clever and intentional. The Jews misunderstood Jesus' prediction concerning his death and related it to the reconstruction of the second temple that had been in the process of building for forty-six years (2:20), which puts the time of the discussion at about A.D. 26 or 27 (since construction began under Herod the Great in 20–19 B.C.). The post-resurrection perspective in the Gospel is then inserted by the evangelist as he indicated that after the resurrection, the disciples remembered and believed (2:22).

But then comes the hook. John says that at Passover, many "believed" in his name when they saw his "signs" (note the plural here), but Jesus did not "believe" (in their believing) because he clearly "knew" how to evaluate humans (2:23–25). Often humans think that they are in charge of believing and that God will accept any believing. But a reexamination of such an idea is necessary. God does not play games with humans, and neither did Jesus!

The third story in this section concerns the Jewish leader, Nicodemus, who approached Jesus at night (an indication of his spiritual condition). Jesus wasted no time with the introduction but honed in immediately on the problem by telling the Pharisee that he had to be born from above or anew (*anothen*, 3:3). This "Nick" tried to install that idea into his mental computer, but he could only envisage physical birth. The religious leader/teacher needed a lesson in the reality of the divine/spiritual world. "Birth" in the context of water and spirit did not refer to physical birth. It was the picture of new life in Christ involving the intersection of baptism and the gift of God's Spirit. Nick's physical/fleshly thinking could not work in this discussion. Jesus challenged him to believe (recognize) not merely in earthly realities but also in the heavenly realities that were presented by the Son of Man, who came from heaven (3:5–13). Moreover, he gave this "learner" a verbal sign to the effect that as Moses erected a brass serpent in the wilderness to heal the "snake-bitten" Israelites, so Jesus would similarly be hung up in order to heal sinful (snake-bitten) humans in order that those who believe might have eternal life (3:14–15; cf. Num 21:8–9).

The mention of eternal life introduces the best-loved verse in the New Testament. But in order to gain the full implications of the message,

John 3:16 should never be separated from verses 17 and 18. As I have repeatedly indicated to my students, it is evident in verse 16 that God has loved his created world and graced humanity with his one and only Son. Accordingly, God expected humanity to believe and accept his gift. God's purpose was obvious, namely that he wanted to save humans and not condemn them (3:17). But the tragic side to the story of humanity is the reality of sin. As a result, whoever does not believe in God's gift is "*already* condemned" (3:18). Indeed, God's stern justice awaits such a one, but eternal life is given to the one who believes because the Son fully represents the decisive perspectives of God (3:34–36).

The fourth pericope (4:5–42) takes us to the region of the despised Samaritan "half-breeds" and a woman of loose morals. While the disciples went looking for acceptable (kosher) food, Jesus waited at the common meeting place (the local well that tradition indicated went back to the patriarch Jacob). When Jesus asked for a drink from the woman who came to the well at an unusual time (high noon), she slyly queried why a Jewish man (!) would talk with a Samaritan woman. The conversation quickly turned to a comparison of the water she came to draw in the heat of the day and the living water Jesus offered her. When she requested it, Jesus probed her sad, immoral life pattern. In defense, she sought to switch the conversation to a typical argument about the best place to worship. When Jesus focused on the spiritual nature of worship, she tried again to move the discussion by raising the eschatological question of the coming Messiah (Prophet/*Tahib*) who would know about such matters. To her amazement, Jesus announced that she was talking to that Messiah (4:26).

When the disciples returned, they were shocked that Jesus was talking to the woman! Nevertheless, rather than pressing such a question that might lead to some sort of censure, they turned to the practical food concern. Jesus, however, did not let them move the conversation to a mere physical plane and turned their attention to the important issue of ministry (4:31–38).

In the meantime, the woman had left her water jar, found the men (*anthropois*) of the town, and told them that a stranger she met knew everything about her! Clearly that remark pricked their ears. Then she queried, "Could he actually be the Messiah?" Their attention (conscience?) was aroused, and they sought him (4:28–30). In fact, John indicated that many Samaritans believed him both because of the woman's testimony and later when they heard him themselves. Then John added their powerful confession: they "knew" that he was "the Savior of the world" (4:39–42). It is rather intriguing that John chose the Samaritan rejects to pronounce this all-encompassing confession. Those who think the Gospel of John offers little in the way of ethical implications for Christianity need to ponder the full implications of this story.

The fifth and final pericope in this section takes us back to Cana in which a political official begged Jesus to heal his son. When Jesus began to critique the people's need for "signs" in order to believe, the man refused to enter into a mere theological discussion and concentrated on the immediate reality of life and death. In response, Jesus told him to return home because his son would be well. The man "believed" and went back to his family (4:50). On the way home, he was met and informed that his son was well. He then asked at what time the boy began to heal. When he learned it was at the same hour that Jesus had made the declaration, he "believed" and was joined in the believing by his household (4:53). The point of course is that from the first Cana story to this last one, believing is not a once-for-all event. Believing is a process in John just as salvation is understood as a three-stage process in Paul involving justification, sanctification, and glorification (cf. Rom 5:1–5; 6:19–22).

4. The Festival Cycle and the Fulfillment of the Jewish Religious Calendar: John 5:1–11:57

There is little doubt that in the Johannine Gospel Jesus is portrayed as completing all the expectations of the Old Testament and of Judaism. In the Cana Cycle, for example, he is the Lamb of God, the new temple, and the new uplifted healing sign in the wilderness. In the Festival Cycle, he is pictured as the fulfillment of the religious calendar. By the time of Jesus, the "calendar" had expanded beyond the major Mosaic festivals of Passover (in Nisan); Pentecost/Weeks or the waving of the first ripe *omer* (a sheaf of about 3.4 quarts) of wheat (in Sivan); and the day of Atonement along with Tabernacles or Booths (in Tishri). To them were added Dedication or Hanukkah (in Kislev) and Purim (in Adar). John chose to focus his attention on Passover (ch. 6), Tabernacles (chs. 7–9), and Dedication (ch. 10), and he closed the cycle by returning to Passover (ch. 11). For a long time I sensed that chapter 5 concerned Sabbath (not Pentecost as Bultmann argued), yet I struggled for a rationale until my Old Testament colleagues reminded me of the Mosaic calendar in Leviticus 23. When I reread that important text, all of a sudden I had my answer: each of the festivals is regarded as a *Shabbat* (Sabbath) to the Lord! John understood the calendar better than some of his later interpreters!

The first pericope in this section concerns Jesus' healing on the Sabbath. A paralytic had suffered for thirty-eight years (the length of time Israel was in the dessert from Kadesh to Zared; cf. Deut 2:14), and he had lingered with other indigents in the porches of the great pool of Bethesda (Bethzatha) north of the temple. When Jesus asked him if he wanted to be healed, his bitterness was evident, and he blamed others for not helping him into the pool when it bubbled so that he could be healed.[5] Jesus merely told him to get up, gather his bedroll, and depart. Since the healing occurred on the Sabbath and the man was carrying his bedroll, the Pharisees condemned the man for working. In his defense, he blamed the unknown man who healed him (John 5:1–10). When Jesus later found the man in the temple, he warned him about his sin. Instead of heeding the warning, the man blamed Jesus for healing him. As a result, the Jews turned their condemnations on Jesus.

What follows is a series of legalistic arguments. The first one involves the Jewish decision to kill Jesus not only for breaking the Sabbath (cf. Exod 31:12) but also for blasphemously calling God his Father (John 5:16–18). Jesus' defense was that he was obedient to his Father and that the hour was coming when he would be their judge and would separate people into two different types of resurrection: some to life and some to judgment (5:19–29). Jesus then continued his defense by

---

[5] Periodically when the pool fills, a siphon action takes place below the surface and the water begins to empty. A myth developed that at those times, an angel would descend and bring healing to the waters. Neither Jesus nor John asserted this myth. It was an early theory and was later incorporated by scribes as a textual addition at 5:3b–4 to explain the man's statement.

calling on four witnesses: (1) John the Baptizer, who bore witness to him; (2) Jesus' works, which should have indicated his power and relationship to God; (3) the Father whom they did not even know; and (4) the Scriptures on which they relied but did not understand. They all bore witness to Jesus, and Moses' words would actually condemn his religious critics (5:30–47). Conflict with the Jewish leadership was obvious, and their approach to the Sabbath highlights the clash.[6]

The second segment involves Passover and is introduced by the only two miracles in John that are common to the Synoptic Gospels. But in John the term "miracle" is not used. Instead, the term employed is "sign" because John's focus was on the fact that Jesus' works pointed to who he was. Chapter 6 opens with the feeding of the five thousand from five loaves and two fish, which add up to seven. Twelve baskets of remains were recovered. Both numbers as I indicated earlier are composed of three and four and theologically relate to perfection or fulfillment (seven) and to God's people (twelve). The second story continues with Jesus' control over the sea as he walks on the water. It is imperative for the reader to understand that in the union of these two signs, John saw a reflection of God's acts in the exodus.

It is no surprise, therefore, to find that in the theological reflection on the exodus, the Jews argued that Moses provided bread in the wilderness. Jesus countered that it was not Moses but the Father who gave and was continuing to provide bread because he, Jesus (!), was now the bread who actually came down from heaven (6:31–34). Indeed, he made the connection clear when he declared, "I am the bread of life" (6:35, 48). The Jewish grumbling or murmuring that followed (6:41, 43) only solidified the identification of this story with Israel's earlier wilderness experience. To emphasize the point, Jesus contrasted their eating of manna and dying in the wilderness with the ingestion of this new bread (Jesus) and the gaining of eternal life (6:47–58).

Nevertheless, this passage that deals with the eating of Jesus' flesh and drinking of his blood is for many readers a difficult text to understand and accept (6:53–57). As I have repeatedly insisted, John's

---

[6] For rabbinic views on the Sabbath, see *The Mishnah*, trans. H Danby (London: Oxford University Press, 1933) 100–21.

Gospel is symbolic and the text undoubtedly was John's method of reflecting on the magnificent symbolism that is present in the Lord's Supper. To refer to the Supper as a "mere" symbol (as some of my Baptist colleagues often do) is a catastrophic error. But to use this text (as others do) for a justification of humans turning the elements into the actual body and blood of Jesus is no less a tragic error.

The grumbling served to indicate the division Jesus created by this teaching in the synagogue in Capernaum (6:59; notice the move in locations). Many who had been his disciples found it difficult to continue after that discussion. As a result, he posed for his inner core of disciples the question of whether they too would abandon him. Peter's response confirmed their commitment, but Jesus indicated that one of them was devilish and would betray him (6:60–71).

In the next (third) segment involving Tabernacles or Booths, the evangelist brought together a series of pericopes (chs. 7–9) that focused on a number of issues related to this feast that many regarded as the most popular of the early Jewish festivals. Coming at the end of harvest and soon after *Yom Kippur* (Atonement), it was regarded as a time for vacation. That people constructed temporary shelters as a reminder of their exodus pilgrimage, when they followed God's leading by smoke and fire through the desert, only added to the festive spirit. Since it was such a popular time, many people expected the Messiah to appear. Moreover, it was also a time when the city-dwelling Pharisees prayed for rain to fill their cisterns after a hot summer, an urbanite addition to the Mosaic feast that in the reign of Alexander Jannaeus (second century B.C.) led to a mortal conflict with the sociologically conservative Sadducees. Each of these elements is clearly represented in this group of Tabernacle pericopes.

First, Jesus' brothers did not believe his claims and challenged him to reveal his messianic intentions during the festival (7:3–5). He refused to yield to the temptation for public display (cf. the temptation on the pinnacle of the temple in Matthew and Luke) and instead went up privately to the feast. While he was there, the waiting crowds were not given the show they expected but were informed of his impending departure (7:25–36). Second, during the last "great" day of the feast that brought the water ceremonies to an end, Jesus announced that he would supply them with living water that would flow from their hearts when the Spirit would come to those who believed (7:37–39). When the authorities tried to arrest Jesus, confusion reigned. Nicodemus, the man in transition, sought to defend Jesus in the council (7:50–52; cf. 3:1–2 and 19:39–40) but was rebuked by the Jerusalemites as a deluded Galilean. Third, Jesus announced in one of his declarative *ego eimi* ("I am") statements that he was the "light of the world," and—like the ancient Israelites who followed the pillar of fire at night—he declared that those who followed him would not be guided into the wilderness of darkness (8:12; 9:5). But the Jewish authorities (Pharisees), who should have recognized their leader, failed to understand "where he came from and where he was going," so they refused to acknowledge his divine sonship. Yet many who heard him believed (8:13–30).

The stage was set for Jesus' well-known call to freedom through knowing the "truth." To know the truth in John means to know Jesus, the one who sets people free (8:32). The authorities, however, responded defensively that they were free sons of Abraham and had never been in bondage. That statement was misconceived, and Jesus showed them they were both slaves of sin and hardly represented the perspectives of father Abraham. Instead, Jesus designated them as devilish children because of their desire to kill him (8:34–44). The argument degenerated, and they categorized Jesus as a demonic Samaritan, an indication of their ethical perspective about other people (8:48). The exchange continued on issues of life and death and focused on Abraham, over whom Jesus claimed superiority. They finally had enough and sought to stone him (8:51–59).

The perspectives on Tabernacles are conclusively epitomized in chapter 9 with the healing of the blind man and the issue of theodicy. The disciples questioned Jesus by posing the alternative: Who sinned—the man or his parents—that he was born blind? They anticipated an easy answer of attributing guilt. Jesus refused the alternative and focused on the potential for God's action through the power of the one called to be the "light of the world" (9:1–5). Then he made mud from clay and his spit and put it on the man's eyes (like God breathing into the red dust that became man [*Adam*] at creation). Then Jesus sent the blind man to wash in the Pool of Siloam. Miraculously, the man was able to see (9:6–11).

The face-off with the Pharisees continued in earnest because the healing occurred on the Sabbath! Unlike the paralytic in chapter 5, however, the blind man did not play the blame game. He was amazed that the Jewish leaders could not understand that they placed their rules above the gracious work of God in the healing. The man's parents declined to become involved in the entire investigation for fear of being excommunicated from the synagogue (9:18–23). But when the man himself refused to condemn the one who had healed him, even though he had never seen his healer, he was summarily thrown out of the assembly as guilty of sin from birth (9:24–34). After Jesus found him, the man finally learned who had healed him, and he believed. Jesus concluded the scene by issuing his stern judgment: those who "think" they see will remain blind, but those who are blind and recognize their blindness can be made to see. The Pharisees quickly realized that Jesus was referring to them as being "guilty" before God (9:35–41).

The fourth festival, Dedication, is focused on Jesus as God's good shepherd in John 10. It reminds the reader of the false shepherds (leaders) of Israel who were condemned by God, and of God's decision to be (or supply) the true shepherd (cf. Jer 23:1–6 and Ezek 34:1–24). In this Johannine *mashal* (extended parable), Jesus declared himself in two new *ego eimi* ("I am") assertions to be both the "good shepherd" and the "door" for the sheepfold (namely, a protective gate against thieves and wolves). Those who have lived in Israel and watched shepherds in the morning call out their sheep from among others in the pen by singing to them, or watched a shepherd lead his sheep even through busy traffic in Jerusalem, will understand the close relationship between the shepherd and his sheep that is pictured in this pericope (10:1–18).

The intense division of opinion signaled in 10:19–21 prepares readers for John's announcement that it was Hanukkah/Dedication. But it was not party time; it was winter (10:23)! Of course the 25th of Kislev was in the winter, but time and temperature notations in John are symbolic spiritual keys for understanding the story. What follows confirms that hostility was boiling as the Jews demanded Jesus reveal to them if he was the Messiah. But Jesus knew they did not really want his answer, so he told them his sheep heard his voice and followed him. Moreover, he said he gave eternal life to them, and no outside force could steal them (10:27–28). Indeed, if the Jews had understood the prophecies of Jeremiah and Ezekiel, they would have known that he and the Father were one! The Jews recognized clearly that Jesus condemned them, and in response they grabbed stones to kill Jesus as a blasphemer. He was able to depart from Jerusalem, yet many believed and came seeking him on the other side of the Jordan (10:30–42).

In the next (fifth) story, John (ch. 11) concludes the Festival Cycle, bringing us back to Passover. The story begins in the north where Jesus was teaching when he received an urgent "telegraphic" message from Martha and her sister Mary (the one who anointed him, cf. 12:3) to the effect that his friend Lazarus was ill (11:3). Instead of responding immediately, however, Jesus completed his mission and then announced that he was headed back south to Jerusalem and Judea. That announcement did not sit well with his Galilean disciples, who feared the hostile south. Also, they reasoned that if Lazarus were merely ill or sleeping, he certainly would wake up. But to the disciples' dismay, Jesus told them that Lazarus was dead. Thomas voiced the distress for them when he blurted out, "Well, let's go and die with him!" Society seemed so overpowering that Thomas could hardly recognize that the "Lord" was with them. But to his credit as a realist, he at least expressed his continuing firm commitment to God's special agent (11:14–16).

When Jesus arrived near Jerusalem, the distressed Martha went out to greet him and wearily voiced her sense of hopelessness. "If only" he would have come earlier, her brother would not have died. The well-meaning Martha asserted some confidence, but this situation was different. Her brother was dead! Like any person from a good Pharisaic tradition, she responded to Jesus' concern that she knew her brother would rise at the end of time (11:21–24). Then Jesus issued one of his crucial *ego eimi* statements to the effect that he was "the resurrection and the life," and he asked Martha if she believed him. After she confessed that he was the Christ, the Son of God (11:27), the scene changed and Mary repeated the same refrain, "if only." But naturally it was then too late! When Jesus saw all the crying that was taking place, the text indicates that "Jesus wept." Why? The friends, seeing him weeping, asked a crucial question: Could not this miracle worker have "kept"

Lazarus from dying (11:32–37)? Now ask yourself: Was Jesus weeping because he was powerless in this situation?

With this exchange, the scene again shifted, but this time it was to the tomb and a confrontation with the reality of Jesus. "Roll away the stone," Jesus told them. Martha protested that the body had been in the tomb four days and would stink! Just stop and compare Martha's statements: "I believe!" and "He stinks!" Human verbal confessions are easy to make, but they often do not correlate with actual believing. Yet human believing was not the measure of Jesus' power. He shouted to Lazarus, "Come out!" (11:38–43). I like to imagine what happened to the mourners when the wrapped-up body came out of the tomb! What do you think you would do if a corpse came out of a tomb bound up in grave wrappings?

The Pharisees could not help finding out what happened, and they were frustrated by the turn of events. It was at that point that the high priest issued his decision that "it was necessary for one man to die for the people" (11:50). John realized that his ruthless means and ends argument was virtually an "inspired" statement that signaled the end of Jesus' public ministry since it was the time for the climactic Passover (11:51–57). The Festival Cycle is thus completed, and Jesus' Farewell and Death lie just ahead.

5. The Centerpiece of the Gospel: The Beginning of the End: John 12:1–50

The evangelist employed the familiar stories of the anointing and entry into Jerusalem to underline the arrival of the culminating events in the story of Jesus. By placing these two events together, John focused not on the triumph of Jesus but on his preparation for death at Passover.

The *litran* (12 ounces) of nard/myrrh (from the "spike" or root of the Indian plant) used by Mary for the anointing was extremely valuable (approximately a year's wages) and could easily have represented her "bride price." Judas's stunned reaction at what he termed a waste would probably not have been an unusual response in that company. But John had no love for Judas, whom he regarded as a thief, and refused to affirm him. Jesus, however, set Mary's sacrifice in context as the sign of his coming burial (12:1–8). John also added the brief note that the Jewish leadership considered the elimination of Lazarus to be a probable necessity as well since people believed in Jesus because of him (11:9–11). The death of Jesus was thus on the horizon!

With the above introduction in mind, the evangelist presented his version of the entry story. The reader should notice the various perspectives that are present: (a) the people shouted their hosannas to the King of Israel (12:12–15); (b) the disciples were confused because they could not understand the mixed messages they were getting (12:16–18); (c) the Pharisees were frustrated because the world seemed to have gone overboard after Jesus (12:19); and (d) the Greeks (probably Hellenized Jews and proselytes) wanted to get in on the action and sought assistance from Phillip (12:20; he had a Greek name and was from Hellenized Galilee). But when Jesus viewed what was taking place, he had an entirely different perspective. The Son of Man's "hour" had arrived to "be glorified." Jesus then defined what that troubling reality would mean. He would be like a seed that was planted and needed to die in order for it to bring forth fruit. Moreover, his servants would have to follow in his footsteps (12:23–26).

Unlike the Synoptic accounts, John includes no extended discussion of Jesus wrestling with his forthcoming death in the Garden of Gethsemane. Instead, the wrestling is reported in this context. Furthermore, the voice from heaven that affirmed Jesus' relationship to God at the baptism in the Synoptics is used by John at this point since there is no specific account of Jesus' baptism in John. In the light of these events, John testified that Jesus declared the time for the judgment on the world had arrived and the evil prince of the world would be defeated. The people, however, had difficulty understanding Jesus' perspective because their view was that the Messiah and the Messianic Age was to last forever. A dying (lifted-up) Messiah was hard for them to imagine. It did not compute. So Jesus informed them that they had only a little time to believe as children of the light because the darkness was ready to descend (12:27–36a).

This centerpiece of the Gospel concludes with summary remarks of the evangelist on how difficult it was for the people to believe, and even though many did so, their fear that the Pharisees would also excommunicate them was so great that they kept their views to themselves. In this comment, John was also probably reflecting on the many nominal believers in his day who were fearful of taking a stance for Jesus (12:36b–43). This section closes with Jesus reasserting that his purpose was not primarily to judge but to save the people of the world and bring them to eternal life. Yet John reasserted the stark reality of judgment (12:44–50; cf. 3:16–18).

6. The Farewell Cycle: The Model of Jesus and the Promise of the Spirit: John 13:1–17:26

This major section of John is a masterpiece of construction. As I indicated in my larger commentary, it can be compared to a bull's-eye (target) that scholars might designate as a "chiasm" (an X form of argument). The structure is as follows: (a) the modeling of Jesus in the foot washing and in his magnificent prayer (chs. 13 and 17) serve as the outside ring in the presentation; (b) the two pericopes on anxiety and loneliness (14:1–14 and 18:16–33) form a ring inside the outer one; (c) the discussions on the Holy Spirit or Paraclete (14:25–31 and 15:26–16:15) are the next inside ring; and (d) finally, the core or crossing point (15:1–25) involves John's second *mashal* (extended parable) that deals with the well-known pericope of the vine and the branches.[7] Bearing this structure in mind, I turn to discuss the content of the chapters in succession.

The first segment (ch. 13) contains a phenomenal interplay of ideas as both Peter and Judas are contrasted with Jesus. The scene opens with the announcement that Passover was almost upon them and that Jesus knew his "hour" had arrived (13:1). In that context, he stripped his outer clothing and, wrapping a towel around himself, he began to wash the feet of his disciples. He was making good progress until he came to Peter, who refused and chided him for acting like a lowly servant (cf. John 1:27). When Jesus replied that failure to have his feet washed meant that Peter would have no part with Jesus, Peter responded rather comically and virtually asked for a shower. To this reply Jesus answered, "Feet are enough!" Then Jesus interpreted the situation. They had been calling him "Teacher and Lord," and those designations were correct,

---

[7] For a longer discussion of this construction in John, see Gerald Borchert, *John 12–21*, 73–75.

but if he washed their feet, then his actions should be a model for them to do likewise to others. As followers of Jesus, they were not more significant than their Lord (13:3–16).

Yet they were not all his loyal servants because one of them, Judas Iscariot, was a traitor, a devil man (13:2; note 6:70) who had plotted to betray him—had lifted up his heel against him (13:11, 18, 21). As Judas was eating next to Jesus, the Lord handed him a sop (from the sour dip, identifying his treachery). Reclining next to Jesus' back on the other side from the beloved disciple (symbolic of his stabbing Jesus in the back), Judas received the sop, and Satan took over the devilish thief (13:27–29; 12:6). Then, as Judas left the final dinner, John noted that "It was night!"—a symbol of the spiritual evil that had descended on them (13:30).

The attention then narrowed as Jesus notified them that the time had arrived for him to be "glorified" and issued what has since become known as a key Christian dominical command: "to love one another just as I have loved you." It is by love, he said, that "all people would recognize" that they were his disciples (13:31–35). Sadly, Christians often find it easier to talk about "love" than actually to practice the command. Based on this command of Jesus, the church has instituted the solemn celebration of "Maundy[8] Thursday" prior to "Good (Black) Friday." When Jesus indicated that they would then be unable to follow where he was going, Peter again responded confidently that he would lay down his life for Jesus. In a rhetorical reply, Jesus asked, "Will you?" Instead, he announced that Peter was mistaken and would deny him three times before the time of the cock crowing (13:36–38)!

With chapter 14, the focus shifts to the second segment, the anxiety of the disciples and the announcement that Jesus was going to the Father and preparing for them. This important promise is repeatedly used at funerals as a means of comfort for those who are mourning and wondering what comes next for them. But the discussion that follows is intriguing. Did the disciples know where Jesus was going? The realist Thomas replied that they did not have a global positioning satellite

---

[8] "Maundy" is derived from a defective form of the Latin verb *mando* ("I command").

reader or a "TripTik" to the place, so how could they join him (14:1–5)? Jesus responded with another pertinent *ego eimi* saying, specifying that *he* was "the way" as well as "the truth and life." Reaching the destination with the Father was done through him. This double-level discussion was too much for the disciples, and finally Philip blurted out, "Just show us the Father!" He hardly realized what he was asking. Yet the Jews knew that to see God meant that they would die (cf. Isa 6:5)! Jesus tried to help them understand that encountering Jesus meant meeting God. If they had trouble understanding his "words," Jesus enjoined them to believe his "works." Who could do such works but God? Indeed, through him, he said, they would be able to do similar works and more—if they were praying and acting in the spirit and nature of Jesus (John 14:6–14).

Into this discussion on anxiety and grief at Jesus' near departure, the evangelist added a new focus, the third segment, and inserted the first two of the Paraclete sayings. If they loved him and obeyed him, Jesus promised to send "another Paraclete"—supporter, counselor, or advocate. He had been "*with*" them, but the "other one" would be "*in*" them (John 14:15–17). Some Charismatics have misunderstood this verse as two stages of a relationship with the Holy Spirit rather than two evidences of God's presence (Jesus and the Spirit) among humans. Instead, Jesus assured the disciples that just as he and the Father were in close relationship, in the days to come he would not leave them orphaned, but they would experience a close relationship of love with him (14:18–22). The second Paraclete saying then emphasizes the role of the Spirit as a teacher or interpreter of the significance of Jesus. In recognizing his purpose and presence among them, they should no longer be anxious but find his peace and joy since they would realize that the devilish prince of the world had no power to conquer Jesus or defeat his purposes (14:25–31).

John 15:1–17 then forms the fourth segment, the core or heart of this section, which involves the second of the great Johannine *mashals*—the vine and the branches (cf. the shepherd and door at 10:1–21). Each verse is loaded with significance, but I have space only for a summary. The parable begins by comparing the Father to a caring gardener and Jesus to the authentic vine—the replacement for unfaithful Israel as God's vineyard (cf. Ps 80:8; Isa 5:1–7; 27:2–6; Ezek 15:1–8; 19:10–14; Hos 10:1–2).

The text makes it clear that his followers are purified through Jesus and that the task of the branches is bearing fruit. The disciples were to be clear on their identity and never confuse their role with the foundational vine (John 15:3–5; cf. the basic problem of Adam and Eve in Gen 3:5). Those who fail to continue in the proper relationship with the vine are like useless branches that are removed, die, and are burned. But the fruit-bearing, obedient branches are invited to make their prayers known to God and are viewed as true disciples who bring glory to God. Christian life can thus be viewed as (1) founded in the love of Jesus and (2) marked by obedience that (3) results in a life of joy through him (John 15:6–11).

Having thus given an exegesis of the vine motif, the evangelist returned to the dominical command of loving one another (cf. 13:34–35) based on Jesus' prior, selfless love. True relationships with Jesus lead to being designated as "friends of Jesus" (cf. the Roman designation "friend of Caesar" at 19:12). This embracing term is rooted in the Lord's prior calling and is evidenced in obeying Jesus' directions. Such a relationship enables disciples to make appropriate requests of God, just like Abraham, the "friend of God" (15:12–17; cf. 2 Chr 20:7; Isa 41:8; Jas 2:23).

I next turn to the mirror side of this major section and the fifth segment, which begins with the last three Holy Spirit assertions. The third Paraclete saying has been the focus of controversy. It occurs in the context of Jesus' announcement that since the disciples were not part of the world's pattern of behavior, the world would hate them as it hated him. Since it persecuted Jesus, it would persecute them. They needed to know that since his opponents hated Jesus without justification, they were in reality condemned. But the Holy Spirit *whom Jesus would send to the disciples from the Father* would give them the truthful witness (15:26). Such a verse has caused a controversy in Christianity as to whether the Holy Spirit was sent from the Father only (Eastern church) or the Father "and the Son" (the *filioque* clause; Western church). The point here, though, is not to distinguish Father and Son but to enunciate the Spirit's purpose. The Paraclete's role was intended to keep Christians from being "scandalized" (*skandalisthete*, "stumbling" or "falling"; 16:1). This text along with the removal of the branches in 15:6 has caused another problem for Christians who cannot envision the possibility of "falling" (cf. 1 Cor 10:6–10; Heb 2:1; 3:12–19; 6:1–6; 10:26–31) in the light of Jesus' promised protection in John 10:28–29. The reader should remember that the Bible is filled with tension between both wonderful assurances and resolute warnings. Christians, therefore, must be responsible![9]

The fourth Paraclete saying then reminded the disciples that it was a benefit for Jesus to go away because he would send them the Spirit who would serve as a prosecuting attorney against their enemies, namely (a) to identify their sin; (b) to make clear the righteous standards of God; and (c) to render judgment on them in light of the divine standards (John 16:7–11). The fifth and final statement then presented the Holy Spirit as their personal guide in the world, declaring the will of Jesus to them and bringing glory to him (16:12–15).

The second mirror text and the sixth segment (16:16–33) focuses again on loneliness and abandonment but with a different twist. Clearly the disciples would be in mourning, but this experience would be short lived. Like a woman who suffers pangs for a short time in giving birth but rejoices afterward, so the disciples would soon again rejoice. The post-resurrection perspective was clearly in John's mind. The disciples declared that Jesus came from God, but did they really believe? It was time for straight talk. Jesus said they would all abandon him, but he would *never* be abandoned by the Father (16:32). This text, accordingly, supplies the Johannine perspective on the human agony of Jesus and the difficult cry of dereliction in Mark 15:34.

The concluding segment in the Farewell Cycle returns to the modeling pattern of Jesus. Instead of having Jesus wash the disciples' feet (cf. 13:3–5), here the evangelist provided a structural masterpiece and a model of relationship with God through Jesus' magisterial prayer. The basic key is to recognize the use of *pater* ("father"), which signals the prayer petitions of Jesus in John (cf. John 11:41; 12:27). The first petition here focuses on his "hour" and his glorification so that he could glorify the Father and provide eternal life. It reflects the Johannine purpose of Jesus (17:1–3; cf. 20:20–31). The second petition involves restoring Jesus to his prior glory and role before creation and the knowing and receiving of him by the disciples. It reflects the assertions of the Prologue

---

[9] For my further discussion on this topic see G. L. Borchert, *Assurance and Warning* (Nashville: Broadman, 1987; Singapore: Word N Works, 2006).

concerning his role in creation and salvation and highlights the concern of the Cana Cycle concerning knowing and believing in Jesus (17:4–8; cf. 1:1–18 and 2:1–4:54).

The third and fourth petitions beseeching protection of his faithful disciples and his own consecration are introduced by a single "Holy Father" (*pater hagie*; 17:11). These petitions parallel the Jewish hostility and the presence of Judas, the devil man, in their midst (6:70) as well as Jesus' insistence on his integrity in the Festival Cycle (17:9–16; cf. 5:1–11:57). It is interesting to note that this concept of his and their holiness in the face of repeated hostility in these petitions (17:11, 17, 19) is found earlier only in the hostile Festival Cycle at 10:36!

The remaining three petitions involve three emphases in the Farewell Cycle. The fifth petition concerns the hoped-for oneness of Christians and the recognition that in order for worldwide mission to be accomplished, they needed to act like loving brothers and sisters modeled on the Godhead (17:20–23; cf. 15:5, 12). Sadly, Christians often seem to act like squabbling, accusing siblings rather than self-giving and praying family members. In the sixth petition Jesus prays that they would see his glory and realize their ultimate destiny that he earlier had promised them (17:24; cf. 14:1–7). Finally, the seventh petition following his heart-wrenching and culminating "O Righteous Father" is an implied request that the disciples would truly represent the love of God and fulfill Jesus' new command "to love one another" (17:25–26; cf. 13:35–36).

7. The Johannine Death Story: John 18:1–19:42

The death story in John is another uniquely constructed section in this amazing testimony. It begins with a clear focus on Jesus in the betrayal and arrest, continues with a brilliant interweaving of stories in the trial, and ends with highlighting who Jesus is in his death and burial. As I have stated many times, there is no prayer in Gethsemane in this section (agony was treated in 12:27–33), no kiss of Judas (he is not in control) and no further mention of him besides leading the arresting group, no allowing Pilate to escape guilt by washing his hands, no assisting of Jesus in carrying his cross, no focus on those who were crucified with him (except their mere mention), no cry of abandonment (that matter was settled at 16:32), no shredding of the temple veil (his body was the new sanctuary that was ripped; cf. 2:19–21), no confession of the centurion at the cross (that confession belonged later to Thomas; cf. 20:28), and no guard at the tomb as though humans could prevent God's power. The focus is instead on Jesus, the Lamb of God and the King of Israel (cf. 1:29, 49)!

The arresting band led by Judas came to the garden in "darkness" with torches and weapons as though seeking an armed rebel by stealth. Instead of hiding, Jesus stepped forward and asked whom they were seeking. When they said "Jesus of Nazareth," he responded with *ego eimi* ("I am"). On hearing the divine assertion, the arresters fell on the ground (no one stands before God; 18:3–6)! After repeating the earlier exchange, Jesus yielded but commanded the captors to let the disciples go free (he cared for them). Well-meaning Peter, however, interrupted the arrest by cutting off the priestly servant's ear. But Jesus promptly halted the assault by reminding Peter that the divine Son was in charge, and he would drink his bitter cup (18:7–11).

At this point the evangelist introduced a series of alternating scenes that revealed the serenity of Jesus and the lack of integrity of all the other characters in the story. The arresters took Jesus captive to Annas, the "godfather" high priest whose son-in-law used expediency to condemn Jesus. Peter then entered the scene and gained admittance to the compound of the high priest through the other disciple, but he denied knowledge of Jesus before the charcoal fire (*anthrakian*) with his categorical *ouk eimi* ("I am not"; 18:17–18). Then the high priest questioned Jesus and when Jesus insisted he had done nothing in secret, he was unjustly struck. But Jesus challenged the attack, and since the hearing accomplished little, Annas sent Jesus to Caiaphas. It was then Peter's turn again, and he failed two more times—after which the cock crowed (18:19–27).

Attention next shifted to the praetorium and the Roman investigation, but because the Jewish authorities did not want to "defile" themselves before Passover, they refused to enter the procurator's chambers. So Pilate went outside and asked what Jesus' crime was. The Jews punted the question back to him, whereupon Pilate told them to judge Jesus themselves. When they insisted that Jesus should die, Pilate reentered his chamber and decided to examine Jesus. The questioning centered on if Jesus were the "king of the Jews," which could bring a charge of *maiestas* (treason). After Pilate learned that Jesus' kingdom was not an earthly realm and that Jesus was talking about religion and truth, he returned outside and announced that he found "no crime" present (18:28–38). But thinking to appease the crowd, he gave them an option of releasing Jesus or the traitor, Barabbas. The primed crowd chose Barabbas (18:38–40). Since his ploy failed, Pilate tried to assuage their call for death by having Jesus beaten and adorned with a mock robe and a crown of thorns and declaring the wounded figure not guilty. They were not moved by his mockery and called for Jesus' crucifixion because he made himself the "Son of God." That remark sparked fear in Pilate, and he returned to discuss the matter in his chamber. When Pilate claimed power over Jesus, his prisoner informed him that he was not the source of power (19:1–11).

With that exchange, Pilate attempted to release Jesus, but the Jews were savvy to Roman politics and knew that his patron had been named a "friend of Caesar." Such was also Pilate's goal, so they confronted him with the challenge of reporting him to Caesar. Justice was therefore sacrificed, and the Jews committed the ultimate blasphemy by claiming that Caesar was their only king (cf.1 Sam 8:4–9). Jesus was delivered[10] to be crucified on the Day of Preparation (the day when the Passover lambs were slaughtered). Then Jesus carried his cross to Skull Hill (Golgotha) and was crucified (19:12–18). The charge read, "Jesus of Nazareth, the King of the Jews," which John saw as a universal proclamation since it was written in Hebrew/Aramaic (the language of the Jewish faith), in Latin (the language of the Roman government), and in Greek (the language of commerce). Jesus' accusers tried to change the charge to a mere claim, and John pictures Pilate as finally having found a backbone. Pilate refused to acquiesce (19:19–22).

The death scene includes the dividing of Jesus' garments and two of the few fulfillment texts in John (19:23–24; cf. Ps 22:18; see also John 19:36–37). Jesus, as the oldest son, discharged his caring role for his

---

[10] *Paradidonai* ("hand over" or "betray") is the same Johannine Greek verb used for the actions of Judas, the high priests, and Pilate. They were all guilty in the mind of the evangelist.

mother by transferring her to the custody of the beloved disciple. At that point, the mother fades from view. Then, receiving the sour vinegar, Jesus uttered his final words, "It is finished," and died—delivering (*paradoken*) his spirit (John 19:25–30). The question has often been asked: Where was God when Jesus died? Even though pain must have made Jesus feel abandoned, John is clear that God never turned his back on his Son (cf. 16:32).[11]

Because the Sabbath was approaching, in order to have the bodies removed from the cross, the soldiers were instructed to administer the *crucifragium* (breaking the legs to complete the death process so that victims could no longer use their legs to support the rib cage and gasp for breath). But Jesus was already dead! The evangelist wanted the reader to realize that Jesus was in charge, even in his death. Like a perfect Passover lamb, his legs were not broken. But to make sure he was dead, they pierced him, and water and blood (symbolic of his life given for believers[12]) poured from his wounded side. The disciple who witnessed this strange phenomenon took a solemn oath concerning what he had seen, and scriptural support was added as a confirmation (19:31–37). The death scene is thus portrayed as theologically astonishing.

At the burial by Joseph of Arimathea (mentioned in the other Gospels), John added that the transformed Nicodemus brought a hundred Roman pounds (75 pounds by our calculations) of spice to anoint the body of Jesus. That amount was enough to bury a king! Yet Jesus was more than a king. The day of Preparation thus ended with the Passover lambs being killed, but the Lamb of God had also been sacrificed for the sin of the world (19:38–42; cf. 1:29)! Most stories would end at that point, but there is still one more section to this phenomenal testimony.

7. The Amazing Resurrection Stories: John 20:1–21:25

[11] See also my comments in footnote 79 of Mark, including the tearing of the veil in that Gospel.

[12] John's Gospel is symbolic, and therefore water and blood may also be understood as symbolically referring to baptism and the Lord's Supper.

This section opens with Mary Magdalene coming to the tomb early on the first day of the week. The focus here was not on her carrying spices but on her mourning. When she found the tomb empty, she quickly sought Peter and the other disciple, who immediately ran to the tomb. The comparison between these two disciples is made clear since the other disciple outran Peter, but even though he saw the empty grave clothes, he did not rush into the tomb. They entered the tomb together. Some interpreters highlight the fact that Peter entered first, but the emphasis falls on the fact that it was the other disciple who "believed," although neither yet understood the implications that Scripture was being fulfilled (20:1–9).

Next, Mary Magdalene (20:1, 11) again takes center stage and becomes the focus. When she returned to mourn at the tomb, she assumed that the person in the garden was a caretaker and begged him to reveal where they had hidden the body of Jesus. Her weeping was cut short when Jesus simply called her name, "Mary." In her bewildered excitement, perhaps she thought she had a bad dream, that everything would continue as it was before, and that she could "hold on" to Jesus' presence. But everything had changed, and holding on to the earthly Jesus was impossible. So Mary returned and reported her encounter to the disciples (20:11–18).

That evening the disciples gathered and, fearing the Jewish secret police, they locked the doors of the place. But physical doors were no impediment to the risen Jesus, and without much ado he appeared in their midst. Like the Old Testament theophanies (appearances of God), when God or the Angel of the Lord appeared and told people not to fear, Jesus calmed his frightened disciples by pronouncing divine peace on them. Then, showing them his scarred hands and side, he invested them with the Holy Spirit as he had earlier promised (cf. 14:16–17). In the manner of those earlier theophanies, he sent them on a mission and charged them with the task of proclaiming the forgiveness of sins (20:19–23). This mission is virtually the same as the charge Jesus delivered to Peter and the other disciples in Matthew 16:19 and 18:18.

The realist Thomas was not present for that meeting, and when he heard about their excitement, he responded doubtfully that unless he could physically touch those wounds, he would "not believe!" One week later when they met again, next "Sunday" or Lord's Day (eight days later by their reckoning[13]), Thomas was present, and Jesus again appeared in their midst. Can you imagine what went through Thomas's mind as Jesus confronted him with his wounds? The realist had his answer, and the result was the most important confession in the history of Christianity: "My Lord and my God!" (20:24–29; cf. 14:20). Again, try to imagine the implications of an ancient God-fearing Jew confessing that someone who had walked with him, talked with him, and eaten with him was "his God"! That confession represented a revolution as significant as the transformation of Paul from a persecutor to a proclaimer!

With that pericope, John originally moved to finish his Gospel and state the purpose for his magnificent testimony: namely that his selection of events from the Jesus story were chosen to provide a basis for believing that "Jesus is the Christ, the Son of God." To believe in him would mean nothing less than new life (20:30–31)!

The Epilogue: 21:15–25

The Gospel of John was indeed complete at that point, but something still needed to be added, and the evangelist did so, apparently to the original manuscript because there is no record that this Gospel ever circulated without the Epilogue. What needed to be added was the restoration of Peter, which was done carefully and definitely nuanced. Peter had denied Jesus three times at a charcoal fire (18:17–18, 25–26). Peter had to return to another charcoal fire (21:9), but not before he and the disciples had reassumed their occupation as fishermen.

The story of the great catch of fish here mirrors Luke's account of the great catch and the early call of the disciples (Luke 5:1–11). Some interpreters, based on form criticism, have judged it to be the same story. In this present pericope, the disciples had trolled all night around the Sea of Tiberias (Galilee or Kinereth) and caught nothing. Someone on the land then told them to throw their nets on the right side of the boat. What about a landlubber making that suggestion to fishermen? But they

---

[13] The Semitic writer begins counting with the current day, not with the next day as we do.

obeyed, and the net filled with fish. The beloved disciple was the one who identified the person as the Lord, and in his enthusiasm Peter jumped overboard to get to Jesus (John 21:1–8).

On land Peter was in for a surprise. After breakfast Jesus asked Peter three times if he loved Jesus. At this point many preachers and interpreters with a little knowledge of Greek try to distinguish the Greek verbs for "love" here (*agapan* and *philein* at 21:15–17) as the key to understanding the text, little realizing that John uses such words interchangeably (cf. for example the use of *philei* at 5:20). Instead, the story itself tells you how to interpret Peter's grief. It was the "third time" Jesus asked him about his love before a charcoal fire. According to John, Peter could not help remembering his three denials before a charcoal fire (*anthrakian* is used only twice in the New Testament 18:18 and 21:9). In each of the three cases here, Jesus called Peter to care for his sheep. That this encounter made a lasting impression on Peter seems clear because the same idea is used in 1 Peter 5:2.

When Peter was informed that he would suffer and be stretched out as Jesus was, Peter asked a very human question: "What about the other disciple?" At that point, Jesus virtually told him, "That is none of your business. You follow me!" (21:18–22). The next statement that the other disciple *might be allowed to live* until Jesus returned obviously caused confusion when that disciple became old. So this Gospel corrects any idea that the disciple would not die (21:23).

The Epilogue is brought to a conclusion with a classic authentication by the community. They confirmed that the witness of this Gospel was "true." Indeed, so much more could have been written about Jesus, it was thought, that the world could hardly contain all the implications (21:24–25).

Thus ends one of the most magnificent testimonies of Jesus ever written. But not merely is its magnificence of significance. What ultimately is of importance is whether or not the reader will recognize that this testimony (as well as each of the three others) was written as an instrument for bringing transformation and new life to the people of the world.

Recommended for Further Study

Beasley-Murray, G. R. *John*. WBC. Waco TX: Word, 1987.

Borchert, G. L. *John 1–11* and *John 12–21*. NAC. Nashville: Broadman & Holman,1996, 2002.

———. "John." *MCB*. Macon GA: Mercer University Press, 1995.

Brown, R. E. *John i–xii* and *John xiii–xxi*. AB. Garden City NY: Doubleday, 1966, 1970.

Carson, D. A. *The Gospel According to John*. Grand Rapids MI: Eerdmans, 1991.

Culpepper, R. A. *Anatomy of the Fourth Gospel*. Philadelphia: Fortress, 1983.

Haenchen, E. *John 1* and *John 2*. Hermeneia. Philadelphia: Fortress, 1984.

Koester, C. R. *Symbolism in the Fourth Gospel: Meaning, Mystery, Community*. Minneapolis: Fortress, 1995.

Schnackenburg, R. *The Gospel According to John*. 3 volumes. New York: Crossroad, 1987.

7

Non-canonical and Rejected Witnesses to Jesus

The current era has seen the mushrooming of newspaper articles, blogs, books, and movies attempting to offer "newly discovered" witnesses (such as the Gospel of Judas; see below) or critiques exposing the Jesus of the New Testament who is proclaimed by Christians. Fictional treatments such as *The Da Vinci Code* by Dan Brown and musicals like *Jesus Christ Superstar* that rework the story of Jesus into legendary reconstructions sometimes cause consternation among believers who wonder at their possible truthfulness. Such works merely prove again and again that there is no end to the imagination of humans or their capability of manipulation.

But such creative presentations about Jesus are not new. They have existed for centuries. As we look back to what we have called the dawn of the Christian era, we can discover many such attempts at a rewriting of the stories and teachings of Jesus. These creative presentations have all been rejected, whether they were considered hostile manipulations of Jesus and the Christian kerygma or merely fanciful stories. I turn first to the recently discovered (though not unknown) hostile presentations and then to some segments of other "gospels" that have been available for many years and published repeatedly in New Testament Apocryphal collections.[1] Here, it will suffice to give attention only to a few of the many extant documents.

---

[1] For further information, see either Montague R. James, *The Apocryphal New Testament* (Oxford: The Clarendon Press, 1955) or Edgar Hennecke, Whilhelm Schneemelcher, and R. McL. Wilson, *New Testament Apocrypha*, vol. 1 (Philadelphia: Westminster Press, 1963).

A. The Coptic "Gnostic"[2] Gospels

Some of the so-called Gnostic "gospels" that were originally written in Greek came to light in their Coptic versions in December 1945 through discoveries of fourth-century (etc.) codices uncovered at Nag Hammadi.[3] These engaged my interest in dissertation writing while at Princeton decades ago.[4] Although these new discoveries have enabled us to gain insights into early distortions of Christianity and Judaism by mixing them with foreign dualistic perspectives, the existence of such writings has been known for centuries through the critiques of their early Christian opponents (known as the heresiologs) like Irenaeus, Tertullian, and Ephiphanius. Irenaeus, among the early (second century) Greek critics, inveighed against these Gnostic distorters of Christianity by likening them to a person who takes a beautiful picture of a king, disassembles it, and reassembles it into a fox.[5] Tertullian followed by arguing that the Gnostics mixed philosophy with Christianity and almost screamed, "What indeed has Athens to do with Jerusalem? What concord is there between the Academy and the Church? What between heretics and Christians?...Away with all attempts to produce a mottled Christianity of Stoic, Platonic and dialectic composition."[6] I now turn to several of these documents.

1. The Gospel of Thomas

The Coptic *Gospel of Thomas* (GT) is composed of a series of sayings that some readers at first hastily suggested was the supposed "Sayings

---

[2]The term "Gnostic" is a slippery term since it can refer to a variety of theological and mythical structures of explaining the problem of evil or tendencies toward deviation from the canonical Christian proclamation. It can also be used to encompass concepts of Iranian dualism as well as less metaphysical concepts. It is a general term that is used here for convenience.

[3] For English translations of these documents, see James M. Robinson, ed., *The Nag Hammadi Library* (San Francisco: Harper & Row, 1981).

[4] See Gerald L. Borchert, "An Analysis of the Literary Arrangement and Theological Views in the Coptic Gnostic Gospel of Philip," Ph.D. diss., Princeton Theological Seminary, 1967.

[5] See Irenaeus, *Adversus Haereses* 1.8.1.

[6] Tertullian, *On Prescription Against Heretics* 7.

Source" ("Q" from the German *Quelle*, "source") that stood behind the canonical Gospels of Matthew and Luke. After others reflected on this document, however, it became clear that such an idea was a bit whimsical. This "gospel" contains 114 sayings involving alleged brief statements and answers of Jesus as well as comments and questions that are made by such persons as his disciples (e.g., 18, 20), his opponents (e.g., 91, 100), and on two occasions women such as Mary (21) and Salome (61b). The existence of such a document was known earlier since we had two Greek fragments (Oxyrhynchus Papyri 654 and 655) that contain "sayings" (logia) that are quite similar to logia 5, 30, 31, 36, 37, and 77b of the GT.

The Coptic GT forms a composite collection of logia in no definable order except that there are a few word connectors. It reflects a knowledge of the canonical Gospels, but it clues the reader at the start that the sayings are esoteric since they are "the secret sayings" of "the living Jesus" (obviously using a hint from the parables concerning the "secret" [*mysterion*] of the kingdom and the idea that Jesus' meaning was not understood by most people; cf. Mark 4:11, 34). These sayings were supposedly recorded by "Didymos Judas Thomas" (Thomas, the twin), a mysterious figure supposedly identified with the canonical Thomas who gave the climatic Christian confession (see John 20:28), whom tradition suggests went to India and whose name was used for several non-canonical books since he did not leave a canonical work of his own.

Some of the logia are fairly close to the canonical sayings. They include a sower (9), mustard seed (20), a mote in another's eye (26), blaspheming against the Holy Spirit (44), hating father and mother and taking up the cross (55), excusing an invitation to a dinner (64), tenant farmers who refuse to pay rent and kill the owner's son (65), the harvest is great but the laborers are few (73), my yoke is easy (90), and those doing his will are his brother and mother (99).

But there is in the GT a clear underlying current representing a Gnostic-like rejection of the world and a condemnation of the flesh or anything that affirms the created order. Indeed, even "God" is rejected because, in the scheme, the "Creator" is regarded negatively as an instrument of the demiurgical (dividing) process, whereas Jesus is the mysterious agent from the Ultimate Depth or Ultimate Unity (who is unknowable except through revelation from outside the created universe).[7] Examples would be logion 100 concerning taxes where Jesus replies, "Give Caesar what belongs to Caesar, give God what belongs to God, and give Me what is Mine!" or 61, "I am he who exists from the Undivided" (namely, from the "Pleroma," or "Ultimate Fullness" where the light particles are not divided). Accordingly, the true believer/"Gnostic" is predetermined by the "light" in him. Note logion 10, "Blessed is he who came into being before he came into being" (also in logion 18 the "beginning" determines the "end"), and logion 49, "Blessed are the solitary and the elect.... For you are from [the kingdom], and to it you will return." Speaking of the "flesh" in 29, Jesus said, "I am amazed how this great wealth has made its home in this poverty."

In stark contrast to Paul (see 2 Cor 5:1–5), the Greek Philosophic or "Gnostic" expectation involved shedding the elements of the human body (just a tomb) and ascending through the realms of the planets to the Ultimate "Pleroma" (or the All) beyond the created order. Compare logion 37, "When you disrobe without being ashamed...place your [garments] under your feet like little children and tread on them, then [will you see] the Son of the Living One and...not be afraid." But note the strange mixture that almost verges on a kind of pantheism in logion 77, "It is I who am the All. From Me did the All come forth and unto Me did the All extend. Split a piece of wood, and I am there. Lift up the stone and you will find Me there." Yet perhaps the most interesting logion for readers today (by contrast to Paul's egalitarian view in Gal 3:28), is the Gnostic view of males over females (epitomized in the fall and redemption of the female "god," Sophia). In the GT it is evidenced in the discussion of the final logion 114 where Peter says, "Let Mary leave us, for women are not worthy of Life." But Jesus responded, "I myself

---

[7] While April D. DeConick has called into question the generally accepted designation of the GT as Gnostic, I find her argument concerning it having a more "Christian" source to be less than convincing. See her views in *Recovering the Original Gospel of Thomas* (New York: T & T Clark, 2005) and *Seek to See Him* (Leiden: Brill, 1996). It is certainly possible that an earlier version of the GT may have been used by the Gnostics, but it is still moot what would have been in such a version.

shall lead her in order to make her male…. For every woman who will make herself male will enter the Kingdom of Heaven."

2. The Gospel of Philip

The Coptic Gospel of Philip (GP), unlike the GT, is a mixture of sayings and theological discourses. Scholars, patterning the early translations of the GP after the GT, at first labeled the statements as logia. Later versions of the GP, however, have abandoned such designations and merely refer to the plate or page numbers of the manuscript. Since Philip is also a rather shadowy figure in the canonical Gospels, his name offered Gnostics another means for delivering a message of deviant Christian perspectives.

The GP frequently uses Christian terminology, but great care must be taken not to confuse the understandings of the GP with those of Christian views in the canonical Gospels. The GP itself forewarns the reader to be alert (plate 53) because names are "deceptive" in the world. So when the Philip uses "Father," "Son," " Holy Spirit," "life, ""light," "resurrection," and "Church," he does not mean what people usually perceive by those names "[unless] they have come to know what is correct." Names are instead merely temporal, and they will cease or "end in [this] eon." Yet "truth" provides meaning for those who understand that names are given primarily for the purpose of teaching (54).

As far as the Ultimate Divine in the GP is concerned, it/they dwell in the "Holy of Holies," in the Divine "bridal chamber" (69) into which the lower Godhead or the powers of the lower heavens (the Demiurge and the Archons) cannot enter (84). These "powers" have no power against the "[flawless] Pleroma" or "fullness" (84–85). Then, using a familiar Gnostic parody (from the Hebrew) as a play on the Greek for "Sophia," Philip refers to the demiurgical enemy as "Echamoth" or the "Wisdom of death" (60).

Concerning creation and the demiurgical creator (with the powers), Philip states that "The world came about through a mistake. For he who created it wanted to create it imperishable and immortal. He fell short…. For the world never was imperishable, nor…was he who made the world" (75). Not only is that God incompetent but Philip argued that "God is a man-eater. For this reason men are sacrificed to him" (62–63).

Not only is that demiurgical God an eater but "the world is a corpse-eater," consuming everything in it that is unable to resist (73). Humans in the world, therefore, need help. Jesus came on the scene as the secret agent of the Ultimate and "took them all by stealth." Yet he revealed himself "as great to the great" (57). The Gnostics are "the disciples" whom "he made...great, that they might be able to see him in his greatness" (58).

Without help from this agent of the Ultimate (Jesus), a human is unable to ascend at death to the "resurrection" or the Pleroma and is doomed to remain trapped in the horrible "places" that are "in the Middle" (with the Demiurge/Echamoth), of which Philip says, "God forbid that I be found in them!" (66) and "Only Jesus knows the end of this person" (76). "[B]ut when Christ came, the perfect man, he brought bread from heaven [so] that man might be nourished." That bread, of course was knowledge (*gnosis*). Clearly, however, "[t]he powers thought that it was by their own power that they were doing what they did, but the Holy Spirit in secret was accomplishing everything..." (55). But those powers did not control the one who had knowledge, and such a one "can no longer be detained" in his ascent because "He is master over [nature or creation]" (65).

Unlike most "Christian" Gnostic documents that have survived, the GP has a five-fold developed pattern of "sacraments," as is evidenced in "The Lord [did] everything in a mystery, a baptism and a chrism and a eucharist and a redemption and a bridal chamber" (67). The bridal chamber is undoubtedly the sacramental epitome, and Philip has a great deal to say about sexual activity. Whether such activity was actually prescribed for the Gnostic devotees (as some of the heresiologs forcefully argued) or was merely a way of communicating a spiritual concept of union is not certain, but the language in the GP is suggestive. For example, "A bridal chamber is not for the animals, nor for the slaves, nor for the defiled women; but it is for the free men and virgins" (69). The reader must remember that in interpreting such a text, the Gnostics had no hesitation in referring to some humans as animals. Note also the following, "For it is by a kiss that the perfect conceive and give birth. For this reason we also kiss one another. We receive conception from the grace which is in each other" (59).

The concept of union is further expanded in these words: "When Eve was still in Adam death did not exist. When she was separated from him, death came into being. If he again becomes complete and attains his former self, death will be no more" (68). Philip also added, "Christ came to repair the separation…and unite the two…the woman is united to her husband in the bridal chamber. Indeed those who have been united in the bridal chamber will no longer be separated. Thus Eve separated from Adam because she was never united with him in the bridal chamber" (70). Note the undertone that separation (and thus sin) is a female problem, which mirrors the Gnostic blaming of Sophia for the problems in creation because of her straying from her male consort.

Finally, secrecy and confusion were crucial to Gnostic methodology. Therefore, Philip insisted that the name "the Father gave to the Son" cannot be uttered because "those who…know it…do not speak it." So outsiders cannot learn it (54). Furthermore, Gnostics twisted the Christian understanding of reality and theology to confuse those with whom they argued. For example, they contended that knowledge of one's origin was determinative for salvation. Thus, because of their adherence to a strict predestination, they alleged that the Lord said, "Blessed is he who is before he came into being" (64). Similarly, Philip stated that " those who say that the Lord died first and (then) rose up are in error, for he rose up first and (then) he died" (56). And playing on the Hebrew feminine gender for *ruach* (spirit), Philip argued, "Some said, 'Mary conceived by the Holy Spirit.' They are in error…. When did a woman ever conceive by a woman?" (55). The GP then continues, "Mary is a virgin whom no power defiled." Instead, the "powers defile themselves." And "The Lord would not have said 'My Father who is in heaven'…unless [he] had another father" (55).

For the average early Christian, the GP (and GT) must have appeared to be "Christian" in name. Yet as "gospels," they were strange and troubling. With our knowledge today of the variety in such systems as Gnosticism, however, we can judge them as beyond the boundaries of canonical Christianity. Shortly after the Nag Hammadi documents were discovered and first translated for our contemporaries, J. Baur concluded of the GP that "non sit evangelium, sed florilegium textum ad usum videlicet gnosticorum" (it is not a gospel, but a florilegium [composite] text that, based on our experience, is evidently Gnostic).[8] That judgment of these portraits of Jesus still stands. They are misrepresentations!

3. *The Gospel of Truth* (Evangelium Veritatis)

A work known as the Gospel of Truth (EvV) was mentioned by the early heresiologs as far back as Irenaeus, but little of its content was known until a work by that name was found among the Coptic documents at Nag Hammadi. The significance of finding such a document can hardly be underestimated because Irenaeus seemed to suggest that such a work could have been written by none other than Valentinus. Since he was vying for the post of bishop/patriarch of Rome (but lost), finding such a document had promised to be invaluable.

The document (with the exception of a few pages) was cleverly smuggled out of Egypt and later purchased on the open market by none other than the Jung Institute of Zurich (frequently called the Jung Codex). The interest of a renowned psychological institute in such a document attests to the importance of Gnosticism as a way of humanity dealing with struggles concerning the problem of evil and employing escapism as a way of overcoming guilt and suffering. After the manuscript was copied, translated, and united with the missing pages of the original document, the entire manuscript was returned to Egypt as an act of good will.

But going back to the Coptic documents themselves (there are two copies; one is fragmentary), the EvV begins with the words, "The gospel of truth is joy," which has given the name to this manuscript, but the work is hardly patterned on the canonical Gospels, which describe the acts and teachings of Jesus. Instead, the EvV employs the term "gospel" in the general sense of the "good news." It is more of a theological dissertation or academic homily on the fact that "the Word" that "came forth from the Pleroma" provided "the redemption of those who were ignorant of the Father" (16–17).

After detailing the nature of "ignorance" as the result of the typical Gnostic "fog" of forgetfulness, the writer indicated that the saving

---

[8] See J. Baur, "Evangelio secundum Philippum coptico," *Verbum domini* 41 (1963): 290.

revelation came through "the hidden mystery, Jesus Christ...[who] was nailed to a tree" (18). He "stripped himself of the perishable rags...put on imperishability...entered the empty spaces of terrors...[and] proclaim[ed] the things that are in the heart of the Father" (20–21). "Those who are to receive teaching...are inscribed in the book of the living" (21). When such a one "comes to have knowledge, his ignorance vanishes of itself" (24). Thus "deficiency...will vanish in the fusion of Unity" (25).

Continuing to manipulate the meaning of words, the author indicated "Truth came into the midst" and "all its emanations knew it" (26). Then he added the typical Gnostic theme concerning the ignorant as "he who did not exist...will never come into existence" (28). But of the Gnostics he said that they "cast ignorance aside like sleep, not esteeming it as anything" (29). "The knowledge of the Father," however, "they value as the dawn" (30). Concerning Jesus who came in the flesh, the writer noted that "the material ones were strangers and did not see his likeness" (31), but of Jesus' follower(s) he added that this messenger "gave life to the sheep, having brought it up from the pit" and warned them, "Do not return to what you have vomited" (32–33). So "the word of the gospel" is identified as "the discovery of the Pleroma," and the Gnostics are "those who await the salvation which is coming from on high" (34–35). "Perfection" is therefore viewed as vesting "in the thought of the Father" who is "incomprehensible"; apart from him "nothing happens" (37). Moreover, "the end" involves "receiving knowledge about the one who is hidden...[the Father] from whom the beginning came forth, to whom all will return" (37–38). The Father also established a "resting-place" and brought forth the Son "to glorify the pleroma" (40–41). The goal of the Gnostics, accordingly, is to "come to be in the resting-place" as the Father's children whom "he loves" (43).

I have provided the above set of brief quotes from the EvV to enable the reader to sense the pattern of manipulation of words that were employed by the writer. When one reads such a document, it becomes a little clearer why Irenaeus and Tertullian were frustrated by such writings.

4. Other Gnostic Documents

Many other works could be detailed in this brief review, but I will mention only a few. *The Gospel of Mary* (two brief extant segments), found in the Berlin Gnostic Codex 8502, comes immediately to mind. The Gnostics and others loved to employ the resurrected Jesus as an agent for delivering a special communication. Here the woman Mary becomes the alter ego of Jesus! In the first segment, Jesus had enunciated the typical Gnostic view about creation when Peter raised a question concerning sin. Jesus responded that sin did not exist but was part of "adultery" (7) and that peace (or the Son of Man) was "within you" (8). After Jesus departed, the disciples grieved, but it was Mary who comforted and encouraged the disciples. In the second segment, Mary continued her instruction concerning the ascent of the soul through the seven levels of the powers, but the disciples were perturbed that she supposedly knew more than they did. Andrew responded, "I...do not believe the Savior said this...these teachings are strange." Peter agreed, asking, "Did he really speak privately to a woman [and] not openly to us? ...Did he prefer her to us?" (17). Levi countered, "I see you are contending against the woman like the adversaries...who are you indeed to reject her...the Savior...loved her more than us. Rather let us be ashamed and put on the perfect man...and preach the gospel" (18).

Briefly, other documents include the Coptic *Gospel of the Egyptians*, which is a Sethian Gnostic document that details Gnostic cosmology. In it, Seth (like Jesus) is featured as the agent from without (the Pleroma). Next, the *Sophia of Jesus* is found in both the Berlin manuscript and in the works from Nag Hammadi. What is interesting about the Sophia is that it is a "Christianized" version of an earlier work known as *Eugnostos the Blessed*. It serves as a witness to the fact that the Gnostics used other earlier documents and edited them for their own purposes. Here again, sex and procreation are featured. They are seen as the basis that the powers employ for spreading and weakening the divine light particles (from the errant Sophia) in humans. Thus, procreation further subjugates the weakened light particles within "created" flesh.

B. The Infancy Gospels

Some of the most fascinating works are the so-called infancy gospels that attempt to detail events in the life of Jesus between his birth (even before his birth) and ministry. Since not much is known about this period in the life of Jesus, these works provided opportunity for vivid speculation to "enhance" and develop (not necessarily acceptably) the canonical portraits of Jesus and Mary.

1. The Protoevangelium of James

The so-called Protoevangelium is a document that provides support for the view that Mary was a specially chosen agent of God from her birth. This work proposes not only that Jesus was born from God but that Mary also had a special birth. Thus, when Joachim bemoaned that he had no children, he went off into the wilderness to fast and pray for a child. His wife Anna likewise lamented her state. But the Lord heard her pleading, and an angel told her "your offspring shall be spoken of in the whole world" (4). Two messengers also came to Joachim and announced that his wife had conceived. When Mary was born, Anna praised the Lord for her child with a canticle (much like those in Luke 1). Also in this work, the parents presented the child to the temple when she was two years old, and she "danced for joy" (7). Mary was thus nurtured in the temple and received food from the hand of an angel (8). When Mary was twelve the high priest received a command from the Lord to find a husband for her through a miraculous sign, and Joseph was chosen by the flight of a miraculous dove. Even though Joseph already had sons by a previous wife (note the protection of Mary), Joseph received Mary to protect her and keep her pure (9–10). During this protection time, an angel appeared to Mary and indicated she would "conceive of the Lord" and that the child would be called Jesus (11). Then Mary visited Elizabeth, as indicated by Luke, but here James adds that she was sixteen years of age at this time (12). When Mary was six months pregnant, Joseph realized her state and bemoaned the situation to the Lord, fearing what he should do. But an angel assured him that the child was of the Holy Spirit (13–14). Joseph was then charged by Annas with violating his sacred trust of Mary. When Joseph denied wrongdoing, both he and

Mary were given "the water of the conviction" and sent off into the wilderness as a test. After they were both found to be whole, they were not condemned by the high priest (15–16). En route and following the trip to Bethlehem, Joseph experienced several miracles and found a Hebrew midwife to assist in the birth. She came and praised God, but another woman, Salome, was doubtful that Mary was a virgin. She demanded to use her finger to test Mary's condition, whereupon Salome's finger began to burn and fall off. When she prayed to the Lord and confessed her doubt, an angel told her to touch the child and be healed. Miraculously, she was healed (19–20). The rest of the story involves Herod's killing of children and his searching for John the Baptist. Elizabeth tried to hide herself and her child (John) from Herod and prayed for the mountain to help. Amazingly, it miraculously split open and hid them (22–23). (Note: While Matthew records the fact that Herod sought to kill the baby Jesus and Luke mentions the birth of John, neither Gospel has any reference to Herod's searching for the baby John. But the deaths of infants must have begged the question for some early Christians about how John survived, and the result was this speculative and mythical idea.)

It should be clear to the reader that this work is filled with strange, miraculous events that enhance the story and that also assist in establishing the legitimacy of the perpetual virginity of Mary.

2. The Gospel of Thomas the Israelite: Concerning the Childhood of the Lord

This work, another attributed to Thomas, purports to report "all the works of the childhood of our Lord Jesus Christ" (1). It is filled with the miracles, but unlike those in the canonical Gospels, they generally lack theological purpose except to prove that Jesus was a powerful miracle worker even as a boy. For example, Jesus was at a brook playing on the Sabbath. He made a pool of clear water from the stream and fashioned mud sparrows. When a Jew saw him doing so, he called Joseph. Joseph came and confronted Jesus as to why he was breaking the Sabbath. To the amazement of the Jews, Jesus simply clapped his hands and the mud sparrows "took flight and went away chirping" (2). Then the son of Annas destroyed Jesus' pool and Jesus cursed him. Immediately the boy "withered up" and his parents carried him away. Joseph therefore scolded him (3). Subsequently, another lad bumped Jesus so Jesus cursed the boy and he died. The parents told Joseph that unless he taught Jesus "to bless and not curse," he could not live in their village (4). The parents who accused Jesus were thereafter struck blind (5). As one reads such stories, it is easy to understand that they hardly represent the canonical Jesus.

This work shows that not only did Jesus amaze people with his power but he also dumbfounded Zacchaeus, a revered scholar. The teacher offered to teach Jesus concerning Alpha and Beta (note the Greek and not the Hebrew alphabet). When Jesus told Zacchaeus the details concerning Alpha, the scholar was shamed for his lack of knowledge and told Joseph to take the boy away. After this, Jesus laughed and said, "I have come from above to curse them...." As a result, no one "dared to provoke him" (6–8). Later, as Jesus matured, Joseph took him to another teacher to learn his letters. After a time Jesus, told the teacher that if he would tell Jesus the meaning of Alpha, then Jesus would instruct him about Beta. Annoyed, the teacher struck him on the head, so Jesus cursed him and he fell down on his face (14). Subsequently, Joseph took Jesus to another teacher, but instead of reading a book on the desk, to the amazement of all, Jesus "by the Holy Spirit...taught the law" to those around him. After the incident, the teacher confessed to Joseph, "I took the child as a disciple; but he is filled with grace and wisdom." When Jesus heard his answer, he not only affirmed the instructor for his honesty but also healed the previous teacher (15).

Perhaps two of the best-known stories from this work are the following: First, Jesus was playing with friends on the upper floor of a house, and one of the children fell off the roof and died. When the other children witnessed the event, they fled, leaving Jesus alone. The parents came and accused Jesus "of having thrown him down." When the accusations did not cease, Jesus jumped down from the roof and cried to the boy, "Zenon...arise and tell me, did I throw you down?" As you might expect, to the amazement of everyone, the boy arose and said, "No Lord...but [you] raised me up" (9). Second, Jesus' mother sent him at the age of six to fetch water in a pitcher, but Jesus fell and broke the pitcher. Not to be upstaged, he merely spread out his tunic, filled it with water, and carried it home. Thomas then added that Jesus' mother "kept within herself the mysteries" she saw him do (11).

Thomas concludes his stories with three other healings. The first involves James, the son of Joseph, who was bitten by a viper and was healed. In the second report Jesus brings a child back to life. In the third he raises a dead man. After the third healing the people confessed, "This child is from heaven, for he has saved many souls from death, and is able to save them all his life long" (16–18). The document closes in paragraph 19 with a restatement and expansion about the story of Jesus in the temple recorded in Luke 2:41–52 and with the words, "To him be glory for ever and ever. Amen."

C. Conclusion

1. The Fiasco Concerning the Gospel of Judas

It is important to add an example here for readers to realize that scholars and publishers can and do make major mistakes, but that other scholars are usually ready to confront such errors. This example involves a recently revealed work called the Gospel of Judas that was hastily published with great notoriety by the usually respected National Geographic Society. The claim was that the picture of Judas in the canonical Gospels was in error and that the Tchacos manuscript[9] revealed a true portrait of him. The hype was so great that the work made the *New York Times* bestseller list.[10]

The work in actuality is just another Gnostic document. Clearly Irenaeus knew the Gnostics used the name of Judas, and in fact he said they fabricated a work that they called "the Gospel of Judas."[11] Whether the present work represents Irenaeus's Gospel of Judas is still questionable because in this present document, Judas may not be a

---

[9] Known as such because of the work of Frieda Tchacos Nussberger in the preservation of the document.

[10] See Birger A. Pearson "Judas Iscariot Among the Gnostics: What the Gospel of Judas really Says," *Biblical Archaeology Review* 34/3 (May–June 2008): 52–57.

[11] See *Adversus Haereses* 1.31.1.

totally positive figure for the Gnostic writer. Indeed, in this manuscript, only Judas apparently knew who Jesus was, namely that he descended from the Ultimate reality here called Barbelo (35), a well-known designation among some Gnostics. But instead of honoring Judas, Jesus laughed at him because he was identified as a "demon" or "evil spirit" (*daimon*), one of the thirteen such spirits that belong to the created realm of the planets ("error of the stars," 46). Unfortunately, the scholars charged with translating the text were not permitted by the publisher to share their work with others prior to publication (for economic reasons!), and as a result they made major errors in translation, apparently in an attempt to paint a new, acceptable picture of Judas. For example, they treated *daimon* as a positive word and omitted a crucial "not" in the discussion concerning the supposed assent of Judas (46–47), which changed the document's entire representation of Judas to positive.

Fortunately, such errors have now been recognized, and the document has been republished in a more accurate version. But this fiasco only confirms the fact that there is significant financial gain and prestige for those who can impugn the canonical message (kerygma) in the four accepted portraits of Jesus.

2. A Summation

By making the above statements, I do not intend to decry academically respectable scholarship or the development of new methods for understanding the canonical books of the New Testament. Careful research is essential to provide us with the most accurate assessment of Jesus and the Gospels that is possible to attain at this point. We need to use various methodologies in this process, some of which are briefly discussed in the next chapter.

Finally, while there are many more documents that could have been included in this brief review, those discussed above should provide readers with a sufficient sampling of the literature available in the field. Reflecting on these representative documents, however, should make it patently clear why none of them are part of the New Testament canon. They either present portraits of Jesus that assert a theology that is partly at odds with or completely opposed to the life and teachings of Jesus pictured in the canonical Gospels, and/or they are to be regarded as so highly fanciful that they leave no doubt as to why they were rejected by the Christian church. Still, they make interesting reading if one is ready to ponder the nature of such writings and the reasons why they have attracted or intrigued people in the past and still continue to do so. Understanding their phenomena will help to clarify why the canonical portraits of Jesus are the true measure of the authentic Jesus. New information is welcomed in scholarship, but it is highly unlikely that any such information will change our canonical picture of Jesus.

Recommended for Further Study

Grant, R. M. *Gnosticism: A Source Book of Heretical Writings from the Early Christian Period.* New York: Harper & Brothers, 1961.

Jonas, Hans. *The Gnostic Religion.* Beacon Hill/Boston: Beacon Press, 1958.

Robinson, J. M., editor. *The Nag Hammadi Library.* San Francisco: Harper & Row, 1981.

Hennecke, E., W. Schneemelcher, and R. M. Wilson. *New Testament Apocrypha.* Volume 1. Philadelphia: Westminster, 1963.

Pagels, Elaine. *The Gnostic Gospels.* New edition. New York: Vintage-Random House, 2004.

PART III

AN INTRODUCTION TO GOSPEL METHODOLOGY

METHODOLOGICAL TOOLS FOR THE
STUDY OF JESUS AND THE GOSPELS

We come now to a somewhat difficult but crucial part of our study that involves the way we read the Gospels.

1. Concerning Presuppositions

Each person comes to the stories of Jesus with a set of presuppositions that determines the way he or she will read them. These presuppositions are based either on naively imbedded theologies or on those formulated over years of being socialized to think in certain ways. My purpose in my writings has not been to deny the importance of presuppositions or foundational commitments (Bultmann and others have made their existence in everyone clear). Instead, my goal has been one of seeking to assist people in developing conscious, deliberative suppositions or theologies that will supply them with a basis for approaching new and challenging ideas without fear.[1]

Let me pause for a brief personal comment. After having finished the study of law and having served in a well-known Canadian law firm for a short time, I felt impelled by a sense of God's leading in my life to enter seminary and prepare for some form of ministry. When I informed my pastor, he gave me a piece of advice that I have never forgotten. He told me, "Take up your theological studies with zeal, and remember that truth wears no labels. It is neither conservative nor liberal. Truth is truth. Commit yourself to God and truth!" Therefore, one of the great themes

---

[1] See for example my study, G. L. Borchert, *Worship in the New Testament* (St. Louis: Chalice Press, 2008) 2.

or commitments of my life since that time has been "Still I am learning!" As a result, I try to weigh my presuppositions within the context of a clear Christian commitment to the existence of God and to the divine purpose in sending the "one and only Son," Jesus, into the world to transform and renew humans with new life and offer the world's inhabitants divine direction through the creative power of the Holy Spirit. That people misunderstand or reject God's directions here on earth is quite evident. But since God gave humans the freedom to make personal and corporate decisions that can and do run counter to God's intentions for them, their choices lead to significant consequences either for good or evil.

With this personal reflection in mind, I return to the issue of developing an adequate, deliberative approach to the Gospels. In moving forward with this task, we should not close our minds to questions or doubts. Doubt can be a powerful incentive for learning. To confront queries and challenges honestly and perceptively within the Christian life requires both faith and the realization that some methodologies can enable us to sort out and find at least partial answers to difficult issues, always recognizing that as humans we may not gain final perspectives in this life.

I suggest you ponder the fact that while the Gospels were written in an oral culture, they are genuine literary documents. We may confess that the Gospels are inspired, but they do not claim to have been written in heaven and delivered without human involvement to other humans (see for example Luke 1:1–4). Moreover, they do not even claim to be like the tablets containing the simple ten Hebrew words (commandments) that Moses received at Mt. Sinai. Nor are they like the far more complex message on the so-called ethereal golden tablets of Mormonism given by an angel to Joseph Smith, or even the more transcendent Koran delivered to Mohammed. During my study in the Middle East with a Muslim professor, I early learned that the Koran cannot in actuality be translated or in fact fully interpreted by mere humans. It is best understood as a static, frozen document, behind which is the transcendent "Allah" who cannot actually be known; only his will in part can be sensed. Some of the rabbis of the Tannaim (around the first and second centuries B.C./B.C.E. and A.D./C.E.) came close to such a claim for the Torah and verged on a somewhat similar status even for the Oral Law, which later was written as the *Mishnah* (see my earlier comments). Some Christians might also be tempted to give the Bible such an ethereal status, even attributing to an English version of the Greek and Hebrew such transcendence. Yet Christians ought to know that the Bible is not God, but a special vehicle to lead us to a closer walk with God (2 Tim 3:17), who revealed God's self most fully in the incarnation of Jesus. Many Christians would confess that the evangelists were truly inspired human writers, but they should be careful not to identify the Gospels as written substitutes for a pope whom some Christians believe speaks *ex catherdra* for God.

What about the people who wrote these Gospels as testimonies? They were not divine but were servants of the living God. They wrote their testimonies about the divine Jesus who became a human and about his significance for humanity. The texts themselves do not tell us the writers' identities, but early tradition tells us who the authors probably were within their communities of faith. Moreover, in the Fourth Gospel especially, the community confirmed for readers that this testimony was true or authentic (cf. John 21:24). These four testimonies then became the standard (canon) for judging all other testimonies concerning the life and teaching of Jesus. Understanding the nature of these Gospels as witnesses is foundational to a correct perception of them.

In the study of these Gospels, scholars often define the various methods of analysis using the technical term "criticism." Thus, students of the Bible will read about "textual criticism," "form criticism," "synoptic criticism," "literary criticism," "narrative criticism," "sociological criticism," and others. The combination of these expressions is often designated as the "historical, critical method." The term "criticism" often connotes to some people a sense of rationalistic hostility to the Bible, but when the term is used without prejudice, it merely means that the study is being conducted in an analytical fashion. For example, one of my colleagues suggests that most people want a surgeon who has critical skills for detecting problems in the human body. The German term that is used in place of criticism is -*geschichte* (history) as in *Formgeschichte*, which likewise may lead to some misunderstandings. Instead of using either "criticism" or -*geschichte*, however, I prefer to use the term "analysis" to avoid any misconceptions concerning the methodologies that are being used. Therefore, since you have already read about the Gospels, I invite you to a brief introduction to aspects of the "historical analytical method" in the study of these Gospels.

2. Orality and Deconstruction

First, I remind readers that the Gospels were written in a time when, as I indicated in the introduction, the preferred method of communication was oral.[2] Materials were written primarily as a method of keeping a record or for confirmation of decisions (e.g., Acts 15:22–29), but people would have preferred to hear the stories of Jesus rather than read them. The early Christians loved to hear people tell them the stories of Jesus like some of our songs or hymns indicate. Accordingly, the early evangelists had assistants who traveled with them and orally taught or catechized new Christians. It is probable that John Mark served in such a capacity when he traveled with Paul and Barnabas and was designated as their *hyperetes* ("assistant," Acts 13:5). That experience would have prepared him for the writing of our first Gospel when the firsthand witnesses began to pass from the scene. Christians should be grateful to Barnabas for rescuing Mark after the dispute between Paul and Barnabas when Mark left the other missionaries (see Acts 13:13; 15:37–39).

The opening verses of the book of Revelation remind us that literature was scarce, and the written messages of the church were also read orally (Rev 1:3). The problem is that it becomes difficult for us to imagine being part of a culture where silent reading was not one of primary methods of communication. Even though we have cell phones, we use them to text-message others visually, as I reminded pastors in Singapore a number of years ago when I watched their young people text-messaging each other while the sermon was taking place. Since I teach in seminaries and colleges in both the developed world and also in various developing countries, I have become far more conscious of patterns of communication and ponder frequently what it must have been like to live at the time of Jesus and the evangelists. We are certainly

---

[2] See M. Rex Miller, *The Millennium Matrix* (San Francisco: Jossey-Bass, 2004) 19–34.

living in a different world where communication patterns seem to change overnight.

These reflections have alerted me to the fact that our analyses and critiques of the Gospels are often based on our assumptions of living in very different contexts. Some of our methods of analyzing the Gospels assume that we can deconstruct the texts and recover the actual *Sitz im Leben* (the life setting) behind sections or even small parts of pericopes. We assume that we are able to identify which portions of the testimonies go back to Jesus and which go back to periods in the early church's life. I am not arguing against being able to do so in some isolated cases, but we need to be aware of the subjective nature of such processes. This caveat (warning) applies particularly to methods like form analysis and redaction analysis, which I shall note hereafter.

From my perspective, I find some methodologies to be much more helpful and less subjective than others. Textual analysis works with actual documents where we can see some variations that have occurred in the transmission of the texts over a period of time. Synoptic analysis helps us compare how each writer of the Gospels used the pericopes or Gospel segments differently in the development of his testimony. Narrative analysis generally takes the documents as a whole and seeks to understand what literary tools and patterns the author used in writing. Sociological analysis seeks to describe the social settings that are evident in the texts. Of course, each analyst has presuppositions of what that study can accomplish. It is the reader's task to evaluate each scholar's analysis and each method being used to determine its value for understanding both the Gospel texts and the portrait of Jesus that emerges in that study. With these brief remarks, I turn to the various methods used in the study of the Gospels.

3. Textual Analysis

Although we do not now have any original manuscripts of the Gospel writers, textual analysis seeks to determine as closely as possible what their original words were. It involves analyzing the multitude of early Greek manuscripts of the Gospels written either on papyrus or vellum (skins of animals), and it uses the various versions (translations such as Latin, Syriac, Coptic, Ethiopic, etc.) and even commentaries or other works of the early Church Fathers who cited Gospel passages. The Greek manuscripts are either written in the early capital-letter format (uncials) or in lowercase letters (minuscules). Each document is then collated against the Textus Receptus (the so-called later majority text that is somewhat like the Greek behind the KJV). Differences that are thus revealed often indicate an earlier form of the text since scribes tended to add words or change ideas that they thought would help clarify the earlier texts. These "variants" (not usually called mistakes) are then listed and analyzed into families of texts as we seek to determine the earliest words that were written.

Generally speaking, among the manuscripts that have been significant in our attempt at the restoration of the Gospel texts are the papyri #52 (the early Rylands fragment that destroyed arguments for the late dating of John), #42 (Chester Beaty), #75 (Bodmer), and #76 (Vienna); the uncials Aleph (Sinaiticus) and B (Vaticanus); and the minuscule #33 (often designated as the queen of the cursives or minuscules). But there are literally thousands of other manuscripts (some rather fragmentary) that have been collated into various families of texts, and some of them have been important, including A (Alexandrinus, which tends to use more classical or Alexandrian Greek), D (Bezae/Cambridge, which tends to add words, e.g., Luke 6:4), and W (Freer Gospels/Washington, which has the longer ending of Mark).

I offer here a few other examples concerning this tedious yet crucial work of scholars that should provide some clarification for the reader if one compares the KJV with later translations: (a) In John 5:4 a scribe later tried to give a reason why invalids gathered around the pool of Bethzatha (Bethezda) by adding the mythical view that the troubling of the water was caused by an angel stirring the water and in the process bringing healing. (b) Mark 16:9–20 was undoubtedly added by later scribes who were dissatisfied that the Gospel was left without any resurrection appearances (see my comments above in Mark concerning the probable loss of the beginning and the end). (c) A Syriac manuscript later tried to change Matthew 1:16 to read, "Joseph, to whom Mary the virgin was betrothed, begat Jesus who is called the Christ." This reading suggests a later Ebionite view of Joseph as the father. (d) I add an important example of what I call textual interference from 1 John 5:7

where scribes added in the Latin version a Trinitarian heavenly statement (the Father, the Word, and the Holy Ghost) to the so-called parallel three earthly witnesses of 5:8. Erasmus in the first edition of his analytical Greek text omitted verse 7, but the church hierarchy was livid with what they considered the elimination of their best verse on the Trinity. So Erasmus, on pain of punishment and excommunication, promised to put that verse into his next edition of the Greek text if the authorities could produce one Greek text with that verse. Suddenly, a late minuscule copy of the New Testament appeared with that verse included, which forced Erasmus to add it in his second edition. Unfortunately, a copy of that edition made its way to England and became the basis of the King James Version. When the political situation changed, Erasmus deleted that addition from his third edition! But the damage was done for the English translation.

Many other examples of less import could be added here and can be found in most Greek texts printed by the United Bible Societies and in the Textual Commentary of Bruce M. Metzger.[3] While the task of textual analysis is tedious and does not make headlines, the examples I have given are glaring problems. But this painstaking type of work is being conducted by scholars in order to provide students of the Bible with confidence that their New Testaments are trustworthy and that no theological doctrine is threatened because of a textual error! What scholars and readers do with the New Testament texts, however, may be another matter.

4. Source or Synoptic Analysis

If a reader briefly scans a copy of parallel texts of the four Gospels, it should become clear that the Gospels of Matthew, Mark, and Luke have many identical words but that the Fourth Gospel is generally quite independent of the other three.[4] There are, of course, a few exceptions in

---

[3] I had the delightful privilege of working a little with Professor B. M. Metzger in the initial stages of this detailed work that was finally published as *A Textual Commentary on the Greek New Testament* (New York: United Bible Societies, 1971).

[4] See K. Aland, ed., *Synopis of the Four Gospels: Greek–English Edition*, 3rd ed. (New York/London/Stuttgart: United Bible Societies, 1979).

the first half of John, such as the importance of John the Baptist (John 1) or the feeding of the five thousand and Jesus walking on the water (John 6, the only parallel miracles/signs of Jesus in John). The cleansing of the temple (as I indicated above in John) has been moved purposely into the first half of that Gospel. Similarities in the second half include the entry into Jerusalem (John 12), Peter's denials, and the accounts of the arrest, the trials, and the death and the resurrection stories (John 18–20). The major catch of fish (John 21) is somewhat similar to Luke 5. But even in these similar stories, the Greek words employed in the descriptions are not often parallel. The opposite, however, applies to the other three Gospels. Because of their close parallelism, they have been designated as the "Synoptic Gospels."

That statement, however, does not reflect the whole picture because of the following: (a) Clearly, nearly 97 percent of Mark's 661 verses seem to have been used in the other two Gospels: about 500 of those verses are basically shared in some form by both Matthew and Luke with roughly another 70 different verses each (140) that are used by Matthew or Luke, leaving only about 21 verses of Mark that at least in part are not utilized by the other two. The use of the Marcan verses by Matthew and Luke is generally close, yet it is not always an exact word-for-word copying, which could suggest that there may even have been an earlier edition of Mark. (b) In addition to the phenomenon involving Mark, Matthew and Luke contain at least 235 (some suggest 272) verses that are common to both of them but not present in Mark. Much of that material involves the teaching of Jesus or his "sayings." This phenomenon has led to the theory that there must have been available to both writers a "Sayings Source." Whether this source (usually called "Q" from the German *Quelle*) was oral or written is not clear, but it is difficult to account for this commonality without such a source. As I indicated in the discussion on the Gospel of Thomas (GT), some scholars at first were tempted to designate the GT as the missing Q, but even though the structure of GT may have been like somewhat like what might have been Q, the content was hardly Q. (c) The result would mean there are roughly 263 (or 226) verses in Matthew and 344 (or 307) verses in Luke that are independent of the other Gospels. The exception might be the likeness between Luke 5:1–11 (the call of the disciples) and John 21:1–8 (the resurrection appearance), which some have suggested are displacements of the same event.

How then are these phenomena to be explained? As early as Papias in the second century, there was a theory that Matthew first "wrote the oracles [*logia*] in [the] Hebrew dialect [*dialecton*] and each one interpreted as he was able."[5] As noted in my discussion on Matthew, it is highly unlikely that he wrote in Hebrew. This theory was followed by Jerome, but he did not know how Matthew came to be in Greek (*non satis certum est*).[6] By the time of Augustine, the tradition was regarded as confirmed until the late eighteenth century when J. J. Greisbach developed a theory of Marcan priority and suggested a proto-Mark theory. But then he promptly reversed himself and argued that Matthew was written first, then Luke, and finally Mark.

Scholars, however, found his early Marcan priority theory to be more satisfactory and refined it so that, by the early twentieth century with B. H. Streeter and his Oxford colloquium, a composite argument known as the "Four Source" theory was enunciated.[7] It was posited (a) that Mark (or Proto-Mark) was the earliest source that Matthew and Luke used; (b) that Matthew and Luke also used Q; and (c) that Matthew, "M," and (d) Luke, "L," each added their own additional information. This theory has convinced most current scholars with the exception of a few who have followed W. R. Farmer and consider that there is no such "document" as Q.[8] They have sought to revive the later "Griesbach theory" and have posited that Luke used Matthew and that Mark was a later edited version.

Although the revised Griesbach theory eliminates the need for a Q, it fails to take seriously some of the unique aspects of both Matthew and

---

[5] See the report in Eusebius, *Hist. Eccl.* 3.39.16.

[6] See *Prolog in Matt.* 3 in D. J. Theron, *Evidence of Tradition* (Grand Rapids: Baker, 1958) 66–67.

[7] B. H. Streeter, *The Four Gospels: A Study of Origins* (London: Macmillan, 1924).

[8] For a review of these views, see W. R. Farmer, ed., *New Synoptic Studies: The Cambridge Conference and Beyond* (Macon GA: Mercer University Press, 1983). For a thorough critique of the theory see C. M. Tuckett, *The Revival of Griesbach Hypothesis; An Analysis and Appraisal* (Cambridge: Cambridge University Press, 1983).

Luke: (a) How could Luke avoid not using some of the major themes and organization of Matthew (even a so-called Proto-Matthew) if he copied him and not Mark? (b) How can you explain the organization of Luke, who seems to alternate his writing between using a Marcan source and a Q source in a different order than is in Matthew along with interspersing his own L materials? Farmer has not convinced most New Testament analysts. The "Four Source" theory seems at this point the best in explaining the relationship between the three Synoptic Gospels. Moreover, for students—once they perceive the genuine reality of both similarities and differences in the parallel Gospels—it offers the best format to explain the uniqueness of each witness.

5. Form Analysis (or the Analysis of Pericopes)

Form analysis presupposes that the stories of Jesus were told orally before they were set down in the written form of the Gospels. In the oral culture of the first century, people preferred for the witnesses of Jesus to "tell" them stories about Jesus. It was only later that these stories were put in writing when the original witnesses began to die. Mark, as I have argued, was probably the first to do so, not likely before the mid-sixties of the first Christian century. How then were these stories told? As in any oral culture, certain forms are adopted, much like we expect a children's fairly tale to start with "Once upon a time..." and end with "They lived happily ever after."

In reflecting on form analysis, it is usually presupposed that these stories of Jesus assumed certain forms shaped by the church's telling and retelling as they circulated for some thirty years in various contexts before they were written down. Often it is thought that the contexts of the telling affected the development of their forms. To what extent those stories were altered in the telling is a matter of significant debate. In the case of the canonical Gospels, we can recognize certain forms such as parables, miracle stories, conflict stories, proverbs, sayings, and pronouncements.[9] Perceiving these forms is a helpful tool in the hands of

---

[9] I have avoided using terms like "legends," "myths," and "tales" since they conjure in the minds of many non-technical readers forms that are untrue. While M. Dibelius, who formulated the term *Formgeschichte*, would have had questions

a wise biblical interpreter who attempts to understand the point of a story or pericope.

While we can recognize such forms, we must interpret them with great care and not assume that when we have identified the form, we necessarily also understand its original *Sitz im_Leben* ("setting in life"). For example, form analysts often proceed beyond the question of the meaning of the story in a Gospel to the issue of the historical context represented in the story's present form. Thus, interpreters often ask particular questions concerning the setting of a pericope: Does it actually go back to Jesus? Or does it represent a context in the early church's preaching? Or, finally, is it simply the work of a creative writer (as editor) of the story? It may be possible to see in a story both a context from the life of Jesus and a related context in the life of the early church (e.g., Matt 10:16–23; Luke 12:1–12). We would consider that such an evangelist has seen a connection or relevance to both settings. Moving to this later stage, however, *unless* it is so indicated *in the story*, means that the interpreter assumes an ability to trace the history of the story's use behind the text itself. Such an assumption concerning the need for the deconstruction of texts, however, is fraught with subjectivism, especially should a commentator decide that a story in a Gospel did not go back to Jesus but went back to some setting in the later life of the church. The commentator then presupposes that the story was read back by the writer into the mouth or the activity of Jesus (once again I refer to the so-called parallel fishing stories in Luke 5:1–11 and John 21:1–8).

In such a case, the interpreter has done far more with the methodology than to use it in understanding the meaning of the form in its present context. Instead, he has presumed to tell the reader that he has a historical perception behind the text or has isolated the "history" of that story's form before it became part of the canonical Gospel. Such a pattern would certainly then be related to the German designation of the

---

concerning the reliability of some canonical stories, the more skeptical R. Bultmann did so to a greater extent. But the method of form analysis does not need to imply skepticism. The major work on this subject is R. Bultmann, *History of the Synoptic Tradition*, trans. John Marsh (New York: Harper & Row, 1963). For a contrast see G. R. Beasely-Murray, *Preaching the Gospel from the Gospels* (London: Lutterworth, 1965).

methodology as "form"-*geschichte*. The interpreter may be correct, or he may be in error. But the burden of proof is upon the one who makes such a statement. It is not on the text itself! This presumption of the burden of proof has not always been admitted by form analysts (critics). It is also true that playing loosely with this burden has engendered significant negative *criticism* about form critics.

While the value of form analysis can both be overstated and understated, progress can be made in interpreting the canonical Gospels by developing a keen sense of the various forms that appear in them. One does not need to adopt a sense of skepticism concerning the Gospels or the methodology of form analysis.

6. Redaction Analysis and the Quests for the Historical Jesus

Redaction analysis generally presupposes form analysis and moves the methodological concern one step further into the process by concentrating on the evangelist's activity in his role as an "editor" of tradition. He controls what is being presented and can add his comments, thus focusing the reader's attention on his particular concerns. Thus, throughout Mark one notes that things happen "immediately" in the presence of Jesus, that people are "stunned" or "shocked" by his activity, and that there is a definite emphasis on Jesus not allowing people and the spirits to identify him as divine. Luke periodically mentions Jesus' activity in prayer and his concern for the marginalized, Matthew frequently mentions fulfillment sayings and the importance of mountains, and John notes the "I am" sayings of Jesus (or "I am not" sayings by John, the witness, and by Peter). These particular comments or notes reflect a special interest of the author, and in their repetition they are unique to that writer. Accordingly, they provide the reader with an insight into the type of portrait the evangelist wants the reader to have of Jesus.

In the nineteenth century, many scholars, particularly in Germany, focused on finding the possible "kernel of truth" in the Gospels that would reveal the "historical Jesus." Albert Schweitzer designated this focus as "the quest for the historical Jesus." Briefly stated, following the absolute skepticism of Bruno Bauer, scholars busily searched to find a basis for uncovering who Jesus was. They decided that a form of Mark was the primitive Gospel and revealed a true picture of Jesus and that the other evangelists had added to this early portrait.[10]

Unfortunately for those "questers," Wilhelm Wrede discovered in Mark a theme of the "messianic secret," which suggested that Mark also was involved in presenting a theological picture of Jesus.[11] Wrede's work was like a bombshell that devastated these questers, and it led to great skepticism concerning research into studies of the "historical" Jesus. Rudolph Bultmann emerged in that period and declared in a famous dictum, "We can now know virtually nothing concerning the historical Jesus."[12] As a result, his little work on *Jesus* (translated as *Jesus and the Word*) contains only a few sayings that he considered went back to Jesus. Since that time many scholars have struggled to overcome the skepticism by launching into the "second" and "third" quests in an endeavor to find a "real historical Jesus" devoid of "theological accretions."[13] The result has been the development of new methodologies such as redaction or editorial analysis.

From my perspective, I consider most of these so-called "quests" to be hopeless because to discover Jesus apart from a Christian theological confession about him in the Gospels will not work. It is still like peeling an onion to discover the core. You keep peeling until there is really nothing left. Of course Jesus lived. Of course he taught. Of course he died. But he also did the miraculous, and he rose from the dead to the astonishment of even his disciples! That resurrection is foundational to the Gospel presentations of Jesus. Without the resurrection, there would be no Gospels (cf. 1 Cor 15:14). The remembrances of Jesus are all

---

[10] Albert Schweitzer provides an excellent review of this early history of the so-called quest in his work *The Quest for the Historical Jesus* (New York: Macmillan, 1910).

[11] Wrede's 1901 German work was finally translated into English and appeared as *The Messianic Secret* (London: J. Clarke, 1971).

[12] See his German work, Rudolf Bultmann, *Jesus* (Tübingen: J. C. B. Mohr-Paul Siebeck, 1951).

[13] For reviews of the various recent quests see L. T. Johnson, *The Real Jesus: The Misguided Quest for the Historical Jesus and the Truth of the Traditional Gospels* (San Francisco: HarperCollins, 1996) and M. J. Wilkins and J. P. Moreland, *Jesus under Fire: Modern Scholarship Reinvents the Historical Jesus* (Grand Rapids MI: Zondervan, 1995).

presented in the light of the resurrection. See for example the editorial comment in John 2:22. Confession and the portraits of Jesus are inseparable. Scholars have tried to get to Jesus apart from the confessions, and what results is virtually nothing but speculation. *As a former lawyer, I have tried.* I have used the methodologies that I have listed here and others. They are helpful in revealing various aspects of the Gospels, but I cannot get behind these Gospels (as many have tried) to uncover a different picture of Jesus. Frankly, any such results are predetermined by the presuppositions of the scholar. As of now, I consider that the "questing" task is not productive, although I do attend meetings regularly in the Society of Biblical Literature where such methodologies are used because I am interested in any new insights I can gain from others.

These methodologies can be helpful in the study of the Gospels, and I encourage students of the Bible to use a marking pen and check each time they find an editorial note or particular repetition in a Gospel. It is one way to discover the focus of the Gospel and the portrait of Jesus that is being presented by the evangelist. Such a use of redaction analysis can be an enlightening exercise.

7. Narrative Analysis

Narrative analysis assumes a basic coherence in a written document and focuses on the various aspects of a text. These aspects include plot, characterization, types of scenes in the story (such as pericopes that involve recognition or betrayal), literary features such as irony and tensions, use of symbolism and metaphor, the role of a narrator or implied author over against the real author, and the use of themes and various hermeneutical emphases that provide focus to the document. Among the innovators in this enterprise has been my former colleague Alan Culpepper, whose significant work, *Anatomy of the Fourth Gospel*,[14] directed attention away from deconstructive analysis to a more holistic

---

[14] Alan Culpepper, *Anatomy of the Fourth Gospel* (Philadelphia: Fortress Press, 1983).

treatment of a Gospel text and affirmed me in my concentration on thematic and characterization studies in John.[15]

In the study of the Gospels, bringing to bear various tools learned from literary studies can be enlightening. But the point or focus of the analysis is not the tools or the method itself; the method is employed as a servant to a better understanding of the text. Thus, while certain patterns of reading may provide new insight into the texts, the commitment is not to adopting a specific hermeneutic such as employing counter-cultural, gender-specific, or post-colonial patterns of reading the Gospels. Such matters lead naturally into the next topic, which is sociological analysis.

8. Sociological Analysis

While I could mention a number of other methods of study, I come finally to a methodological concern that has engaged my interest for some time. I think it offers students of the Bible possibilities for considerable enlightenment of the biblical texts. But just as with all contemporary tools, social investigation must be used with a clear recognition of its limitations.

As I indicated in my 1990 article in *Mercer Dictionary of the Bible*, because of writers from the nineteenth century such as F. C. Baur and Adolf Harnack, scholarship was primed to consider some facets related to the social dynamics of New Testament Christianity. But lurking within such studies has been the tendency to assume that background matters (in Hellenism, Judaism, Gnosticism, the Mystery Religions, or even the Roman Imperium) determined meaning for the early Christians. Thus, reductionism has been a constant danger in such studies when they overlook "originality in the shaping of the early church."[16] Such a danger must be recognized because foundational in this "shaping" was the unique person of Jesus (in his incarnation, death, resurrection, and expected *parousia*). He was not simply a first-century wandering charismatic who had little intention to form communities of faith, as

---

[15] G. L. Borchert, *John 12–21* (Nashville: Broadman & Holman, 2002), esp. at 345–80.

[16] See G. L. Borchert, "Sociology of the New Testament," *MDB* (Macon GA: Mercer University Press, 1990) 832–35.

Gerd Theissen argued.[17] Jesus was the initiator of a new way of life, a new community, and even a new worldview.

But bearing in mind this caveat, I turn to the nature and benefits of sociological analysis for the study of the Gospels. The field can be divided into a number of areas or concerns, some of which impact our study of the New Testament: (a) socio-linguistics, the use of words (or more significantly in the use of phrases as argued by James Barr), is significant[18] because their meanings may have changed and words naturally lead to specialized *descriptions* of the social facts in the Gospels; (b) social history involves understanding the background matters and the historical context related to the Gospels; (c) social organizations involve institutions, structures, and forces that have emerged as a result of the incarnate Jesus; and (d) social or symbolic worldviews were created and given meaning by Jesus and early Christianity. Obviously in this brief statement it is impossible to detail these matters but perhaps listing some of them will stimulate further investigation.

In this type of study, one analyzes geographical, archaeological, economic, political, social, and religious factors in an attempt to determine how people lived, organized their institutions, and related to one another in their social contexts. For example, consider this problem that we face: because the United States is so large, Americans often have difficulty envisaging how Jesus could have lived his entire life in a small area. Perhaps some can grasp that most people in Israel lived with great poverty; that there was virtually no health care, no retirement, and not even Social Security; that communications were vastly different and maybe even nonexistent (with no telephone and certainly no cell phones); that travel was hard (no packing and getting into a car) and it took a great deal of time to go five or ten miles; that ships depended on the weather for sailing; that goods were limited and there were no

---

[17] Gerd Theisen, *Sociology of Early Palestinian Christianity* (Philadelphia: Fortress, 1978) and *The Shadow of the Galilean: The Quest of the Historical Jesus in Narrative Form* (Philadelphia: Fortress, 1987).

[18] See J. Barr, *The Semantics of Biblical Language* (London: Oxford University Press, 1961); E. A. Nida and J. P. Louw, eds., *Greek-English Lexicon of the New Testament Based on Semantic Domains*, 2 vols. (United Bible Societies, 1988); and J. P. Louw, ed., *Sociolinguistics and Communication* (United Bible Societies, 1986).

supermarkets, let alone many places that we would identify as actual stores; that bartering was common as Boaz did for Ruth (even bartering with God like Abraham did over Sodom); that most farms were tiny; that entertainment was basically for the rich; that many did not live to thirty years of age; and that security for most was hard to imagine.

Do you wonder why Jesus' confidence was regarded as fascinating? Why did his message seem to be an unbelievable answer to the people's dreams? Why did he seem to be different from most religious people? Why were many threatened by him? When you think about Jesus, remember that he was not an American, a Canadian, or a European. You might even think he was strange. Would you like to meet someone who seems to know what you are thinking and tells you that your institutions will soon be destroyed? Consider Jesus seriously in his context. Do not isolate him or his words from his time and place.

Social analysis of the Gospels forces you to move outside your current social context and impels you to envisage the ancient context in which Jesus lived. You have to read the Gospels from a Roman-Jewish frame of reference. But be forewarned that you may have trouble doing so. Even if you succeed, you have to remember that Jesus did not actually receive his perspectives from the Roman-Jewish context. He brought the perspectives of God into that time frame. Thus, while Jesus was formed in that time frame, he and Christianity could not be captured in it no more than he can be imprisoned in the twenty-first century. The task of sociological analysis can be an exciting way to study the New Testament.

9. Conclusion

Welcome then to the various methodologies, those here listed and those not discussed, such as canonical analysis (how the texts fit into the overall strategy and perspectives of the church that accepted the documents as the standard for authentic Christian faith) and many methodologies yet to be formulated. Do not fear using them. These methods of study are merely tools. They can be used by skeptics, rationalists, and believers alike. The user's presuppositions determine how the methods are used. May you use them wisely, and may you learn that truth is never to be feared. Embrace learning with confidence!

Recommended for Further Study

Black, D. A., and D. S. Dockery, editors. *New Testament Criticism and Interpretation*. Grand Rapids MI: Zondervan, 1991.

Childs, B. *The New Testament as Canon: An Introduction*. Philadelphia: Fortress, 1985.

Culpepper, R. A. *Anatomy of the Fourth Gospel*. Second edition. Philadelphia: Fortress, 1983.

Evans, C. A., editor. *Routledge Encyclopedia of the Historical Jesus*. London: Routledge, 2008.

Johnson, L. T. *The Real Jesus: The Misguided Quest for the Historical Jesus and the Truth of the Traditional Gospels*. San Francisco: HarperCollins, 1996.

McKnight, E. V. *What Is Form Criticism?* Philadelphia: Fortress, 1969.

———. *The Bible and the Reader: An Introduction to Literary Criticism*. Philadelphia: Fortress, 1985.

Metzger, B. M., and B. D. Ehrman. *The Text of the New Testament: Its Transmission, Corruption, and Restoration*. Fourth edition. New York: Oxford University Press, 2005.

———. *The Bible in Translation: Ancient and English Versions*. Grand Rapids MI: Baker, 2001.

Thiselton, A. C. *New Horizons in Hermeneutics*. Grand Rapids MI: Zondervan, 1992.

Thatcher, T., and S. D. Moore, editors. *Anatomies of Narrative Criticism*. Atlanta: Society of Biblical Literature, 2008.

Tidball, D. *The Social Context of the New Testament*. Grand Rapids MI: Zondervan, 1984.

Wilkins, M. J., and J. P. Moeland, editors. *Jesus Under Fire: Modern Scholarship Reinvents the Historical Jesus*. Grand Rapids MI: Zondervan, 1995.

PART IV

CONCLUDING REFLECTIONS AND IMPLICATIONS

THE SIGNIFICANCE OF JESUS:
CONSIDERING HIS IMPORTANCE

A. What about the Context and Time?

Jesus was born in what was then a tiny village in an out-of-the-way, troublesome sub-province of the great Roman Empire. He came into a poor family, and although the arrangements had been made for the couple's marriage, the woman was uniquely pregnant before the final ceremony took place. What kind of a beginning context was this for the coming of the "Savior of the World" (John 4:42)? Should he not have been born in a palace? Did not the stargazers come to the Jerusalem palace to find him (Matt 2:1–2)? Why were insignificant shepherds the ones to hear the angelic message and the first to visit the baby Jesus (Luke 2:8–18)? Could not God do any better? I ask you to think about the expression, "But God…." Perhaps God is actually wiser than humans.

Major parts of the world had been subjugated and united by Rome, a strong nation that was skillful, even though it was not kind, in the realm of political administration. It was masterful in providing for freedom of travel by subduing the pirates on the Mediterranean and building roads (a little like our interstate highways for transporting its military), thereby connecting the provinces with the capitol. Rome inherited the Greek common language of commerce and communication from the Macedonians and Alexander. Because of the failure of the Greek and Roman Pantheon of gods to provide the answers to questions of life, the Roman world was open to the religions of the east. The Christian gospel was waiting in the wings. Maybe it was an appropriate time for the coming of God's messianic answer (Gal 4:4)—even though some might think the modern world would have been a far better time and context!

But why did Jesus concentrate on people who hardly counted in society? Why did he choose the first disciples from the lower class? Did not the upperclass religious crowd regard the disciples as completely untrained in matters of religion (Acts 4:13)? How could they have the answer? Yet they were undauntedly persuasive, and they did some amazing things. Indeed, they had "been with Jesus," and they did care about people in need (4:13–35)! Could one of the leading Jewish rabbis, Gamaliel, have been correct (5:33–39)? Could the religious elite have failed to recognize that God might have been acting through these common people? Then, to everyone's shock, the highly educated Saul/Paul became one of Jesus' disciples. He was hardly ordinary or stupid. On the contrary, Ashley Montague, the well-known agnostic, told doctoral students at Princeton that Paul was as great a thinker as Plato or Aristotle. Could he be correct? What was going on with God and the world? Could God have been turning the world on its head (17:6)?

I think you know some of the answers. Many Christians died for their commitment to Jesus, but God did not let their testimonies concerning this Jesus die or disappear. The great Roman Empire certainly died, but not before the powerful emperor Constantine actually espoused Christianity. The result of the so-called "Christendom" that was established has not been the most authentic representation of the witness of Jesus. That witness, however, was carried through the culture of Christendom and has been proclaimed to other cultures as well. Maybe you will agree that there could be some significance to the context and time for the coming of Jesus. Maybe the time was right.

This statement brings me to the confusing issue of chronology. As mentioned in chapter 1 above, a monk in the sixth century by the name of Dionysius Exegium (whom I call "Dennis the Little") took upon himself the task of trying to calculate the time of Jesus' birth and death in terms of the Roman calendar. His efforts led to the establishment of the Christian calendar, but his calculations were hardly accurate.

He thought Jesus was born in 754 A.U.C. (*ab urbe condita*—"from the founding of the city [Rome]"), but Herod died in 750 A.U.C. (4 B.C./B.C.E.)! We do not know exactly when the stargazers visited

Bethlehem (it may have taken them up to two years to arrive from Mesopotamia), so the birth of Jesus may have been as early as 6 B.C. We do know, however, when the plans for the reconstruction of the temple in Jerusalem under the auspices of Herod were being developed—namely in 734 A.U.C. (20–19 B.C.)—although the actual reconstruction on the ground may not have begun for two years. According to the Gospel of John 2:20, the cleansing of the temple in Jerusalem occurred forty-six years after the construction began, which would mean that the end of Jesus' ministry was approximately 780 or 782 A.U.C. (A.D. 26–27 or 28–29). These dates coincide with other dates we know.

We also know that Jesus began his ministry when he was about thirty years of age in the fifteenth year of the reign of Tiberius Caesar (cf. Luke 3:1), which would mean either 780 A.U.C. after Augustus made him co-regent in the provinces (less likely) or in 782 (A.D. 29) after Augustus died. The latter date conforms to the perspectives of the major Roman historians such as Tacitus and Seutonius.[1] Furthermore, Colin Humphreys of Cambridge has argued convincingly that the only day on which Jesus was likely to have died was Nisan 14, the day before Passover, on Friday, 7 April A.D. 30, or Friday, 3 April A.D. 33. Humphreys chose A.D. 33 because he was of the opinion that Jesus' ministry lasted for three years according to the general misunderstanding concerning the use of Passover in John.[2] But while I agree with most of what Humphreys has argued, I would clearly disagree with him on A.D. 33 since I have argued strongly that the Passover in John is a thematic organizing principal and not a series of seriatim chronological statements. In the Synoptic Gospels, the ministry

---

[1] See for example the arguments of John P. Meier in *A Marginal Jew: Rethinking the Historical Jesus*, vol. 1 (New York: Doubleday, 1991) 383–84.

[2] See the important study of Colin Humphreys, "The Last Days of Jesus in John and the Synoptics—the Evidence from Astronomy and Chronology," a paper presented to the "John, Jesus, and History Division" of the Society of Biblical Literature, New Orleans, LA, on 23 November 2009.

of Jesus seems to last for only one year.[3] Accordingly, I am of the opinion that Jesus died the day before Passover on Nisan 14 in the year A.D. 30.

I turn now to a recent phenomenon that has caused confusion and consternation among Christians. While the designations B.C. (before Christ) and A.D. (Anno Domini, in the year of the Lord) have been used for centuries, more recently other designations are appearing in academic writings. These designations are B.C.E. (before the Common Era) and C.E. (in the Common Era). Some Christians have regarded this change as a hostile attack on Christianity. That reaction may be somewhat true, but probably more significant is that the cultural dominance of "Christendom" has ceased, and the new designations are an indication of the contemporary dominance of secularism and the realization that the world is a global community containing many religious perspectives. The contemporary culture may in fact be a culture somewhat like the one when Jesus came into the world. Christians can continue to use the older designations because both represent the same time frames, but everyone should recognize that "time designations" do not belong exclusively to Christians. Nevertheless, "time itself" is not ultimately under the control of mere humans (cf. Heb 1:8–13). Time is in the hands of God and under the co-founder of the world, namely Jesus, the divine agent in all of creation (cf. John 1:2). Moreover, the clear conviction of Christians is that God in Christ Jesus will bring time to a conclusion (cf. 1 Cor 15:22–28; 2 Cor 5:10; Phil 2:9–11; 1 Pet 3:22; 4:12–19; 2 Pet 3:11–13; Rev 7; etc.).

B. Who Is this Jesus?

Among the questions of significance that are frequently asked concerning Jesus is this one: Who was he really (to echo the question of the disciples in Mark 4:41)? To answer this question, when we read the Gospels, we must constantly watch for clues that the New Testament

---

[3] See Gerald L. Borchert, *John 1–11* (Nashville: Broadman & Holman, 1996) 95–97, 145–46, 230; and *John 12–21* (Nashville: Broadman and Holman, 2002) 21–26.

writers and evangelists seek to give us. The writers are in charge of their presentations, and each one prompts readers in slightly different ways by the choice of pericopes and the organization of the materials about Jesus. While Matthew and Luke probably used Mark, we have seen that the focus of each Gospel is slightly different and that John includes a great deal of material that is completely different. Two Gospels have birth stories and two do not. John has only two "signs" (miracles) of Jesus that are in the other Gospels, and yet all four have powerful acts that reveal something about Jesus. Some teachings are parallel in the Synoptics, and yet they are organized differently in each one. The relationships of the disciples to Jesus are similar in their lack of understanding, but the accounts are not always presented in identical ways. They all have climactic death and resurrection stories that provide crucial clues to who Jesus is, but these stories are also different.

With this understanding in mind, I turn to discuss the question of Jesus. I am not attempting another of the so-called quests for the "historical" Jesus in which some scholars have sought to isolate Jesus apart from the confessions about him. Instead, I am interested in reflecting on some things that can be concluded about him on the basis of those four different witnesses or confessions concerning him.

1. The Virginal Conception and the Incarnation

In the inquiry concerning Jesus, there usually resides the desire to determine whether or not Jesus could actually be divine. Could the incarnation (God enfleshed in Jesus) be a reality? That question does not merely involve the modern-day quests or debates concerning the historical Jesus. It has involved debates concerning Jesus throughout the history of Christianity.

The early "adoptionists" proposed that the divine was not actually "enfleshed" in a human Jesus but that the divine Spirit merely adopted his body for a time. Many Gnostics had a similar view. Clearly, a concept of the complete harmonious meshing of the divine and the human in Jesus has been difficult for humans to comprehend and accept. The Gospel of John makes that claim clear in the statement that the divine Word became flesh (John 1:14). To reassert without hesitation that complete co-mixing of the divine and the human in Jesus, the Nicene

Creed (found in Epiphanius, A.D. 374) declared that Jesus was "begotten, not made" and "of one substance with the Father." Then the Council of Chalcedon (A.D. 451) permitted no misunderstanding or compromise and thus described Jesus as the "only-begotten, recognized in two natures, without confusion, without change, without division, without separation."[4]

Why did the early church fathers debate this issue so intensely? It was because they honestly believed the Gospel writers asserted that God did something unusual and miraculous in sending Jesus. They took seriously the uniqueness of the "virginal conception" (a better phrase than the "virgin birth") of Jesus. They recognized that God had acted miraculously in the birth of Isaac by opening the womb of Sarah so that she could have a son through Abraham (Gen 17:17; 18:9–15; 21:1–7) and that God acted similarly in the births of Samuel (1 Sam 1:9–28) and John the Baptist (Luke 1:5–25). But they confessed that it was different with Jesus. He was not the son of Joseph, but the Son of God (Luke 1:26–38; 3:23; Matt 1:18–25). Throughout his ministry and even at the point of his condemnation to death (cf. Mark 14:61), the Gospel witnesses indicate repeatedly that Jesus clearly insisted on his direct filial relationship to God.

These Gospel witnesses did *not*, as some have suggested, create the virginal conception from Old Testament texts such as Isaiah 7:14 (used in Matt 1:18–25) and 2 Samuel 7:13–14 (the Son of God is referenced in Luke 1:32–35 and elsewhere). Those texts in their settings would hardly have suggested the event to the writers because even the Hebrew word *alma* in the Isaiah context does not have to mean "virgin." Instead, it was the reality of the virginal conception itself—supported by the earlier Greek word *parthenos* in the Septuagint (LXX) for the Hebrew *alma* of the text—that undoubtedly suggested to Matthew that the verse in Isaiah could be used as a fulfillment text. Without the reality of the event, the writers would hardly have thought to use the ancient texts. It is clearly similar to Matthew's report of the flight of Jesus to Egypt that suggested to him the use of Hosea 11:1. or the murder of the Bethlehem infants that suggested

---

[4] See H. Bettenson, *Documents of the Christian Church* (London: Oxford University Press, 1956) for these statements and many others.

Jeremiah 31:15 (cf. Matt 2:15, 18). For the evangelists, the genuine events surrounding the birth of Jesus gave rise to an understanding of the biblical significance of the events in the plan of God for humanity!

Similarly, contrary to the demythologizers, the community of faith hardly created the idea of the virginal conception as a mythological base to support what is called a falsely conceived idea that Jesus was somehow divine. In response, as a former lawyer, I turn to discuss this matter. For the early Christians, was the deity of Jesus based on the virginal conception? The answer must be negative. If the virginal conception were considered such a basis, then every book in the New Testament would trumpet that idea. Instead, it appears only in the beginning of Matthew and Luke, and it is not mentioned thereafter in either Matthew or Luke as a foundation for any major theological idea. And, I repeat, neither is it mentioned in any other New Testament book. Then is the sinlessness of Jesus dependent on the virginal conception? I will discuss this matter shortly, but again the answer must be negative. Would the virginal conception guarantee for the disciples an assurance of the divinity of Jesus? Once again, the response must be no.

Instead, Jesus' calling the disciples to follow him and their experience of sensing God's presence in him gave them a resulting conviction of his uniqueness prior to his death. His divinity was not really understood by them prior to his resurrection. Thus, Peter's confession at Caesarea Philippi did not mean that they thought Jesus was divine, although the experience of the cloud and the voice must have left them with a sense of wonder and curiosity (Mark 9:6–8). Only after the resurrection appearance does John provide a clue for us that Thomas confessed: Jesus was in actuality his "Lord and…God" (John 20:28)!

The Prologue of John (1:1–18) certainly implies the highest Christology in the Gospels, but at that point there is no mention of the virginal conception. Does the lack of its presence elsewhere in the New Testament mean, as sometimes argued, that (a) the other disciples were unaware of it, (b) thought it was unimportant, or (c) thought it was a mistaken idea? Each of those options implies an argument from silence and a pre-assumption of the answer. Well then, was the virginal conception a later mythological development to prove the deity of Jesus? Again, if it was a crucial part of such an argument for the divinity of

Jesus, why did the evangelists not use it as a proof for that purpose? They merely indicated that God was at work in the birth of Jesus. The basic problem is a rationalistic mind-set that attempts to disprove the reality of the incarnation by attacking a simple story.

One might then ask, Why did Mary and the disciples not make more of that part of Jesus' story? Can you imagine the response that would have been engendered? Who would believe that a woman could give birth without the sexual act of the husband? I realize there are strange stories of births in Greek, Roman, and Semitic literature. But think about the implications for Mary. Would she not have been treated as an immoral woman? Did Joseph not at first think of such a possibility? Did Matthew not also think of that possibility (see Matt 1:19–25)? Naturally, when the later enemies of the Christians learned of the claim, they did in fact circulate ideas that Jesus was an illegitimate son (*ben Pandera* and other ideas) in an effort to discredit Christianity. The virginal conception was hardly a necessity for the messiahship of Jesus in the minds of the Jews, and it is hardly necessary for the theological significance of Jesus. For that reason alone, it seems overly skeptical to reject it as a literary creation.

Finally, then, was the virginal conception merely an epiphany tradition created by a group of ill-informed believers to substantiate their commitment to the incarnation of Jesus? I doubt that a group ("mass minds") of bewitched Christians created the Gospels of Matthew and Luke or even created the whole idea of the incarnation. Unless one is a rationalist and thinks an event must be repeatable to be believed, it would appear that it requires more confidence to trust such arguments than to consider that the virginal conception might actually have been plausible and therefore was included by two of the evangelists.

2. The Issue of Temptation and Sin Concerning Jesus (and Others)

The temptation stories of Jesus often raise another question in the minds of readers. There is no doubt that human beings succumb to temptation. What about Jesus? The preacher of Hebrews[5] proclaims that

---

[5] See G G. L. Borchert, *Worship in the New Testament* (St. Louis: Chalice Press, 2008) 176–77.

Jesus was "a great High Priest" who was "tempted in every aspect" as other humans, but "he did not sin" (Heb 4:15).

This statement has led to much speculation concerning the sinlessness of Jesus. The Latin theologians developed a means to reflect on this issue by formulating a threefold set of options. They are (a) *non posse non peccare*—"not able not to sin," (b) *non posse peccare*—"not able to sin," and (c) *posse non peccare*—"able not to sin." The first option obviously applies to human beings in general, but the question is whether the second or the third option applies to Jesus. If the second applies to him, then the temptations of Jesus would become merely a charade. So, for the writer of Hebrews, the answer must be the third.

But that option means the reader must take seriously the temptation stories as real temptations. For convenience, I use the Matthean order to provide an understanding of the temptations of Jesus (Matt 4:1–11; cf. Luke 4:1–13). They are (a) turning stones into bread, (b) jumping down from the pinnacle of the temple while expecting God's angels to rescue him, and (c) bartering with the devil to gain authority in the world. These temptations would hardly represent temptations to most humans, but that realization is the point of their significance for understanding Jesus according to the Gospel writers. Temptations are a clear indication of who the person actually is!

If the preacher of Hebrews is correct, then, how can the temptations Jesus faced be similar to the ones faced by humans in general? The answer lies in their nature. First, people are tempted to use whatever power or authority they have for their own benefit, especially if they are desperate. And they readily exclude God in the process. Second, humans long for recognition, and they will seek to achieve it by any means at their disposal. Indeed, they will even try to use God to attain it. Third and finally, the human race is bent on obtaining power and authority over others, whether it is physical, economic, psychological, or social and whether it is in a family, business, politics, international relations, or religion—even within the church! This insatiable appetite for dominance almost inevitably is accompanied by corruption. Jesus was not deceived by the devil's temptations, and neither should his followers be deceived by them.

Now watch for the clues. Each of the Synoptic evangelists had his own way of indicating the significance of temptation in their witness concerning Jesus. By concluding the temptations the way he does, Matthew uses his order to emphasize that Jesus is God's agent in the world, "fulfilling" God's purposes, and that Jesus is completely unwilling to turn over the world to the devil or his evil forces. Luke, on the other hand, concludes the temptations with the Jerusalem temple because the temple is the symbolic center of Luke's thinking. Even though the temple had become corrupt and Jesus wept over it twice (not merely once as in the other Synoptics; Luke 13:34–35; 19:41–44) and since the temple was regarded by the Jews symbolically as the presence of God, the point of this temptation, especially for Luke, is that Jesus not only eschews showmanship in worship but would also never give up on the presence and authority of God in the world.

Mark is much shorter and has a different focus (Mark 1:12–13). His emphasis in the temptations is on the awesome power of Jesus to control the spiritual forces of evil represented by Satan and hostile animals. Much like God controlled chaos in the creation story, Mark highlights the victory of Jesus by noting that angels (representing the divine presence) cared for Jesus in his chaotic experience. At this point it is important to pause for a moment and ask, Do you think God actually abandoned Jesus on the cross (cf. Mark 15:34)? Such a pattern would violate the nature of the caring God. But did Jesus have a sense of aloneness in his suffering on the cross and even in his temptations? How could it be otherwise? His suffering was an indication of his humanity. In this respect he was like us! Yet do you think he was actually and totally abandoned by God? Do you think it would have been possible? Check out John 16:32–33!

With that comment, I turn to John, whose focus is completely different. As Judas is not presented as identifying Jesus with a kiss at the betrayal (Jesus identifies himself with "I am," 18:5), and Pilate is not portrayed as washing his hands in a symbol of innocence, so the temptations of Jesus are not mentioned in this testimony concerning the eternal Word who became flesh. But the devil and his forces of evil are nevertheless identified as a serious reality in John (e.g., 6:70; 8:44; 12:31; 13:27; 16:11). Yet, in addressing a group of suffering Christians, John's purpose focused on God's power through the Spirit (the Paraclete) for dealing with temptation and persecution (16:1–2, 31–33; 17:14–15; 21:18–19). For John, Jesus is the model of total reliance on God (John 5:19).

By way of contrast, I must add comments concerning the rather "mythological" developments of tradition concerning temptation. (I use the term "myth" here carefully in the technical sense of trying to explain a theological concept through a physically oriented story.) In making the following observations, I honestly do not wish to offend any Christians who might genuinely find consolation from God through doctrinal developments on this subject. I merely include my comments here by way of illustration concerning Mary and sin.

Although the Gospel writers themselves did not use the virginal conception to make doctrinal assertions concerning the sinlessness of Jesus, some Christian theologians and church leaders have done so. They have even gone far beyond the Gospels and included doctrinal developments concerning Mary. In order to affirm the sinlessness of Jesus from birth, various stories were developed concerning Mary's uniqueness (as I indicated in the non-canonical gospels discussed above). Moreover, since the sexual act was regarded by these fathers of the church as being related to sin, the perpetual virginity of Mary was espoused. Statements in the Gospels concerning the "brothers" of Jesus were accordingly reinterpreted, even though it seems hard to argue against the meaning that Mary had other natural children after Jesus was born (e.g., Mark 3:31; John 7:5). But the sense of these statements was later altered to mean that the "brothers" were either so-called sons of Joseph by an unknown earlier marriage or were cousins of Jesus. Then, since Mary was declared perpetually sinless, it was natural to remove her from earth in a miraculous manner so that her sinlessness would not be contaminated by a normal death. The result was the further doctrinal assertion of Mary's bodily assumption. Along with this development, the statement Elizabeth made to Mary that she was "the mother of my Lord" was developed into a confession that Mary was "the Mother of God." Since she was sinless, bodily assumed into heaven, and the Mother of God, she could easily be regarded as a co-redemptress with Jesus and honored as a kind of queen of heaven to whom prayers could legitimately be offered.

These developments, I remind readers, are not found in the canonical Gospels but are later declarations made by some church leaders who insist on their validity as necessary aspects of church doctrine. Despite any declarations of their legitimacy and any spiritual feelings they may engender, these ideas are in fact to be regarded as later accretions to the canonical witnesses concerning Jesus.

On the other hand, I would strongly protest the tendency of some Protestants to degrade Mary or Peter. Neither of them is ultimately condemned in the Gospels for their misunderstandings or attempts to "protect" Jesus. Their efforts were part of human frailties that they, like us, also possessed. Instead, Mary, Peter, Thomas, and the other early disciples should be highly respected as the forebears of our faith, but they, like angels, should never be worshipped (cf. Rev 19:10; 22:8)!

3. The Dependence of Jesus on God (the Father)

The above discussion leads naturally to the next question: According to the canonical Gospels, did Jesus act on his own during his life on earth? Was he self-motivated, self-directed, and independent of God the Father? The answer to that question is a resounding negative. The repeated insistence in the Gospels is that Jesus was totally dependent on God, his Father, for direction. Here is a clue: Jesus was the unique agent of God on earth, and he would not act apart from the Father's guidance. John stated this close oversight of the Father emphatically as "the Son can do nothing on his own (*poiein aph' eautou ouden*)," but only "what he sees the Father doing" (John 5:19).

Luke expresses this idea of divine superintendence in the life of Jesus with his emphasis on the theme of Jesus at prayer. Repeatedly, at strategic moments in Jesus' life, Luke portrays Jesus at prayer—e.g., at his baptism (3:21), before choosing his disciples (6:12), before asking the disciples whom people said he was (9:18), before his transfiguration and in anticipation of his "exodus" from the world (9:29). Five times his praying is mentioned in the brief Gethsemane pericope before his betrayal and arrest (22:40, 41, 44, 45, 46). Jesus was continually conscious of his need for dependence upon his Father, and he was anxious for his disciples to copy him in order that they might not be led astray (e.g., 21:36; 22:46; cf. the example of the Pharisee and the tax collector at 18:9–

14). Jesus' insistence that his disciples wait on God's presence for correct timing and direction concerning the coming of the Spirit also provides an important perspective on the significance of dependence in Jesus' life (e.g., Luke 24:49; Acts 1:4).

Matthew typically employs teaching sections to highlight some of his concerns—in this case dependence on God. From the perspective of Matthew, Jesus made it clear in the Sermon on the Mount that words and actions can be cheap. Using the patterns of the Pharisees, Jesus demonstrated that piety and dependence on God are not measured by showmanship, whether donating tithes to the temple, praying, or fasting (Matt 6:1–18). True piety is marked by a simple dependence on God. In this context of simple dependence, readers of Matthew will find what has since become known as the Lord's Prayer (6:9–13) to be a model of authentic worship where God is the focus and not human self-centeredness. Remember that Matthew highlights the stern warnings of Jesus against various public evidences of piety (6:1–7; 23:1–36).

To find examples of the significance of Jesus' authentic dependence on God, look at his prayers. In this respect, the magisterial prayer in John 17 comes immediately to mind.[6] Notice again that Jesus' petitions are focused on glorifying God and on his genuine concern for his followers. He was willing to die, but his prayer was that his disciples might be protected, become holy, be united, expect to join him in the presence of God, and love one another. Is it any wonder that the Apostle Paul found in Jesus such a magnificent model that he called on the early Christians to have the "mind" of Christ and copy his pattern of self-giving humility and dependence (Phil 2:5–11)?

4. The Messianic Consciousness of Jesus: A Brief Reflection on His Words and Works

I turn now to the next question: What did the evangelists think about Jesus' self- understanding concerning his messiahship? To begin this subject, we must acknowledge that we cannot psychoanalyze Jesus. We cannot put him under observation. All we can do is analyze the Gospel testimonies about him. A better question may be: Did the

---

[6] For more elaboration on this prayer see G. L. Borchert, *John 12–21*, 185–211.

evangelists consider that Jesus believed himself to be the promised Messiah for Israel and the world?

To reflect on this question, I turn to Mark's early testimony concerning Jesus. As I indicated previously, Mark is not simply a history book about Jesus. It is a theological testimony about Jesus, and, as Wrede discovered,[7] it is laced throughout with the theme of a "Messianic Secret." In other words, Mark consciously wrote his work with the intention of forcing the reader to ask why Jesus forbade the evil spirits to testify concerning him (e.g., Mark 1:25, 34; 3:12) and why he told humans not to tell others that he healed them (e.g., Mark 1:44; 5:43; 7:36). The obvious reason is that Mark, who was an astute writer, wanted to draw his readers' attention to the fact that Jesus believed he was the Messiah! But like Jesus, Mark must also have understood that most people (including his readers) had the wrong idea of what the Messiah should be. Accordingly, although Jesus did wonderful works and taught people about the kingdom of God, he still kept them guessing about his true messianic nature. Instead of calling himself the Messiah, he referred to himself as the "Son of Man." That designation could be understood merely as a "man" (a human), or it could be recognized by the sensitive person as a surrogate for a divine visitor so that "Son of Man" could then be identified with God/the "Ancient of Days" (e.g., Dan 7:13). The crucial question Jesus asked his disciples at Caesarea Philippi concerning who he was (Mark 8:27), therefore, could hardly have been a mere light-hearted query. It was a deep probing of his disciples to determine if they and the people of Israel actually recognized him for who he was.

Similarly, in Matthew (11:1–6) and Luke (7:18–23), Jesus does not answer the question of the imprisoned John the Baptist when, in a sense of desperation, John sends his disciples to Jesus in order to inquire whether Jesus is in fact "the coming one" (a designation for the Messiah). Apparently the Baptizer wondered if his work of announcement had been in vain. Instead of answering John's question, Jesus told the messengers to describe to John what was happening concerning the blind, the lame, the lepers, the deaf, the dead, and the proclamation of

---

[7] W. Wrede, *The Messianic Secret* (London: J. Clarke, 1971) is the English translation of the 1901 German work.

"good news" (undoubtedly referring to the coming of the great day of Jubilee; see Isa 61:12 and Luke 4:18–19). Jesus did not answer the question, but that does not mean he did not know the answer. It means he wanted people to reflect on the issue and realize that "the coming one" had indeed come!

But I return to Mark's story of Jesus' healing of the paralytic (Mark 2:1–12). When Jesus saw the sick man and the friends who with great effort and faith brought him to Jesus, he said to the man, "Your sins are forgiven." The stuffy religious leaders were shocked and charged him with blasphemy because only God could forgive sins. Jesus responded, "Which is easier?" The obvious answer is that only God can both forgive sins and tell a lame man to get up and walk. Did the Gospel writers think Jesus knew who he was? What do you think?

I will not leave that question hanging because Mark actually answers it. When Jesus appeared before the hastily called Sanhedrin meeting, a series of false testimonies were leveled at him in an effort to condemn him. After hearing the conflicting witnesses, in frustration the high priest demanded an answer from Jesus to a point-blank question: "Are you the Messiah (Christ), the Son of the Blessed One?" (Mark 14:61). Since Jesus was confronted by the religious leader of the Jews with the ultimate direct question, he did not back down but gave a direct answer: "I am!" And he did not stop with that simple response. He continued and asserted that he was indeed the great eschatological "cloud rider" of Daniel 7:13 who was expected to bring in the Day of the Lord!

The Johannine evangelist confirms such a high messianic/christological understanding on the part of Jesus when the Jews interrogate Jesus at the festival of Hanukkah (Dedication). To their hostile questioning, Jesus responded, "I and the Father are one" (John 10:30). The Jews clearly understood the significance of Jesus equating himself with God, and their response was an attempt to stone him for blasphemy (10:31–33). Moreover, in a previous argument with the Jews at 5:8–47, the evangelist presents (in the form of a legal defense brief) a telling response concerning Jesus' identity and status with the Father. Jesus called to witness John the Baptist, Jesus' powerful works, and the Father himself, and the coupe de grace of the argument was Moses and the

Scriptures that the Jews attempted to use to condemn him (5:18–47). Finally, the capstone clue concerning this evangelist's knowledge of Jesus' self-understanding is found in Jesus' acceptance of Thomas's confession that he was "My Lord and my God!" (20:28). For a Jew to make such a statement concerning a human who walked and talked with him is nothing less than revolutionary!

The question then is whether the Gospel writers believed Jesus understood himself to be the Messiah. The answer must be a resounding "Yes!"

5. The Nature of Jesus' Messiahship

Having contemplated with you Jesus' self-understanding, I turn to the next question. What kind of a Messiah was Jesus? Most Jews expected a warrior who would liberate them from outside conquerors—particularly the Romans. Indeed, when Jesus rode into Jerusalem on a donkey and the people waved their palm branches, the participants in the celebration likely anticipated that the time of the Jewish deliverance had arrived and that they would shortly be called to arms. But when Matthew (21:5) quotes the fulfillment text from Zechariah 9:9, notice that he left out the part in which the king would arrive with victorious vindication. Instead, the evangelist only included the section on the rider's humility and his coming in on a donkey. What does that fact tell us about Matthew's perception of Jesus' messiahship?

When you read the brilliant interplay in the Johannine story, remember the reactions (John 12:12–21). The people shouted their "Hallels" but the disciples were confused and, although it was undoubtedly an exciting time for them, it did not seem to compute with the nature of Jesus. The Pharisaic leaders, however, recognized that they were losing control over the people, and they were not the least bit happy about it. Then there was the group of Greeks (perhaps some non-Jews but mostly likely Greek-speaking Jews and proselytes) who figured it was time to join the action. They all misunderstood the event because for Jesus it marked the anticipated time of his ultimate test, the bell toll of his hour (12:27)! That hour was his initiation into death and the conclusion of his messianic ministry on earth. Was death, then, the focus of his messiahship?

For the evangelists, the death of Jesus was and is the climactic symbol of his messiahship. He did not come to fight and win the kingdom by arms. He came to model a different way. When one reads the Beatitudes (Matt 5:3–12), he or she has the strange feeling that being "blessed" or "congratulated" by Jesus would hardly sell on Madison Avenue in the United States or on Fleet Street in London or in any other major context of the world. How can poverty, hunger, or mourning be regarded as positive? Of course, there is also purity, showing mercy, and peacemaking in that list—but then there is persecution! The answer does not lie in the affirmation of degradation but in the fact that when one reaches the end of one's own resources, there emerges a realization of the absolute need for dependence on God. Jesus modeled that way of dependence, but he also insisted that his way must have integrity. Lack of integrity made Jesus very angry and led him to condemn the "religious" Pharisees (Matt 23:1–36). The people's failure to understand God's intentions in Jesus caused him to weep over Jerusalem (23:37–39). Their ancestors had misunderstood the prophets and had killed them. The descendants would do the same to Jesus.

Whom did Jesus help the most? He sometimes healed the powerful and the religious, but most of his attention was focused on the dispossessed who were like scattered sheep without a shepherd (Matt 9:36). Those who did not seem to count in society followed him and gladly listened to him (Mark 12:37). Others followed him in order to criticize him and to watch for opportunities to condemn him. When you read the Gospels, pay particular attention to the recipients of his concern, like the rejected Samaritans (Luke 10:33–37; 17:16–18; John 4:9, 39–42).

The messianic model of Jesus was different from what most people expected. But here is a clue! There were actually some in Israel, like the old priest Simeon (Luke 2:34–35), who understood that Jesus' model from God would cause division in the world. According to the pattern of Adam and Eve in the garden, most human beings would rather choose their own self-centered models that grasp for power, prestige, and dominance rather than the self-giving, humble model of Jesus "who came not to be served but to serve others and give his life as a ransom for many" (Mark 10:45; Matt 11:28).

6. The Death of the Messiah

The conclusion to the previous section leads naturally to the next question. My students often ask me, "Did Jesus, the Son of God, really die?" They follow that question with a second one: "What happened to him between his death and resurrection?" I usually answer that he was "dead-dead." Their response to that statement comes in the form of another question because many of them have been socialized to have difficulty understanding this issue (along with many who follow various folk traditions). Accordingly, they ask, "Since Jesus was the Son of God, how could he really have been dead?" I will save more comment on this second question for the next section when I discuss the resurrection.

That Jesus died a horrible death on the cross is beyond question. Even his enemies would have had little doubt concerning that fact. Moreover, his brutal death has been portrayed by Mel Gibson in *The Passion of the Christ* with extreme vividness and cruelty on giant silver screens in hundreds of theaters. Gibson's work captured the attention and emotions of many who may not have understood that crucifixion was a cruel punishment. But is cruelty the focus of Jesus' death in the Gospels? Rejection—of course! Cruelty? I wonder. Think about people's interests today. Humans are entranced by frightening stories that emphasize hate and cruelty. These characteristics attract followers. The shock of sex, blood, or war tends to provide the kind of catharsis that entertains. Even J. R. R. Tolkien's "hobbit" stories and others that people think are children's tales have large sections on war and violence.

I encourage you to look at the book of Revelation for a perspective.[8] You will discover an interesting phenomenon there. The enemies of God assemble their forces for battle, but there is no battle recorded! There are, of course, brief notes concerning the results of God's victorious triumph (e.g., Rev 14:18–29) so that readers/listeners might take seriously the pointlessness of opposing God. But to most people's amazement, the battle scenes are not described because the focus is not on war but on God's supremacy (notice how even the devil's attempt at war is

---

[8] For my further exposition of this book see G. L. Borchert, "The Book of Revelation," in *The NLT Study Bible* (Carol Stream IL: Tyndale House Publishers, 2008) 2160–99.

described only briefly in Rev 12:7–8). Similarly, the descriptions of Jesus' death in the Gospels are not mere dramatic sub-tales to be read, watched, wept over, and then, after experiencing a cathartic high, put aside to pursue life as usual without much thought of the implications. For the evangelists, the death of Jesus is a major key to unlocking the meaning of the Gospels.

While some of the details in the final few days of Jesus' life on earth are presented with slight variations in the Gospels and with some focal differences, the overall impact is similar in highlighting the fact that his death offers important clues that Jesus was indeed the Messiah they expected, and even more! In Mark 15:33, 38–39, the unusual darkness and the divine shredding of the temple veil are brought to a focus through the centurion's confession that Jesus was "the Son of God," which ensures that the Messianic Secret is actually being revealed. To these clues of darkness, the ripping of the veil, and the confession, Matthew (27:45–54) added the divine response of nature with the earth quaking and mentions the strange appearances of the dead coming from their tombs. According to Matthew, God confronted the death of his Son. While Luke also picks up the darkness and the tearing of the veil, he highlights the theme of innocence in the statement of one of the criminals and of the centurion. The point is that the murderers of Jesus had obviously misjudged who Jesus was (Luke 23:41, 47)! John has none of these clues, but with his stress on symbolism,[9] the Lamb of God is pictured as pierced, and from that wound flowed blood and water, the symbols of death and life (represented in the two sacraments or ordinances of the church). Do you understand the clues?

I will now comment briefly on a few other matters in the death stories. When Jesus entered into Jerusalem for the moment that has become enshrined by Christians in Palm Sunday celebrations, the excitement and expectation of the people soon transformed into the music of a dirge as the drumming incidents leading to Jesus' death marched steadily toward the cross. The "ex cathedra" declaration of

---

[9] For a helpful study see C. R. Koester, *Symbolism in the Fourth Gospel* (Minneapolis: Fortress, 1995).

Caiaphas that "one man should die for the people" represented John's perspective on the death (11:49). Jesus was the self-giving Messiah!

Unlike in the Synoptics, John's description of Jesus' last meal with his disciples was not focused on giving them instructions concerning the elements of eating the broken bread and drinking from the fruit of the vine (cf. Mark 14:22–25; Matt 26:26–29; Luke 22:19–24). Those clues would be established as both a memorial and a proclamation of his return (cf. 1 Cor 11:24–26) in the celebrations of the Lord's Supper. John earlier illustrated his views on these elements in the feeding of the five thousand and his discussion in the synagogue when Jesus dealt with the grumbling of the Jews by reminding them of God's provision in the exodus (John 6:41–59). Instead, John concentrated on modeling Jesus' self-giving for them as Jesus washed their feet and ordained them with a new commandment to love each other as an indication of being his followers (13:34–35). That event (clue) has since become established in the church year as Maundy Thursday.[10]

For Mark, much of the death story is focused on intrigue involving Judas and the Jewish authorities, highlighted in the betraying kiss of Judas while he called Jesus "Master" or "Lord." The slicing off of the ear of the high priest's servant was a human pointless defense that revealed nothing but human frustration, and then Jesus' followers fled in fear, epitomized in the strange note concerning the young man (Mark?) who lost his robe (Mark 16:43–52). Matthew added that Jesus condemned the violent action of the disciple and reminded them all that what was happening fulfilled scripture, but he also informed them that he was not helpless because he had at his disposal the armies of heaven if he needed to call upon them (Matt 26:52–54).

Prior to the arrest, Mark's Gethsemane story centered on the troubled prayer of Jesus and the sleepiness of the disciples (Mark 14:32–42). Luke used this event to focus on his theme of prayer and emphasized the intensity of Jesus' struggle by indicating that the sweat poured off of him like drops of blood (Luke 22:39–46).

---

[10] "Maundy" was derived ultimately from the Latin verb *mandare* (to command).

For John, the death story is cleverly articulated. Judas, who thought he was in control of the betraying process, fades from the scene into insignificance. The arresting band that came with torches in the middle of the night to seize Jesus needed help in identifying him, and when Jesus did so they fell to the ground before the God-man! The fearful disciples who thought they could protect Jesus fled in terror. The Jewish authorities who were supposed to understand God's will revealed that they were merely programmed rebels who condemned Jesus. Dear Peter who tried to follow failed miserably in his time of testing, and Pilate who thought he was omnipotent came to discover he had little power to make decisions. They were all pawns yielding to the power of evil. They were all failures. Only Jesus is pictured by John as serene in this story (18:6–8, 37; 19:11). Even as he carried his cross (19:17) and hung there, he remained in control as he cared for his duty as the eldest son of his mother (19:26). Finally, he decided on the moment he would die, and he gave up (delivered) his life/spirit (19:30), an act that surprised even the soldiers who were sent to administer the *crucifragium* (breaking the legs, 19:32–33). Jesus died as the true King of the Jews (19:22), and in addition to dying for humanity and indeed becoming the Savior of the world (4:42), he provided the ultimate model of confidence in God even in his death.

For the evangelists, the death of Jesus was critical to understanding who Jesus is. But it would have been pointless without the resurrection.

7. The Resurrection of the Messiah

I come now to the crucial question concerning Jesus. As I will indicate in the next section on integrity, this issue has involved my personal academic pilgrimage. There is no question that, for the writers of the New Testament, the resurrection is not merely the happy ending to a sad story. The Gospels are not fairy tales. Every writer of the New Testament presupposed that Jesus rose from the dead. That confession is fundamental to the Christian *kerygma* (preaching), which is perhaps best articulated in the preaching of Peter to the house of Cornelius at Acts 11:34–43. It is the basis for Paul's confidence that humans can receive the forgiveness of sins and that their faith is not an empty (*kenos*) shell (1 Cor 15:12–19).

But having enunciated this foundational thesis about the Christian faith, some readers of the Gospels may still have a perturbing question. If the resurrection is so central, why are the stories of the resurrection of Jesus so different? Mark's story of Jesus affirms the empty tomb, but, while it does indicate that Jesus would meet the disciples in Galilee, it ends without any appearance reports as though the conclusion was lost. Matthew has the appearance stories, but the crucial one takes place on a mountain in Galilee. Luke's appearances are all focused in the Jerusalem area. John's stories take place in both Jerusalem and near the Sea of Tiberias/Galilee, and they both may seem to be initial appearances of Jesus, even though the Johannine Gospel in the Epilogue says that Jesus revealed himself "again" to his followers (John 21:1).

These differences have vexed scholars for centuries, and they have made various attempts at synthesizing the stories. In the twentieth century, many scholars gave up on the task. Among them was Norman Perrin, who basically followed Bultmann in his negative analysis.[11] Reginald Fuller attempted a redactional analysis, but he ended his study with a great deal of skepticism in terms of the process and virtually used Paul's statements on the resurrection as the key to understanding it as a spiritual experience.[12] Grant Osbourne used a modified redactional analysis but ended with a much more positive result.[13] Other works that I will not mention here basically assume that there is no problem. The above representative works provide at least a brief overview of the difficult situation.

One way to approach the problem is to remember that the resurrection was totally unexpected by the disciples. The fact that Jesus appeared to these disciples would have been seared into their memories like it happened yesterday. Moreover, the telling of these stories in an

---

[11] N. Perrin, *The Resurrection According to Matthew, Mark and Luke* (Philadelphia: Fortress, 1977). For the classic article by Rudolf Bultmann, see "New Testament Mythology," in *Kerygma and Myth*, ed. H. W. Bartsch (New York: Harper and Brothers, 1961) 1–44.

[12] R. H. Fuller, *The Formation of the Resurrection Narratives* (Philadelphia: Fortress, 1971, 1980).

[13] G. R. Osbourne, *The Resurrection Narratives: A Redactional Study* (Grand Rapids MI: Baker, 1984).

oral culture would have been the highlight of their testimonies concerning Jesus. That Jesus appeared a number of times over a considerable period is attested by both Luke (Acts 1:3) and Paul (1 Cor 15:4–8). But the telling of the stories about those appearances in an oral culture would *not* have been harmonized into a clear set of calendar dates. Only when the various evangelists put those stories in writing much later and the stories were collected, assembled, and compared would conflicts in the sequences of the appearances have been detected.

The early Christians hardly doubted that the appearances took place. They were willing to die for their testimonies concerning the appearances, but I have grave doubts that they were willing to die for the order of those events. Indeed, one should not read Paul's statements concerning the resurrection appearances mentioned above as a statement of chronological order. The appearances are listed in a logical order for the purpose of argument, and the words *eite/epeite* ("then") are typical connectors in rabbinic arguments. Note particularly the words "received" and "delivered," which are the standard rabbinic terms for the passing on of a strategic, authentic tradition (1 Cor 15:3).

The so-called inconsistent overlaps in the resurrection accounts do not prove that the evangelists cannot be trusted or that they created stories to enhance their faith. If they were merely fabricating the message of the resurrection, they would have certainly made sure to have a consistent and orderly series of reports manufactured concerning the most crucial parts of their testimonies. The resurrection is not a fairy tale. It is a reality upon which the early Christians were willing to stake their lives!

8. The Church and the Return of Jesus in Power

Clearly the Gospel testimonies indicate that Jesus conquered death in the resurrection, but they also indicate that the story of Jesus does not end with the resurrection. Some readers may suppose that Jesus was merely a prophet and that he never envisioned a church being constituted beyond his coming. The book of Acts and the New Testament epistles, however, argue strongly in the opposite direction. The same is true of the Gospels (e.g., Matt 16:18–19; 18:17–20). The kingdom of God was not intended by Jesus to be merely a spiritual idea any more than Israel was intended by God to be merely an idea about a spiritually conceived nation. The church is the people of God, called to be a community of God's representatives on earth (e.g., Eph 4:11–16). The followers of Jesus are not meant to be individual "lone rangers" (John 17:20–21; 1 Cor 12:12–26) doing what is "right in their own eyes" as Israel did in the time of the Judges (Judg 21:25). God intended the people of God, the believers in Jesus, to be a "community of love" demonstrating to the world what it means to live in harmony with each other and in obedience to God in Christ Jesus (John 13:35; 15:12–14; 1 John 3:23).

But Jesus also gave the community an eschatological perspective (e.g., Luke 21:25–36). This life on earth, according to the writers of the Gospels, was not expected to be an end in itself. Jesus is now ensconced at the right hand of God (cf. Heb 1:3). Yet, just as the disciples had seen him leave this earthly realm and be translated into the heavenly one, so according to Luke those followers of Jesus were informed by a divine announcement that Jesus would also come again (Acts 1:11). His followers joyfully anticipate his return, but his return does not promise to be a source of joy and gladness for everyone. At his return there will be a time of judgment when he will separate people according to their life patterns, some to blessing but some to condemnation (Matt 25:31–46).

The Synoptic Gospels describe Jesus' return as similar to that of the cloud rider of Daniel 7:13, when the cosmic structure will collapse and many will experience intense mourning. But his chosen followers will be drawn together from the entire globe ("the four winds," Matt 24:29–31; cf. Mark 13:24–27). Luke identifies this time as the "redemption" (*apolutrosis*) of the believers (Luke 21:25–28).

John indicated that when the disciples contemplated the departure of Jesus prior to the crucifixion, they felt like they were being orphaned (John 14:18), but Jesus promised them that in fact he would be in the process of preparing a new residence for them and that he would return and carry them to his realm so that they would be with him (14:2–3). The book of Revelation describes the abode of Jesus and of God (heaven) in earthly symbols, including streets of "transparent gold" (which no human has experienced), but these symbols are not meant to be taken literally (Rev 21:9–22:5). They are pictorial attempts by John, the great visionary, to describe for mere earth dwellers the realm that is beyond mortal knowledge and imagination.[14]

When will the return of Jesus occur? No one knows. Not even Jesus knew the time while he was on earth (Mark 13:32). Such a statement forewarns his followers against eschatological speculators. That time is hidden in the divine mind. But Jesus also advised his followers to pay close attention to his warnings and not to think that a seeming delay means his return will not happen (13:33–36). Indeed, Paul challenged Christians to be alert and to live not as people from the dark side of reality but as children of light and of the day (2 Thess 5:2–10).

According to the evangelists, there was little doubt that the Lord's return was on the horizon, but apart from providing general signs of its impending nature, these writers refused to give their readers a date. Were they certain of Jesus' return? Yes! Did they attempt to schedule his coming on a calendar? No! Did they model living and proclaiming a message of hope? Absolutely! May the Gospel readers of today follow the pattern of these four great witnesses of the Lord Jesus.

C. Reviewing the Integrity of Our Understanding of Jesus

I now reflect on the integrity of our picture of Jesus. As a young lawyer and a young theologian at Princeton, I felt impelled to follow in the footsteps of apologists like William Paley and others who had taken up the mantel of the second-century apologists or defenders of the Christian faith.[15] When I began to write my first thesis, it became clear to me early in my venture that the hinge point of Christianity was the resurrection of Jesus. With Paul, I agreed that if there had been no resurrection of Jesus, then not only was our preaching in vain or empty (*kenos*) but so was our

---

[14] For my discussion of symbols and the interpretation of the Apocalypse of John, see G. L. Borchert, "Revelation," in *The NLT Study Bible* (Carol Stream IL: Tyndale House, 2008).

[15] For a brief review of the thinking of Paley see my brother's work in A. Castell, D. Borchert, and A. Zucker, *Introduction to Philosophy* (Upper Saddle River NJ: Prentice Hall, 2001) 210–16.

Christian faith (1 Cor 15:14). Such a conclusion also meant that the rationale for the church and the seminary had been destroyed.

In that immature stage of my life, I took upon myself the huge task of trying to harmonize the Gospels on this subject. I began with Tatian's second-century *Diatessaron*, and I wrote what I considered was quite a good thesis, receiving a first-class standing for my second theological degree. But after I finished, I had to admit that just as Tatian could not fully accomplish his goal, neither could this young lawyer.

That realization led me to read everything I could in English and German from D. F. Strauss to W. Wrede to R. Bultmann to K. L. Schmidt to the post-Bultmannians and then back to the Gnostics and their critics, even taking a doctoral seminar with H. Jonas, the Gnostic heir of Bultmann, and eventually writing a second thesis on the Gnostic gospels. That journey brought me to recognize that the canonical Gospels should be understood as testimonies and that attempts at stripping them down until one could find the historical Jesus was hopeless, whatever method one might use. The Gospels are still testimonies, and you can study them to find what we might label as inconsistencies according to our concepts of time and place or the possible use of sources and editorial comments, but you cannot really cross-examine the Gospels and get back to the historical Jesus without sacrificing the witnesses themselves. Bultmann was in part correct when he concluded that "we can now know virtually nothing of the historical Jesus," but I would add that we can know nothing about him *apart from the evangelists' perspectives in the Gospels*! While Bultmann would not agree with my analysis, you can examine the documents, but you cannot examine Jesus! You can evaluate the evangelists' faith but not Jesus' faith. Bultmann was conscious that he was actually analyzing faith, so he gave up and abandoned Jesus for a construct he called the "Christ of faith." I have refused to choose that option of separating Jesus and Christ because "I believe" God sent Jesus to be the Savior of the world. Is my faith flawless? Of course not! I am simply human.

That statement, however, naturally forces the next question. Are the Gospel portraits of Jesus flawless? Each person reading the Gospels will respond to that question as he or she studies them. If we had one gospel like Tatian's attempt to produce a defense of Christianity, we would not have variations in the presentations such as time sequences of when the crucifixion took place. Mark 15:25 indicates that it was at the third hour when Jesus was crucified, but John 19:14 indicates that it was the sixth hour when Jesus was before Pilate. Christian scholars are not ignorant of such matters. They have known of their existence since the second century. Jerome tried to solve the problem by suggesting that in one writer's notes on time there could have been a shorthand flaw between a gamma and a diagamma (a letter no longer used in koine Greek but that could have represented "six"). That argument may relate to a "possible flaw" in an "unknown possible source," but that argument does not deal with the "words" of the Greek text as we have them.

I have already dealt with the differences in the use of the cleansing of the temple pericopes in John and the Synoptics as well as the references to Passover in John as over against the Synoptics. Similarly, as one compares the Gospels, there are differences of when the anointing of Jesus takes place in relation to his entry into Jerusalem. Did the anointing take place before or after the entry? These issues concerning the testimonies are organizational matters in the writing patterns of the evangelists. I could continue listing what western readers might consider flaws in the Gospel records.

Could the early church transcribers have corrected these so-called flaws? Of course! Tatian tried by reducing the four Gospels to one and thereby eliminating any possibility of these so-called flaws. Was his attempt accepted? No! The early Christians did not accept his changes or his construction. Instead, the early church continued to maintain a commitment to the four testimonies as the canonical model or standard for any witness concerning Jesus because they knew that the point of the four Gospels was to provide more than mere literal harmony. What we have are four different but compatible perspectives that testify about who Jesus is and what his significance can be for our lives and our relationships to Almighty God.

The Gospels are not mere history books. They are testimonies structured for a purpose. That purpose is best summarized in the closing verses of John 20 in which the evangelist states that the Gospel was "written that you might believe that Jesus is the Christ, the Son of God, and that believing you might have life in [or through] his name."

Recommended for Further Study

Achtemeier, P. J. *Jesus and the Miracle Tradition*. Eugene OR: Cascade Books, 2008.

Bauckham, R. *Jesus and the Eyewitnesses: The Gospels as Eyewitness Testimonies*. Grand Rapids MI: Eerdmans, 2006.

Beasley-Murray, G. R. *Jesus and the Kingdom of God*. Grand Rapids MI: Eerdmans, 1986.

Blomberg, C. R. *Interpreting the Parables*. Downers Grove IL: InterVarsity Press, 1990.

Brown, R. E. *The Birth of the Messiah*. Garden City NY: Doubleday-Image Books, 1979.

————. *The Death of the Messiah*. 2 volumes. New York: Doubleday, 1994.

Jones, P. R. *Studying the Parables of Jesus*. Macon GA: Smyth & Helwys, 1999.

Yoder Neufeld, T. R. *Recovering Jesus: The Witness of the New Testament*. Grand Rapids MI/London: Brazos/S. P. C. K., 2007.

Osborne, G. R. *The Resurrection Narratives: A Redactional Study*. Grand Rapids MI: Baker, 1984.

Stanton, G. N. *The Gospels and Jesus*. London: Oxford University Press, 1989.

Twelftree, G. H. *Jesus, The Miracle Worker*. Downers Grove IL: InterVarsity Press, 1999.

Implications Concerning this Mysterious Person Called Jesus

1. Doubt and Rejection of Jesus

Why is (was) it so difficult to accept Jesus? Why is (was) it so easy to doubt? Thomas voiced for humanity the natural reaction not only to the resurrection but to the very coming of Jesus itself. The almost immediate response of humanity to the testimony concerning Jesus is that unless I see or unless I touch for myself, I will not believe (cf. John 20:25). There exists within mortals an innate longing to discover God or to be discovered and relate to the immortal, transcendent God, whom some theologians have designated as the completely "Other One." Yet there is also a general suspicion of anyone who claims that such a reality as God can actually be perceived and experienced. Humans continually search for some indication or proof that would enable them to draw aside the curtain that separates the immortal from the mortal in order to believe. Accordingly, all Thomas asked was to see and touch (John 20:25), and then he indicated he would believe. Is it any different for us today?

Penetrating the veil that separates us from the eternal reality, however, is a "spooky" business. It can cause the hair on our necks to stand on end, and it generally terrifies us because it is a fearful experience to fall into the hands of the "living" God (Heb 10:31; Job 25:2). For that reason, the repeated refrain associated with theophanies, angelophanies, and christophanies (appearances of God, an angel, or Jesus) in the Bible brings dread or terror. Such fear begs a response like "Don't be afraid" or "Peace be with you" from these transcendent figures (e.g., Gen 26:24; Deut 1:21; Judg 6:23; Mark 7:50; John 6:20; 20:19–20).

In Jesus, the evangelists proclaimed that the hidden or veiled God (*YHWH*) was enfleshed in a human (John 1:14) who was designated as Emmanuel ("God with us," Matt 1:23). He was clearly compared to God who "tented" (*eskenosen*) among humans like the tabernacle (the tent of God's presence) that journeyed with ancient Israel in the wilderness wanderings (cf. Exod 40:34–38 and John 1:14). Humans saw, touched, and heard (1 John 1:1) this unique (John 1:18; 3:16) embodiment of the divine in human flesh, but his divinity was not apparent to those who met him. He did not wear a sacred halo like pictures in Medieval art suggest. To most observers, Jesus seemed like just another human being who wore clothing like them, needed food and sleep like them, who bled if you pricked him and who had to go to the bathroom just like them. He was a human. So, his critics reasoned, how could he be anything else?

Yet he made incredible claims of divine authority (John 5:19–23) that were crazy unless they represented reality. He also performed deeds that left people aghast (Mark 3:22). How could he do such miraculous acts? Was he using black magic? Was he serving evil powers? The religious leaders certainly leveled such charges at him (Matt 11:24). He was quite mysterious, if his witnesses can be trusted. Or are some contemporary scholars correct in assuming that the stories are merely creative tales written to enhance Jesus' image? His ancient questioners reasoned that he was just "Joseph's son" (John 6:42). Were not his brothers known to the people (Mark 4:31; Luke 8:19–20; John 7:5)? Was he not just a mere mortal? Or was he more than a mortal? This question perplexed people then—and it still does today!

But among those who saw and heard him there were also more intense reactions. The religious elite were enraged because this Jesus challenged the genuineness of their religious practices. In fact, he judged their praying, fasting, tithing, religious clothing, and pious appearances to be nothing but inauthentic, fraudulent religion (cf. Matt 6:1–18; 23:1–36). Moreover, they were frustrated in his acceptance by non-professional, untrained, common people (the *am haeretz*) who willingly followed him and jeopardized their standings as the religious leaders of the Jews (John 12:19). Jesus had to be eliminated for the sake of maintaining the status quo and of course the Roman peace (John 11:49–50)!

The murderous crucifixion of Jesus was a definite reality that does not need further confirmation. Who was responsible for his death and why he was crucified will undoubtedly continue to be debated by those who are unwilling to accept the testimonies of the evangelists. He was eliminated because he could not be tolerated by the religious and political leadership of his day. He died and was buried. He was, as I indicated earlier, dead-dead—really dead. He did not simply swoon and later recover. That he was raised from the dead is the testimony of the evangelists. It was disputed early by his enemies and will undoubtedly continue to be debated (cf. Matt 27:62–64; 28:11–15). Yet his resurrection will forever be the focal point of the Christian faith. Without the resurrection there would be no Christianity and no church, and this book would be irrelevant (1 Cor 15:14–19).

The resurrection of Jesus, the unique agent of God, is the dividing point in the testimony of Jesus. It is the basic canonical presupposition. It implies a real death of Jesus and is a demonstration of a real victory by God over human mortality and the forces of evil. It is not a vacuous dream, nor is it a mere faith in the faith of the early disciples (as some recent writers have argued). It is the foundational element of the Christian faith that God was in Christ providing reconciliation to the alienated and hostile world (2 Cor 5:19).

2. The Worship of Jesus[1]

For Thomas, recognizing and accepting this Jesus for who he is led to a high christological confession of Jesus as both "my Lord and my God" (John 20:28). It does not, however, indicate the Jehovah's Witnesses' misunderstanding of John 1:1 that Jesus (the Word) is merely "a god"[2] as though Christians believed in more than one God. The early Church Fathers, however, wrestled intensely with the relationship of God the Father to Jesus as God the Son. But they refused to accept that

---

[1] For a full discussion on this subject see G. L. Borchert, *Worship in the New Testament: Divine Mystery and Human Response* (St. Louis: Chalice Press, 2008).

[2] See the argument of B. M. Metzger, "The Jehovah's Witnesses and Jesus Christ: A Biblical and Theological Appraisal," *Theology Today* 10 (1953): 65–85. See also G. L. Borchert, *John 1–11*, The New American Commentary (Nashville: Broadman & Holman, 1996) 103–104.

Jesus and the Holy Spirit were merely other forms or "modes" of God. Instead, in early councils of the church, they clearly condemned those who argued for such a view (which we know as "modalism"). So, even though they articulated the idea that Jesus was of one substance with the Father, they did not in fact have adequate language to express how the three so-called *personae* (Tertullian's use of the Latin to designate the three entities) were related. In further attempting to explain the relationship between these three entities, the designation "tri-theism" was also rejected, and the term "Trinity" was developed. But to perceive the depth of this relationship is ultimately beyond definition or human understanding.

What remains clear is that after the resurrection, when the disciples finally understood who Jesus was (note Mark 9:9), the early Christians regarded Jesus as fully God. At that point, the worship of Jesus began (e.g., Matt 28:9; Luke 24:52). On the basis of this new understanding, the early believers began to articulate hymns and confessions that expressed their adoration and worship of Jesus as the Son of God.

Not only is that high christological view of Jesus as divine evident in the Prologue of the Fourth Gospel where Jesus as the Word is presented as being active in all aspects of creation from the very beginning (John 1:1–5), but he is likewise so confessed in the lofty hymn at Colossians 2:15–20. His exaltation to the right hand of God as being on a parallel status with God and high above any angels or other created beings is proclaimed by the Preacher in the introduction to the book of Hebrews (1:1–14). In addition, in the famous Philippian hymn he is given a name that is above every other name in all creation, and it is predicted that before him every knee must ultimately bow and every tongue must ultimately acknowledge that "Jesus Christ is Lord to the glory of God the Father" (Phil 2:6–11). The worship of God's only Son Jesus was the legitimate, natural response to his incredible sacrifice for humanity.

The death and resurrection of Jesus provided the basis for Paul's overwhelming confidence that nothing in all of creation would be able to separate Christians from the love of God in Christ Jesus, the Lord (Rom 8:38–39). But Paul never elevated his understanding or worship of Jesus above that of God the Father. Accordingly, in the end, after Christ had subjugated all his enemies in the created order, Paul announced that the

Son would prove his submission to God's ultimate authority (1 Cor 15:24–28).

The will of Jesus is thus so entwined with that of God (of the same nature / *sui generis*) that the one who worships Jesus can actually be said to worship God. Moreover, in the light of this relationship between Jesus and the Father, the meaning of the seemingly difficult Johannine texts on God's responses to Christians' prayers should become much clearer. When, therefore, the Christian devotee prays "in the name of Jesus" (John 14:14), that person is not using some magical formula to have the prayer answered. Instead, the Christian seeks to pray to God with a commitment to follow the nature or pattern of Jesus, namely to "abide" in him and to obey his leadership (15:7). Accordingly, that devotee's prayers will be answered (14:14; 15:7) because Jesus did not seek his own will but the will of the Father (5:30), as Luke indicated in Jesus' traumatic wrestling prayers in the Garden of Gethsemane (Luke 22:39–44).

3. Living and Witnessing for Jesus

No work on Jesus should end without at least a brief statement concerning the implications of living and witnessing for Jesus.

a. Authentic Living for Jesus. God was not playing games in sending Jesus into the world of humanity, just as he did not play games with Israel when Israel was rescued from slavery in Egypt. Deliverance from Egypt implied that the people should be obedient to the Lord their God and bless the world. Note that the Decalogue does not begin with the ten commands (words) but with the crucial statement that God rescued Israel and therefore they should be obedient (Exod 20:2). That Israel failed to obey God repeatedly did not mean God revoked the commission to obedient living. Likewise, in a more intense way Jesus established the commission for believers to live authentically in the world as followers of their Lord. The Sermon on the Mount in Matthew 5–7 is not merely a set of lofty ideals any more than the Ten Commandments were an idealized set of rules.

To worship God in Jesus Christ means to live a sterling life before God and others, consciously following the pattern of Jesus who came not to be served but to serve others and to give his life to redeem the sinful people of the world (e.g., Mark 10:45; Matt 20:28; Luke 22:27).

When the rich man came to Jesus and asked what he had to do to gain eternal life, Jesus responded by reminding him of the second ledger of the Decalogue concerning his relationship to other people. When the man replied that he had kept all the commandments from his youth, Jesus simply gave him one more requirement: namely, to sell all he possessed, give it to the needy, and follow Jesus. The man's refusal to do so revealed both that he had not kept the first ledger of the Decalogue concerning his relationship to God and that the two ledgers were intimately intertwined—loving God means loving others and sacrificing oneself for them (Mark 10:17–31; Matt 19:16–30; Luke 18:18–30). In his first epistle, John reminded the early Christians that loving God meant loving one's brother also (1 John 4:19–21). Is such an ethic popular? I doubt it.

Jesus demonstrated another aspect of authentic living in the parable about the rich man who had such bumper crops that he decided to tear down his barns and build much larger storage facilities. When he told himself that he was in control of his destiny and could take his ease for the rest of his life, God responded by demanding his life that very night (Luke 12:13–21). Was Jesus saying in this parable that he was opposed to people having riches? I hardly think such was the case, although elsewhere he indicated that it was harder for a rich man to enter the kingdom of God/heaven than for a camel to go through the proverbial eye of a needle (Mark 10:25; Matt 19:24; Luke 18:25). What needs to be understood is that even riches are the result of God's gracious generosity and that all people, both the rich and the poor, are answerable to God for the use of their lives and their resources. Our lives and resources are meant to be a stewardship subject to God. Thus, an accounting of our stewardship will be required when Jesus returns (see the parable of the talents in Matt 25:14–30).

Accordingly, just as our lives and resources are subject to a review by Jesus, so is our relationship between our lives and our worship. As indicated above, Jesus' condemnation of the Pharisees or religious leaders in Matthew 23 is fierce because he understood the self-centered nature of the Pharisees' pious showmanship. His condemnation was fiery because their focus was a demonstration of religious piety that was not directed to God. Instead, it was inauthentic since it was aimed at receiving accolades from other humans. Therefore, Jesus announced that their practices would receive God's searing punishment. God does not welcome pretense in life and patently not in matters of faith and piety.

Similarly, community status did not impress Jesus, who looked to the motivations of the heart. Jesus' affirmation of the caring Samaritan who had little community status and his condemnation of the uncaring priest and Levite who crossed to the other side of the road to avoid assisting an injured man illustrate this perspective in the well-known Lucan parable (Luke 11:30–37). Likewise, in another pericope Jesus commended the prayer of a repentant tax collector who would have been despised by the community, but he rejected the pompous self-centered statements of a proud Pharisee (Luke 18:9–14). Perhaps the most telling is Jesus' whole-hearted praise for a poor widow's donation of two small coins and his contrasting reduction of the significance of the wealthy who gave large sums to temple causes (Mark 12:41–44; Luke 21:1–4). What perspective would be typical of us today? Of our churches today?

John vividly depicted the model of authentic life when he portrayed Jesus washing the feet of his disciples and instructing them to love one another as their pattern for life (John 13:1–17). It was not by power politics or by economic domination that the disciples were to be known as followers of Jesus, but by love and service for others (13:34–35). Love was to be their community emblem, and Jesus earnestly prayed for their unity and oneness so that the world would believe God sent him to provide the world with both a new wholeness and a model for living (17: 20–26). To follow that model is the Christian's summons (cf. Phil 2:1–8).

b. Authentic Witnessing for Jesus. The magisterial prayer of Jesus also reminds us of our associated duty to witness for Jesus. Integrity of life and the way of love are crucial ingredients in opening doors for proclaiming the good news to the world. The gracious gift of the gospel from Jesus was not meant to be hoarded by his followers. The commission of Jesus was not intended for people who merely bask on church pews and never share the message with others. When Jesus committed to Peter (Matt 16:19) and to all Christians (Matt 18:18) the rabbinic commission of binding and loosing, he intended for his followers to share the wonderful message of binding others to the Lord and unshackling them from the power of sin. Jesus' witnesses are to be those who have personally experienced the joy of the resurrection and the power of the Holy Spirit in their lives (John 20:20–23).

The summons for the followers of Jesus in Matthew is to disciple others, to baptize them, and to instruct them in the way of God, knowing that Emmanuel who has all authority in heaven and on earth is with them (Matt 28:18–20). These concluding words of Jesus in Matthew ("Behold, I am with you until the end of time!") are clearly set within the context of the command to "Go!" Failure to take the command seriously may be the reason why so many Christians seem powerless. When God makes covenantal promises, there usually is a concomitant commission. It was so with Abraham (see Gen 12:2), and it continues to be so today. God's promises carry implied conditions, as Jeremiah forcefully stated (Jer 18:7–10).

The departing words of the ascending Jesus in Luke carry a similar import to those of the Matthean statement: namely, the power of the Holy Spirit would be given to his followers for the purpose of extending the gospel (Luke 24:48). That purpose was further defined by Luke in his second volume, Acts. The disciples were to be witnesses in Jerusalem (one's home vicinity), in Judea (one's home state or province), in Samaria (the places one does not want to go), and ultimately to the entire world (Acts 1:8). That text is all encompassing, but it actually begs some questions for today's readers. Have they experienced God's power in their lives? Have they accepted the commission of Jesus? Do they expect Jesus' return in power? Or are they standing staring into heaven and still considering what it all means (Acts 1:11)? When I read these texts, the commission of Jesus to his followers hardly seems to be an option. How do you read them?

4. Conclusion

The Gospels are not merely fascinating ancient stories about Jesus and the early disciples. They are transforming testimonies concerning Jesus, the Christ, that are clearly intended to affect lives like ours today, and they carry enduring imperatives for all followers of this one who was and is called Lord and God (John 20:28). These Gospels provide for Christians a God-given pattern for living in the world until the *parousia* (Jesus' coming in power). In the meantime, the living Lord summons his followers to model faithful obedience, vital worship, and authentic, loving relationships on earth while they live in the expectation of both the "coming of the Lord " (cf. the *maranatha* prayers "Lord come!" in 1 Cor 16:22; Rev 22:20) and the establishment of God's reign and will in the world (cf. the Lord's Prayer in Matt 5:10).

SUBJECT INDEX

abandonment (& cry) 80, 93, 166-67, 170, 222, 236

Abraham 66, 98, 100, 101, 135, 137, 157, 165, 209, 248

Acts of the Apostles 118

Adam 26, 50, 157, 165, 181

adoptionists 217

Aelia Capitolina 36

Alexander Jannaeus 19-21, 23, 156

Alexander the Great 3, 15-17, 66, 213

Allah 194

allegorical 49-50

am haeretz 3, 41, 42, 123, 242

analytical 4

anathema 47

Ancient of Days 226

angels and demons 61, 122-23, 138, 189, 213, 222, 224, 242

Annas (high priest) 32, 62, 126, 168, 185

antithesis 103

Antiochus Epiphanes 17-19

Antipas (Herod) 27-28, 85, 125-26, 129-30

Antipater 19, 21-22

anointing (chrism) 114, 129, 180, 239

anxiety 134, 164

apocalyptic 34, 65, 68-69, 87, 92, 113, 114, 237

Apocrypha (apocryphal) and Pseudepigrapha 18, 47-49, 68, 72, 125

apologist 237

Apuleius 67

Archelaus (Herod) 27-28, 137

Aristobulus 21

Aristotle 16, 214

Augustine 201

Augustus (Octavian) 24, 26, 125, 215

authentication 173

Babylon 17, 71

baptism 79, 101, 116, 148-49, 161, 180

baptism (Taurobolium) 67

Bar Kokbah 36

Beatitudes 103, 229

Beelzebul (see Satan)

believe 84, 147-48, 150-52, 164, 171-72, 218, 220, 226, 239, 241

Bethlehem 124, 215, 218

Binding and loosing 59, 110

birth 150-51, 217-18, 220

birth of Jesus 27, 110, 119, 121, 123, 218-19

blasphemy 81, 94, 154, 159

bodily assumption 123

bridal chamber 179-81

canonical pref., 1, 7, 48, 179, 181, 188-89, 195, 204, 224

catechize 195

Caesarea Maritima 25, 32-33, 40

Caesarea Philippi 40, 79, 87, 110, 219, 226

Caiaphas 32, 126, 168, 232

Cana 125

Capernaum 40, 56, 156

caring 119

Chalcedon 217

charcoal fire 168, 172-73

child/children 88, 89, 100, 108, 111, 131

church/community 111, 140, 165, 235-36, 244

Clement of Alexandria 144

clues to Mark 77-79

Matthew 98-99, 101-02
Luke 120-22
John 144-47
commission/command 107, 245, 248
commitments 194
communication 1-2, 8, 118, 196-97, 208
confession 153, 172, 231
Constantine 214
corban 96
co-redemptress 223
corruption 221
Council of Jerusalem 2
covenant 66
critical 4
crucifixion/cross 94-95, 115, 135, 141,
    169-70, 230-33, 242
curse of the heretics
    (*minim*) 35, 57, 58
cycles in John 150, 153, 159, 160, 162
Darius III 16
Da Vinci Code 175
dead orthodoxy 7
Dead Sea Scrolls 50-51, 64-65
death/dead 66,67, 110, 115, 124, 131m
    136, 146, 153, 167, 180 207, 217, 228,
    230-31, 243-44
Decalogue (Ten
    Commands) 89, 104, 245-46
Decapolis 40, 83, 86, 92, 130, 139
defilement 86
deliberative theology 8-9
Demiurgical creator 177, 179, 180
dependence 224-25, 229
dereliction (cry) see abandonment
desolating sacrilege 35, 119, 139
devil see Satan
devotional 6
Diaspora 3, 47, 49, 69-72
disciple (other/
beloved) 171-72
discipleship 106, 108, 247
Dionysius Exegium 27, 214 (also see
    time)
dispossessed 118, 229
divorce see women

doubt 194, 241
dualism 69
ego eimi (I am) 83, 148, 157, 159, 168, 204,
    222, 227
Elijah 79, 87, 101, 127, 148
Emmanuel 98,99, 113, 116, 242
Emmaus 141
Epiphanius 218
eschatology 51, 68, 139, 227,236
Essenes (*Hasidim*) 50, 64
eternal life (new life) 149, 151, 153, 155
evil 69, 128, 222, 242
ex cathedra 231
exodus 130, 155, 224
Ezra, Nehemiah
    and Zerubbabel 52
factual 7
falling/scandalize 165
fanciful 175
fasting 128, 225
festivals 54-55
filioque (and the son) 165
fog/ ignorance 182-83
foot-washing 162-63, 247
forgiveness 80, 111, 227, 233
form analysis 202-04
freedom 60
friend of (Caesar/God) 28, 165, 169
fulfillment 98, 100, 109, 112, 114, 218,
    222, 228, 232
Gamaliel (Rab.) 214
Gehenna/hell 88-89
genre (Gospels) 3, 73-76
Gentiles (*goyim*) 33, 58, 83-84, 100, 102,
    107-08, 122, 124, 128-30, 142
geographical 3, 38-40
Geschite (history) 195, 204
glory/glorify 124, 138, 148, 183, 225
Gospel of Judas 175, 188-89
Mary 184
Philip 179-82
the Egyptians 184
Thomas 176-79
Thomas the Israelite 186-88
Truth 182-83

Gnostic/Gnosticism 176-84, 188, 207, 217, 238

Haggadah 45-46

Halukah 45-46

Hanukkah/Dedication 19, 55, 154, 158, 227

harmonize 4, 75, see also Tatian

Hasmoneans see Maccabees

hermeneutic 8

Herod Agrippa I 30-31, 126

Herod Agrippa II 31

Herod the Great 24, 27, 30-31, 35, 52, 92, 100, 121, 138, 186, 215

Herodians 3, 29, 60, 91

heresy 114

High Priest 18, 32, 33, 65, 69, 94, 114, 126, 160, 169, 185-86, 220, 227

Hillel (Rab.) 45

Holy Spirit/Paraclete 50, 81, 126-27, 133, 149, 162, 164,-66, 177, 179-81, 185, 187, 199, 223, 244, 248

hour 150, 154, 161-62, 166, 228

humility 111, 149

hymns 123, 244

hypocrisy 133, 135

Hyrcanus 21-22

identity 227, 233

incarnation 207, 217, 220

inn/house 100, 124

innocent/not guilty 140-41, 169

inspiration 107, 160, 195

interference see manipulation

Irenaeus 98, 119, 176, 182, 183, 188

Islam 149

Isis 67

Jacob 152

Jericho 137

Jerusalem, fall 34, 92, 119, 139

Jerusalem/Holy City 70-71, 113, 115, 121-22, 131, 135-36, 138, 141, 142, 162, 166, 213

Jerome 201

Jehovah Witnesses 243

Jesus' family (brothers, etc.) 32, 82, 156, 190, 223

Jewish rebellion 32, 36

John Hyrcanus 19

John the Baptist 79, 85, 100, 108-09. 125-26, 129-30, 146, 148, 155, 218, 226, 227

Joseph 52, 125, 127, 185-86, 198, 218, 220, 242

Josephus Flavius 20,21, 28, 31, 33, 34, 49, 63

joy 103, 124, 165, 182

Jubilee 127-28, 130, 227

judgment/punishment condemnation 67, 195, 113,131, 147, 152, 154, 150, 246, 247

Judas Iscariot 92, 93, 114, 160, 162, 163, 168-69, 188-89, 222, 232, 233

Julius Caesar 23, 66

kerygma 175, 189, 233

King of the Jews/ (of Israel) 94, 115, 140, 161, 169

kingdom of God (of heaven) 82, 89, 103, 105-06, 111, 112, 130, 132, 134, 136, 137, 179

know/knowledge 150, 151

languages (Greek, Hebrew, Latin, etc) 42-43, 47-48, 69-70, 99, 131, 169, 194

Last Suppe/Lord's Supper/Eucharist 93, 114, 139-40, 142, 170, 180, 232

Lebanon 1, 86, 108

Levites 53, 132, 247

light 147, 157, 161

Lord 5, 6, 113, 163, 172, 249

Lord's Day 172

love 91, 147, 163, 165, 167, 173, 183, 232, 246, 247

Luther 144

Maccabees/ Hasmoneans 3, 18, 19, 62, 64-66, 68

manipulation/ interference 175, 183, 189, 198

Mandeans 148

Mary (virgin) 32, 52, 122, 125, 150, 170, 185-87, 220, 223-24

Mary (others) and
 Martha 132, 159-60, 171, 176, 177, 181,
   184
Mark Antony 23-24, 25
Masada 25, 35-36
Mashal/extended
 parable 158, 162, 164
Mattathias 18
"Maundy" 163, 232
manger see inn
methodology 4, 7, 6-9, 193-210
Messiah/One
coming/Christ 1, 51, 79, 87, 98, 100, 108,
   110, 114, 129, 135, 148-49, 152, 156,
   158, 161, 172, 226-27, 228-29, 232
Messianic Secret 78, 80
messianism 19, 22, 41, 68, 129, 213, 220,
   225-26
Mishnah 34, 45, 155, 194
model/example 131, 224-25, 229, 232,
   247
modalism 244
Mormonism 194
Moses 56, 62, 68, 79, 87, 148, 151, 155,
   227
mountains 101-02
Mount Carmel 38, 40
Mount Hermon 38, 160
mystery/secret 87, 177, 180, 183, 226,
   242
Mystery Religions 67, 207
myth 154, 198, 219, 223
Nag Hammadi 176, 181, 182, 184
Nathaniel 149
narrative analysis 206-07
National Geographic 188
Nazareth 100, 127-28
Nicodemus 60, 151, 170
numbers 85, 155
oral/orality 2-3, 77, 194, 196, 202
Oral Law 44-45, 195, see also *Mishnah*
ossuary (bone box) 141
Palestine/*Palestina* 1, 27
Papias 78, 201
parousia/return 236-37, 248-49

passion 115
Passover 54, 93, 95-96, 114, 133, 139-40,
   146, 151, 153-55, 162, 168, 170. 215
Paul (Apostle) 2, 15, 47, 56-58, 61, 119,
   126, 131, 172, 233, 237
peace/*pax Romana* 25, 124, 130, 241, 242
Pentecost 54, 153
persecution 103, 108, 165, 172, 229
Persia 16
Peter 79, 87, 93-94, 110, 114-15, 130-31,
   140, 142, 147, 156, 162-63, 168, 171-
   72, 173, 184, 200, 219, 224, 233, 247
Pharisees 20-21, 32, 42, 50, 59-64, 85, 89,
   91, 109, 111, 113, 118, 121, 129, 133,
   136, 156, 161, 228, 246
Philippi 16
Philo Judaeus 49-50, 69
piety 246
pleroma see Ultimate Depth
Pliny 35
Plutarch 16
Pluto 66-67
Pompey 18, 22, 65
Pontius Pilate 28, 43, 65, 94, 115, 125,
   134, 140, 167-68, 169, 222, 233
portraits 74,78, 189, 204, 206
pray/prayer 9, 41, 88, 105, 122, 126, 128,
   130, 132-33, 139-40, 162, 165-67, 204,
   223-25, 232, 245, 247, 249
presuppositions 8, 193, 107, 206
predestination 181
priest/priesthood 53, 65, 132, 247
procurator/*praefect* 29-31
proof 220, 241
protection 167
Protoevangelium
 of James 185
Prudentius 67
Ptolemy 17
Purim 19, 55
purity issues 86, 229
Q/ *Quella*/"Source" 119-20, 177, 200
Quirinius 29
quests for Jesus 204-06
Qumran/Covenanters 35, 50-51, 64

rabbis/*Tannaim*/
rabbinic traditions 43-44, 47, 50, 59, 70, 110, 194, 235, 247
rationalistic/skeptical 8, 195, 220
reconciliation 243
redaction analysis 204-06
reductionism 207
red-letter Bibles 75-76
religio licita/licensed religion 35, 58
resurrection 63, 78-79, 88, 91, 96, 107, 116, 131, 141, 146, 154, 171, 179-80, 191, 200, 205-07, 217, 230, 233-35, 237, 241, 243, 244
Robert's Fragment 145
Rome/Romans 3, 22, 27, 33, 36, 51, 62-64, 83, 94, 106, 126, 129, 141, 209, 213, 214
Roman Provincial System 28-29
Sabbath/*Shabbat* 58, 61, 71, 81, 96, 115, 128, 134, 154-55, 158, 170, 186
sacrifice 90, 179, 246
Sadducees 20-21, 32, 42, 50, 62-63, 68, 91, 107, 156
Salome Alexandra 19-20
Samaritan(s) 53, 107, 131-32, 136, 152-53, 157
Sanhedrin/council 61, 96, 115, 227
sandwiches (Mark) 84, 89, 90, 112
Satan/devil/enemy 35, 58, 79, 87, 101, 109-10, 121, 127-28, 130, 132-33, 163-64, 221-22, 230
Savior/salvation 5, 153, 179, 233, 238
Scripture 141, 232
Sea of Galilee/ Tiberias/Kinneret 38, 40, 82, 172, 234
secret see mystery
Seleucus/Seleucids 17-19
self-consciousness 225-26
Setuagint (LXX) 42, 69-70, 99
Sermon on the Mount 76, 101-02, 128, 215, 245
Shammai (Rab.) 44
sign 109, 133,150, 153, 217

sin(s) 80, 110, 129, 152, 158, 166, 220, 223, 227, 233
sinless 221, 223
Sitz im Leben 196, 203
shepherds/sheep 107, 118, 123, 158, 173, 183, 213
Son of God 79-81, 83, 88, 95, 97, 114-15, 126, 140, 144, 149, 169, 172, 218, 230, 239, 243-44
sociological analysis 207-09
Sophia 178, 181, 184
spirit world 80, 84, 128, 130, 226
standards 166
stargazers 100, 213-14
storm 82, 106, 130
Suetonius 26, 215
suffer and die 87, 88, 222
symbolic/symbolism 69, 137, 156, 158, 206, 208, 222, 231, 236
synagogue 34-35, 42, 44, 55-59, 80, 81, 84, 109,111, 127, 156, 158, 232
synagogue ruler & *hazzan* (teacher) 56-57
synagogue worship 57-58
tabernacle/tent 148, 242
Tabernacles (feast) 55, 153, 157
Tacitus 215
Talmud(s) 45, 60, 71
Tannaim see rabbis
Targum(s) 58
Tatian/*Diatessaron* 4, 75, 146, 238-39, see also harmonize
teaching (Matthew) 102, 109, 111, 116, 118,126
temple/Temple in Jerusalem 5, 22, 34, 51-52, 54, 63, 65, 90-92, 95, 112, 118, 121-22, 124, 139, 150-51, 154, 156, 200, 215, 222, 231,239
temptation 95, 101, 126-27, 136, 156, 220-24
testimonies/witnesses 5, 9, 73, -75, 98, 132, 172-73, 214, 225, 235, 238-39, 248
textual analysis 197-99
Textus Receptus 198
themes 147, 193

theodicy 157

theophany 181, 241

Theophilis 119, 121

Thomas 159, 164, 168, 172, 176, 188, 219-
    20, 224, 241-42

Tiberius 28, 125, 215

time/calendar/
 destiny 27, 66, 125, 146-47, 151, 153, 158,
    172, 209, 213-16, 225, 237, 239, 248,
    also see Dionysius Exegium

Titus 33-34

Torah (Law) 44-45, 61, 194

Transfiguration 87, 102, 130

treason (*maiestas*) 169

triclinium (u-shaped
 dinning table) 93, 114

truth/true 147, 157, 164, 173, 175, 182-83,
    193, 204, 207

Ultimate Depth/All/
 pleroma 15, 177, 178-79, 180, 182-83, 189

union/community/
 unity 181, 227, 236, 247

uniqueness 219

Valentinus 182

Vespasian 33, 49

Via Maris 39, 41

Virgil 26

virginal conception 217-23

Warrior God 46

water 152, 157

wilderness/desert 79,95, 155, 157

witness(es) pref., 3, 116, 144, 148, 155,
    195-96, 202, 222, 248, see also
    testimonies

women/divorce 63-64, 89, 95-96, 100,
    122, 129, 132, 133, 135, 140-41

worship 57, 104, 116, 128, 146, 152, 222,
    224, 243-45

Yavneh (Jamnia)/
 Bet Din 34, 45

Yom Kippur(Day of
 Atonement) 53, 55, 153, 156

Zealots/Sicarii 35, 36, 65

Modern Name Index

Achtemeier, P 240
Aland, K 199
Alexander, P 48
Atkinson, K 21
Bauckham, R 240
Baur, B 204
Baur, F 120, 207
Barr, J 181-82, 208
Barrett, C 22, 29, 35, 37, 57, 64, 67, 72
Beasley-Murray, G 174, 203, 240
Bettensen, H 35, 218
Birnbaum, P 57
Black, D 210
Block, D. 143
Blomberg, C 117, 190
Borchert, D 237
Borchert, G 15, 25, 54, 57, 73, 74, 89, 104,
    144, 145, 147, 166, 174, 176, 193, 207,
    216,220, 225, 230, 237, 243
Boring, M 117
Bovon, F 143
Brown, D 175
Brown, R 145,174, 240
Bultmann, R 145, 149, 154, 193, 203, 205,
    230
Cadbury, H 120
Carson, D 174
Cartlidge, D 26, 72
Charlesworth, J 23, 49, 68, 72
Childs, B 210
Conzelmann, H 120, 143
Craddock, F 143
Culpepper, R. A 143, 145, 174, 206, 210
Danby, H 45, 72, 155
Davies, W 37, 117
De Conick, A 178

Dibelius, M 202
Erre, M 26
Evans, C 97, 210
Farmer, W 201-02
Finkelstein, L, 60, 62
Fitzmyer, J 143
Flusser, D 72
Fuller, R 234
Garland, D 97
Gibson, M 230
Grant, R 190
Griesbauch, J 201
Guelich, R 97, 102, 117
Gundry, R 117
Haenchen, E 174
Hagner, D 117
Harnack, A 207
Harrington, D 117
Hegel, G 120
Hennecke, E 175, 190
Hengel, M 97
Horsley, R 26, 37
Humphries, C 215
James, M 175
Johnson, L 205, 210
Jonas, H 190, 238
Jones, P 240
Koester, C 174,231
Marshall, I. H 120, 143
Martinez, F 72
McKnight, E 210
Meier, J 215
Metzger, B 199, 210, 243
Miller, R 21, 196
Montague, A 214
Moule, C 78

Mowinkle, S 68
Mueller, T 25
Nickelsburg, G 47, 72
Nida, E 208
Norland, J 120, 143
Nussberger, F 188
Onion, A 31
Osborne, G 234, 240
Pagels, E 190
Paley, W 237
Parsons, M 143
Pearson, B 188
Perrin, N 234
Ramsay, W 120
Rhodes, D 97
Robinson, J 176, 190
Schmidt, K 73, 238
Schnackenburg, R 174
Schurer, E 37
Sxhweitzer, A 204-05
Stagg, F 117
Stanton, G 240
Stott, J 102
Strauss, D 238
Streeter, B 201
Thatcher, T 210
Theissen, G 208
Theron, D 119, 201
Thiselton, A 210
Tidball, D 210
Tolken, J 230
Tuckett, C 201
Twelftree, G 240
Vermes, G 72
Vilnay, Z 39
Votaw, C 73
Whiston, W 37, 49, 72
Wilkins, M 205, 210
Witherington III, B 97, 117
Wrede, W 78, 205, 226, 238
Yadin, Y 36
Yoder, N 240